Deviance in classrooms

Deviance in classrooms

David H. Hargreaves

Stephen K. Hester

Frank J. Mellor

Routledge & Kegan Paul
London and Boston

First published in 1975
by Routledge & Kegan Paul Ltd
Broadway House, 68–74 Carter Lane,
London EC4V 5EL and
9 Park Street,
Boston, Mass. 02108, USA
Set in Monotype Times New Roman
and printed in Great Britain
by Ebenezer Baylis and Son Limited
The Trinity Press, Worcester, and London
© David H. Hargreaves, Stephen K. Hester, Frank J. Mellor 1975
ISBN 0 7100 8275 4

Appreciating a phenomenon is a fateful decision, for it eventually entails a commitment—to the phenomenon and to those exemplifying it—to render it with fidelity and without violating its integrity. Entering the world of the phenomenon is a radical and drastic method of appreciation.

David Matza, *Becoming Deviant*

A new look at teaching, if there is to be one, seems to require us to move up close to the phenomena of the teacher's world. But such a move, though long overdue, is just the beginning.

Philip Jackson, *Life in Classrooms*

Contents

	Preface	ix
1	A critical introduction to labelling theory	1
2	Deviance and education	17
3	Rules in school	33
4	Rules in context	63
5	The imputation of deviance	106
6	A theory of typing	140
7	The typing of deviant pupils	171
8	Reactions to deviance	217
9	Some implications	252
	Notes	265
	Bibliographical index	275
	Subject index	281

Preface

This book was written with two kinds of reader in mind—social scientists and teachers. This double audience has influenced the style in which we have written it, for these two groups have somewhat different working vocabularies. We have tried to write in a way that will make our research and our theory readily comprehensible to both. Social scientists will judge the book by the quality of the social science it contains. We have sought to make a contribution to the theory of deviance and to give insight into our own research procedures and the ways in which we generated theory. Teachers or student teachers will perhaps look at our work in a different way, for they are more interested in the practical applications of theory than in theory in its relation to the social scientific enterprise. They will perhaps expect to be surprised by what they read, for they may be of the view that social scientists should unearth something new, something previously unknown. We have made no great 'discoveries' about classroom deviance. Our object was to attempt to *understand* classroom deviance, and that is an interest shared by both social scientists and teachers. For social scientists, we have sought to generate a more adequate conceptual framework and contribute to the theory of deviance; for teachers, we have sought to elucidate what (in one sense) they already know, and thereby lay some foundations for the development of practical insights into their everyday problems. As Kurt Lewin insisted, a good theory is a practical theory.

A*

We would like to express our gratitude to the headteachers, teachers and pupils of the two schools in which we undertook the research presented in this book, which amply reveals the friendly and co-operative spirit with which they responded to our intrusion into their lives. Naturally we have adopted pseudonyms for them in this book to protect their anonymity.

We would also like to thank Professor Frank Musgrove for his interest in and support for this research project, which is one part of a wider research enterprise into deviance and education being conducted in the Department of Education at Manchester University.

1   *A critical introduction to labelling theory*

Since the 1960s social scientists have been involved in a fundamental and often heated debate about the appropriateness of 'paradigms'[1] for the social sciences. Essentially these paradigms are about the scientific models operated by social scientists and the models of man that are implicit in these scientific models. A paradigm consists of a set of assumptions. Every social scientist works within a paradigm and it is from the assumptions within it that he is able to define certain issues as 'problems', ask certain questions rather than others, adopt certain research methods rather than others, and show a preference for certain kinds of analysis, explanation and theory. The debate, of course, is an exceedingly old one which has been maintained as long as social science itself. The contemporary debate is different in terms of its dominance in the thinking and writing of social scientists and the strength of views of the proponents of different paradigms; the debate is no longer a subterranean specialism of interest to a minority of social scientists and to philosophers of science. All social scientists are, in some way, being affected by the debate.

In an oversimplified form the debate can be characterized as a battle between the more traditional social scientists of this century, who are grouped together under the general label of 'positivists', and the growing supporters of the alternative paradigm, who are grouped together under the general label of 'phenomenologists'. Such labels are inevitably crude since each contains a host of different perspectives, positions or 'schools' in psychology, social psychology and sociology. At its root the debate is between those ('positivists') who believe that social science must be closely modelled upon the natural sciences and those ('phenomenologists') who believe that it should not.

Nowhere has this debate been more sharply felt than in that area of social science, at both the psychological and the sociological level, which is traditionally referred to as deviance. In this book on deviance we have selected certain problems for study; we have drawn on and developed certain theoretical concerns and concepts; we have employed a preferred methodology. In so doing we are working within the 'phenomenological' rather than the 'positivistic' paradigm. It is therefore right and proper that we should explain the differences between paradigms within studies of deviance. Only then can a reader judge what we are trying to do and why we are trying to do it. Only then can the strengths as well as the limitations of our contribution be estimated.

Some years ago the broad differences within deviance studies were analysed by Rubington and Weinberg (1968) in an introduction to their own 'interactionist' approach. They did this by showing the differences in the kinds of question that proponents of conflicting paradigms address themselves to. The more traditional, positivistic-oriented social scientist asked:

Who is deviant?
How did he become a deviant?
Why does he continue in deviance despite controls brought to bear on him?
What socio-cultural conditions are most likely to produce deviants?
How may deviants be best controlled?

From this position, which Rubington and Weinberg described as 'deviance as the given object', we can detect some important assumptions. Deviant acts are treated as relatively unproblematic; we all know what deviance is. The problem is to find those who are deviants, who are then taken to be quite different from 'normal' or non-deviant persons, and explain how they come to be what they are. Given that we have statistics about deviants (records of criminals, records of admission to mental hospitals, etc.), the aim is to provide a causal analysis which will explain how these persons came to be deviant and why they persist in their deviance. This causal analysis would then provide a basis on which we could develop prescriptive policies aimed at the reduction or elimination of deviance. The perspective is, in David Matza's (1969) term, correctional.

The alternative position, which Rubington and Weinberg describe as 'deviance as subjectively problematic', makes very different assumptions. The search is no longer for a strictly causal analysis, for that presupposes a determinism. Instead it is assumed that persons make choices, even though these choices may be constrained by various psychological or sociological factors. The statistics on deviance are no longer 'facts' to be explained; instead the statistics are themselves in need of explanation, for they are seen to represent social constructions, not 'facts'.[2] The deviant person is not seen as inherently different from 'normals': the main difference is that deviant persons have been apprehended and processed (by courts, hospitals, etc.) as deviant, whereas so-called normals have not, in spite of having committed similar deviant acts in many cases. Deviants have been labelled or defined by others. There is less emphasis on providing correctional prescriptions. Rather the aim is, again in Matza's words, to be 'appreciative', that is to understand the experience of being deviant. As much attention must be paid to those who label as to those who are labelled. These different assumptions reveal themselves in the questions posed by those social scientists who share this position.

> What are the circumstances under which a person gets set apart, henceforth to be considered a deviant?
> How is the person cast in that social role?
> What actions do others take on the basis of this redefinition of the person?
> What value, positive or negative, do they place on the facts of deviance?
> How does a person judged to be deviant react to this designation?
> How does he adopt the deviant role that is set aside for him?
> What changes in his group membership result?
> To what extent does he realign his self-conception to accord with the deviant role assigned him?

The social scientists who adopt this second position have come to be known as 'labelling theorists', though because of the misleading implications of this title (label?) many prefer the term 'the interactionist approach' to deviance. Two features stand out in this perspective. First, deviance is seen as a question of social definition. Deviance does not arise when a person commits certain kinds of act. Rather, deviance arises when some other person(s) defines that act as deviant. Second, deviance is seen as a relative phenomenon. If a deviant act is an act that breaks some rule, then since rules vary between different cultures, subcultures and groups, acts which are deviant (i.e. which break rules) in one culture, subculture or group may not be deviant in another culture, subculture or group. It is this which allows Becker (1963) to say, 'Deviance . . . is created by society . . . social groups create deviance by making rules whose infraction constitutes deviance', which at first sight seems to defy our common sense. Yet if we abolish rules we also abolish the deviant acts that break those rules. If we abolished the rules against driving over 30 mph in residential areas people would no doubt continue to drive at higher speeds but such acts would no longer be deviant (criminal) acts. We can now see why these writers are called labelling theorists or interactionists. Deviance arises not when persons commit certain kinds of act; it arises when a person commits an act which becomes known to some other person(s) who then defines (or labels) that act as deviant. On this view deviance is a social, interactional phenomenon.

These ideas were pushed into the mainstream of sociological work in the 1960s—they had been born much earlier—by the writing of Howard Becker (1963). This book is a highly readable account of labelling theory, and it is perhaps this feature, combined with its 'quotability' for students and their examiners, which made this such a popular presentation.

> The person making the judgment of deviance, the process by which the judgment is arrived at, and the situation in which it is made may all be intimately involved in the phenomenon of deviance. . . . Deviance is *not* a quality of the act the person commits, but rather a consequence of the application by others of rules and sanctions to an 'offender'. The deviant is one to whom that label has been successfully applied; deviant behaviour is behaviour that people so label. . . . Whether an act is deviant depends on how other people react to it. . . . Deviance is not a quality that lies in the behaviour itself, but in the interaction between the person who commits an act and those who respond to it.

A year before John Kitsuse (1962) was making the same point, when he proposed that

> deviance may be conceived as a process by which the members of a group, community, or society (1) interpret behaviour as deviant, (2) define persons who so behave as a certain kind of deviant, and (3) accord them the treatment considered appropriate to such deviants.

Erikson (1962), also writing at this same period, takes the same view:

> Deviance is not a property *inherent in* certain forms of behaviour; it is a property *conferred upon* these forms by the audiences which directly or indirectly witness them. The critical variable in the study of deviance, then, is the social audience rather than the individual actor, since it is the audience which eventually determines whether or not any episode of behaviour or any class of episodes is labelled deviant.

All three writers emphasize the 'societal reaction' to the act rather than the act itself in the generation of deviance.

There is an elegant simplicity about the basic ideas of labelling theory. The danger of such simplicity, which is perhaps relatively rare in social science, is that it is easily oversimplified. Such has been true of labelling theory, when it is argued popularly that labelling theory is merely asserting that people or acts are deviant when somebody defines them as deviant. This is not so. We cannot here make an exposition of all the subtle features of labelling theory, but we shall confine ourselves to noting one important concept which we shall ourselves use later in the book. This is the concept of 'secondary deviation' proposed by one of the most original of the labelling theorists, Edwin Lemert (1951, 1967). He noted that:

> There is a large turn away from the older sociology which tended to rest heavily upon the idea that deviance leads to social control. I have come to believe the reverse idea, i.e., social control leads to deviance, is equally tenable and the potentially richer premise for studying deviance in modern society.

It was as a logical extension of this idea that he developed the concept of secondary deviation. He assumes that very large numbers of persons commit various deviant acts, and that they do so in many varied contexts for many varied motives. But the commission of these deviant acts has only 'marginal implications' for the person committing the act, especially when the acts are undetected, or unreported, or are able to be 'normalized' by the offender. This Lemert calls primary deviation. In contrast, secondary deviation arises in certain circumstances when there is a social reaction to the deviance. That is, the social reaction (the labelling) may create a problem for the person who committed the act.

> Secondary deviation is deviant behaviour, or social roles based upon it, which becomes a means of defence, attack, or adaptation to the overt and covert problems created by the societal reaction to primary deviation. In effect, the original 'causes' of the deviation recede and give way to the central importance of the disapproving, degradational, and isolating reactions of society. . . . Secondary deviation refers to a special class of socially defined responses which people make to problems created by the societal reaction to their deviance. These problems . . . become central facts of existence for those experiencing them, altering psychic structure, producing specialized organization of social roles and self-regarding attitudes. . . . The secondary deviant . . . is a person whose life and identity are organized around the facts of deviance.

In other words, the social reaction to deviance (the labelling) creates, under certain conditions, problems for the person who committed the deviant act which can be resolved by the commission of yet further deviant acts and by a self-designation as a deviant person. The paradox is that the social reaction which was intended to control, punish or eliminate the deviant act has come to shape, stabilize and exacerbate the deviance.

This sensitivity to the possibility that social control can in certain circumstances lead to the amplification of deviance has, however, led to an underemphasizing of the idea that social control can lead to the elimination or attenuation of deviance—perhaps because this is the common-sense assumption about the relationship between social control and deviance which was adopted in an unquestioned manner by earlier sociological theories. Nevertheless, there have been far too few studies which demonstrate the attenuative rather than the amplificatory impact of social control.[3]

No one, however, would question that labelling theory has been highly productive in promoting a wide range of empirical research in the USA (e.g. many contributions to Rubington and Weinberg, 1968, 1973) as well as in Britain (e.g. the work of the National Deviancy Conference reported in Cohen, 1971; Taylor and Taylor, 1973; Bailey and Young, 1973). At the same time labelling theory has been the subject of considerable critical controversy. Some of this criticism has been concerned with the scope or range of labelling theory. The question at issue here is the capacity of labelling theory to comprehend and take account of problems, concepts, findings and phenomena that play an important role in other theoretical formulations of deviance, such as functionalist, subcultural, conflict and Marxist perspectives. Essentially this argument centres on the competition between theories. Although some attempts have been made to integrate different theories (notably Erikson, 1962, 1966), an important and often unrecognized obstacle to such theoretical convergence is that different theories stem from different paradigms whose basic assumptions are often incompatible. For instance, it is often alleged that labelling theory fails to give an adequate causal analysis of deviant behaviour.[4] It is certainly true that some accounts by labelling theorists, especially Becker, are notoriously unclear about whether or not a causal explanation is being offered. A positivist critic expects a 'good' theory to provide a causal analysis and a theoretical formulation in a hypothetico-deductive form. A phenomenological theorist, however, would maintain quite different criteria of a 'good' theory and would not expect to create theory in a hypothetico-deductive form or to offer a causal analysis. Since different theorists are in effect speaking different social scientific languages, the ensuing debate is often replete with misunderstandings, misinterpretations, unproductive accusations and the posing of what are (to the other side) rhetorical questions. Some labelling theorists have brought this trouble upon themselves since they—like some of the functionalists before them—have stood in the mid-ground between positivism and phenomenology with the result that the causal status of some of their concepts is left ambiguous. A good example is Lemert's concept of secondary deviation. Clearly a full analysis of this competition between different theories is beyond the scope of a brief introduction to our own work and in any case has been treated extensively elsewhere (Schur, 1971 and 1973; Taylor, Walton and Young, 1973).

Of more relevance to our purposes are what we might call the 'internal criticisms' of labelling theory, that is, those criticisms which are offered from within the same paradigm and which are directed towards the elucidation and extension of labelling theory. The early formulations of labelling theory inevitably suffered from inconsistencies and inadequacies which these criticisms have helped to clarify and overcome. We shall examine selected examples of these 'internal criticisms' rather than offer a systematic survey of them, since our purpose is to convey to the reader—especially to one who is relatively unfamiliar with labelling theory—some insight into the range and subtlety of labelling theory as well as into its continuing evolution.

Labelling theory stands within the 'phenomenological' paradigm. In making this assertion we are using the term phenomenology in a very broad, even simplistic, way to embrace several distinctive perspectives (Natanson, 1963), including symbolic interactionism, the phenomenology of Alfred Schutz, and the ethnomethodological approach stemming from the work of Aaron Cicourel and Harold Garfinkel. (In so doing we are temporarily emphasizing the common ground between these perspectives and ignoring the significant differences between them.) The early formulations of labelling theory are unquestionably rooted in symbolic interactionism and the interactionist social psychology of George Herbert Mead. Strangely, these origins are acknowledged only once—and in a footnote—in Becker's (1963) exposition. Other writers have been more self-conscious of their roots (e.g. Lemert, 1967; Erikson, 1962; Schur, 1971; Schervish, 1973; Denzin, 1974) or have built upon the ramifications of symbolic interactionism at the theoretical level (e.g. Lofland, 1969; Matza, 1969) or at the substantive level (e.g. Humphreys, 1970). Those who have worked in the phenomenological-ethnomethodological tradition have offered very different analyses to the symbolic interactionists, as is shown in the development of Cicourel's work (1963a, 1963b, 1964, 1968, 1973a, 1973b) as well as in the contributions of Garfinkel (1967), Douglas (1967) and Coulter (1973). At the same time it must be recognized that many writers, such as Williams and Weinberg (1971) and Emerson (1969), have drawn upon both perspectives. Inevitably our distinction between these two perspectives is, in the absence of a deeper analysis, somewhat simplistic. But, since our own work also draws upon both perspectives, it does provide us with a useful heuristic device with which we can organize the differences in the problems and questions raised by these different perspectives.

We shall deal first with those criticisms which for convenience can be described as symbolic interactionist. Many critics—not all of them symbolic interactionists—have pointed out a serious logical flaw in Becker's (1963) analysis.[5] Becker accepts the general proposition that an act is deviant when it is reacted to by some audience who perceives that act as rule-breaking. Yet he develops the concept of 'secret deviance' which arises when 'an improper act is committed, yet no one notices it or reacts to it as a violation of the rules'. Clearly if the deviant nature of an act depends upon the social reaction to it, then if the reaction is lacking in the case of a given act, that act cannot by definition be deviant. The concept of the secret deviant is thus an illogical one in Becker's formulation. Had Becker been more sensitive to the symbolic interactionist roots of labelling theory, he would have found the solution to the problem in Mead's conceptualization of the self as reflexive, which is perhaps the most fundamental of the symbolic interactionist tenets. In proposing that the self is reflexive Mead argued that a person is able to treat himself as an object, that is, he can become an internal audience to his own actions. A person's act can become deviant in spite of the lack of a social reaction on the part of other persons provided that the actor reacts to his own act as deviant. In other words, through Mead's conceptualization of the self as social, self-labelling becomes an essential feature of labelling theory, as was fully realized by some subsequent writers.[6]

Some critics have argued that labelling theory offers an unacceptable characterization of the deviant. Gouldner (1968), in a skilful and highly entertaining critique of Becker, argues that labelling theory is excessively concerned with the 'underdog' who is represented as a passive victim of the agents of societal reaction. In Gouldner's view, labelling theory

> conceives of the underdog as a *victim*. In some part, this is
> inherent in the very conception of the processes by means of
> which deviance is conceived of as being generated. For the
> emphasis in Becker's theory is on the deviant as the product of
> society rather than as the rebel against it. If this is a liberal
> conception of deviance that wins sympathy and tolerance for the
> deviant, it has the paradoxical consequence of inviting us to

view the deviant as a passive nonentity who is responsible neither for his suffering nor its alleviation—who is more 'sinned against than sinning'. . . . It is not man-fighting-back that wins Becker's sympathy, but rather man-on-his-back that piques his curiosity.

Similarly, Taylor, Walton and Young (1973) have been critical of labelling theory partly on the grounds that it is not consistent with their desire 'to argue that many people commit deviant acts as a result of making choices'. The criticism is not ill-founded in the case of some labelling theorists, but this weakness arises because of a neglect by some writers of one of the central tenets of symbolic interactionism, and not because it constitutes an inherent inadequacy of labelling theory which these critics mistake it for. The point is made by Schervish (1973), writing from within the symbolic interactionist framework, when he notes that

> With such an emphasis upon the creative yet social character of man, it is strikingly ironic that labeling theorists often neglect their Meadian heritage by speaking of man in a rhetoric more evocative of the determinism Mead sought to deny . . . [who] instead of expanding the scope of interactionist analysis to study the negotiation of labels by aggressive groups, [have] merely repeated documentation of the successful labeling of helpless individuals.

Indeed, it is the negotiative character of deviant acts, and the motives for those acts, which has been such an outstanding achievement of labelling theory as compared with other theories of deviance. To the labelling theorist there are no 'objective facts' of deviance outside the perception and reactions of the actor and his audience. It is *their* perceptions and reactions, not those of the sociologist, which define deviance. It is this which allows the labelling theorist to recognize— and investigate—the ambiguity and negotiative character of deviance, because he does not impose his own definition of deviance upon the world but derives his definition from the definitional work of the members themselves. It was Becker's failure to recognize this which led him to devise his mistaken conception of 'secret deviance', which cannot be a viable concept because it presupposes that Becker as sociologist has some 'objective' means of knowing that the rule-breaking took place which is independent of the members' own knowledge.

Gouldner has further argued that labelling theorists are guilty of what he calls 'a kind of *underdog* identification', by which he means that the 'appreciative' stance of labelling theorists has been excessively and myopically concentrated upon the deviant's point of view at the expense of the agents of social control (the labellers). The accusation is that labelling theorists are one-sided in their analysis. This must be conceded, as Becker (1974) himself has recently conceded, where he rightly notes that it is a basic injunction of interactionists 'to study *all* the parties to a situation and their relationships' (our italics). Once again, the objection does not identify an inherent weakness of labelling theory, but rather highlights an undue specialized research focus in the practices of labelling theorists. This bias, however, is not entirely unjustified since hitherto the deviants' point of view has too often received only cursory attention from social scientists. It is commendable that labelling theorists should help to 'elevate into public view certain underprivileged aspects of reality. These are aspects of social reality that tend to be comparatively unknown or publicly neglected because they are dissonant with conceptions of reality held by the powerful and respectable' (Gouldner, 1968). On the other hand Gouldner is correct in his view that labelling theory has shown its limitations in failing to provide an adequate analysis of the wider structural and political context in which both labeller and labelled are enmeshed.[7]

The most characteristic feature of the perspective of symbolic interactionism is its emphasis on the subjective meaning of action of persons ('actors' or 'members') and the methodological corollary of this. In the well-known words of Herbert Blumer (1966):

> On the methodological or research side the study of action would have to be made from the position of the actor. Since action is forged by the actor out of what he perceives, interprets and judges, one would have to see the operating situation as the actor sees it, perceive objects as the actor perceives them, ascertain their meaning in terms of the meaning that they have for the actor, and follow the actor's line of conduct as the actor organizes it—in short, one would have to take the role of the actor and see his world from his standpoint. This methodological approach stands in contrast to the so-called 'objective' approach [of positivism] so dominant today, namely, that of viewing the actor from the perspective of an outside detached observer. The 'objective' approach holds the danger of the observer substituting his view of the field of action for the view held by the actor.

This emphasis is to a large degree shared by those social scientists working in the phenomenological-ethnomethodological tradition, but they extend, refine and transform the issues. Whilst the symbolic interactionists criticized the positivists for ignoring, rejecting or taking for granted the actors' meanings, the phenomenologists (and we are now using this term in a narrow sense rather than in the broad sense we used at the beginning of the chapter when contrasting paradigms) took to task the symbolic interactionists for what they in their turn took for granted or ignored.[8] In particular, the phenomenologists are concerned with the relationship between the meanings of the actors (what Alfred Schutz calls the 'first-order constructs') and the meanings of the social scientist (the 'second-order constructs') and the way in which the social scientist relates the one to the other. In other words they are concerned with the relationship between 'natural language' and 'social scientific language' or the way in which social scientists make sense of the ways in which the members themselves make sense of their world. On this view the interpretive work of the social scientist by which he assigns and organizes meaning itself becomes the object of sociological scrutiny.

With regard to the labelling theory approach to deviance, the phenomenologists treat as problematic (that is, in need of explication) the ways in which the labelling theorist himself forges a link between the first-order constructs and the interpretive work of the members and his own second-order constructs such as 'deviance', 'rules', 'labels' and 'social reaction'. Too frequently the symbolic interactionists saw their task as identifying the actions of members as exemplifications of the concepts of 'rule-breaking' or 'labelling' without specifying how they knew this. We shall consider an example of this, and it is an illustration which potentially strikes at the very roots of the field we traditionally refer to as 'deviance'. Labelling theorists, having pre-decided that certain social phenomena, such as blindness, are deviant phenomena, then proceed to analyse them without specifying the grounds on which they made such a decision. Since, to the labelling theorists, deviance is about the perception of rule-breaking, they are obliged to specify the members' first-order rules that are allegedly broken by blind persons. Some labelling theorists have recognized that it is very difficult to specify the rules here—and also in many other cases of 'physical disability' that have traditionally been included in deviance studies—but instead of taking advantage of this difficulty to clarify or examine the relationship between members' and sociologists' conception of rules, they 'bent' the definition of deviance rather than risk an analysis of the difficulty which might force them to exclude physical disability from the domain of labelling theory. Schur (1971) writes:

> Indeed it is questionable that the notion of rules itself is broad enough to describe deviation. This point is clearest in the instance of physical disability . . . there are several good reasons for wanting to define deviance to include reactions to certain

personal conditions and disabilities which really involve no rule violation (except perhaps the extremely nebulous 'rule' that one should not be disabled). From this point of view, reference to departures from expectations may be more useful than is reference to violations of rules.

How this transition from 'rules' to 'expectations' is made remains unclear, for Schur explains neither term. Nor does he assess the implications for labelling theory. However, it does allow Schur to make extensive use of studies of physical disability to illustrate labelling theory, which is presumably what he wanted to do.

Other theorists, who similarly wish to retain physical disability within the auspices of labelling theory, find other solutions. Mankoff (1971) devises a distinction between what he terms ascribed and achieved rule-breaking.

Ascribed rule-breaking occurs if the rule-breaker is characterized in terms of a particular physical or visible 'impairment'. He does not necessarily have to act in order to be a rule-breaker; he acquires that status regardless of his behaviour or wishes. Thus, the very beautiful and the very ugly can be considered ascriptive rule-breakers.

This is an extraordinary statement in the light of Becker's (1963) attempt to demarcate labelling theory.

The simplest view of deviance is essentially statistical, defining as deviant anything that varies too widely from the average. When a statistician analyses the results of an agricultural experiment, he describes the stalk of corn that is exceptionally tall and the stalk that is exceptionally short as deviations from the mean or average. Similarly one can describe anything that differs from what is most common as a deviation. In this view, to be left-handed or redheaded is deviant, because most people are right-handed and brunette. . . . But it is too simple a solution. Hunting with such a definition, we return with a mixed bag—people who are excessively fat or thin, murderers, redheads, homosexuals and traffic violators. The mixture contains some ordinarily thought of as deviants and others who have broken no rule at all. The statistical definition of deviance, in short, is too far removed from the concern with rule-breaking which prompts scientific study of outsiders.

Those acts or persons which Becker excludes because they do not meet the definition of rule-breaking, Mankoff seeks to include once again by his device of the 'ascriptive rule'. Unfortunately, this then provokes definitional problems, which Mankoff does not solve, and it classifies as 'deviant' many acts and persons that most deviance theorists have ignored.

The clue to the issue lies in Becker's sentence, '. . . we return with a mixed bag *ordinarily thought of* as deviants . . .'. Is this referring to the conceptions of social scientists, or the everyday conceptions of ordinary people, or both? It is this confusion which is endemic in the symbolic interactionist account, and which has been examined in a most important paper by Pollner (1974), who shows that Becker so confuses the members' model of deviance with the sociologist's model of deviance that in the end neither is adequately conceptualized. Since it is the relationship between these two models that the phenomenologists are anxious to specify, we shall show that the topic of 'physical disability' requires us to provide such a specification—which Pollner does not provide—and that the labelling theorists of the symbolic interactionist school are limiting the theory by their reluctance to do so.

Since hitherto it is not clear at the members' level what rules the blind and the physically disabled imputedly break, the inclusion of such groups within labelling theory's conception of deviance seems to be unjustified. The only other means of including them is for the sociologist to 'invent' a rule which they allegedly break, e.g. Mankoff's 'ascriptive rule'. But we do not know the sources of such a rule—even though we may suspect the motive for its invention—and the relationship between this rule and the members' conduct towards the disabled is, to say the very least, highly problematic. In short, they would be excluded from labelling theory for the present. This would not, of course, involve a denial that the physically disabled share some common problems with those deviants who are included in labelling theory, such as 'stigmatization' or 'exclusion'. But these two groups can be brought together within a different conceptual area—e.g. stigma—which would cross-cut, but not be subsumed by, the conceptual area of deviance.

The classic case of a person who falls within the scope of labelling theory is the criminal, for in this case it is assumed by both sociologists and members that he has broken a rule; that generally speaking he knew about that rule; that generally speaking he intended and chose to break that rule (McHugh, 1970). At this level the members' and the sociologists' models of deviance coincide. But between the criminal (who is clearly within the scope of labelling theory) and the disabled (who in our view are outside the scope of labelling theory) stand the alcoholic and the homosexual. Both have traditionally been included as deviants by the sociologist, long before the birth of labelling theory, presumably on the basis of some common-sense knowledge that 'everybody knows' that they are 'deviants' and 'present problems' for members of society. But if they are to be included within labelling theory it is essential to show that they meet the criterion of being perceived rule-breakers which rests upon the members' knowledge that they broke some rule; that generally speaking they knew about that rule; that they intended and chose to break that rule. Yet some members (and some social scientists) would argue that alcoholics and homosexuals did not have any choice, or had little choice, in breaking the rules; or that they did not break the rules; or that, if they did break someone else's rules they did not break the rules approved by some members. That some members do not define alcoholics and homosexuals as breaking their rules is readily accommodated by traditional labelling theory, which has always assumed the relativity of deviance, i.e. what is rule-breaking to one person or group is not necessarily rule-breaking to another group. But the other two points create more serious problems for labelling theory. For if some members believe that alcoholics do not break any rules (e.g. laws), then although such members may disapprove of the conduct of alcoholics and homosexuals, or object to them, or shun them, they cannot be said to be defining or labelling them as deviants. To such members, alcoholics and homosexuals are being defined as 'abnormals', i.e. as statistical freaks or oddities in a biological or social sense. On this common-sense members' model, alcoholics and homosexuals are being placed in the same conceptual category as the physically disabled. A similar argument applies to those members who believe that alcoholics and homosexuals had no choice in breaking the rules. The rules are perceived to be broken, but it is claimed that the offenders were driven by physiological or biological forces to such acts—which is, of course, the argument used by alcoholics and homosexuals to 'neutralize' the imputations of deviance that are sometimes made against them. At the same time there are some members who believe that there is no distinction to be made between the criminal, the alcoholic and the homosexual.

From this brief analysis we can appreciate that there is not one model of deviance operated by all members of society. Rather, there are multiple models of deviance (and 'abnormality') operated within the common sense of members. It is imperative that the labelling theorist recognize and analyse these multiple models and relate each of them to his own sociological model of deviance. In so doing, he will inevitably have to pay close attention to questions such as the imputation of intent and the imputation of responsibility,[9] for these are an essential part of members' common-sense models of deviance. It is these issues to which the phenomenologists have been most sensitive, whereas the symbolic interactionists have tended to ignore them except in so far as they came to light as part of their examination of the negotiative work between labeller and labelled.[10] Even then the symbolic interactionists have not been willing to recognize the implications of these features of members' practices for the revision of the sociological model of deviance.

The phenomenological approach to deviance draws our attention to the problematic and ambiguous nature of the members' models of deviance and the interpretive work which is undertaken by members in defining acts as deviant. More than this, the labelling theorist's very formulations of members as doing what the sociologist calls 'defining acts as deviant' or 'imputing rule-breaking' or 'making a reaction' themselves become problematic. This is so because the labelling theorist has not explicated his own interpretive work by which he knows that members are performing acts which he calls 'defining as deviant' or 'imputing rule-breaking', etc. In this sense the phenomenologist makes a notable advance on the symbolic interactionist because he is much more self-conscious in creating and specifying the relationships between sociological, second-order constructs (the sociological theory) and the members' first-order constructs (the members' 'practical' theory). Not only does the phenomenologist examine the common-sense knowledge of deviance which organizes the actions of members, but he is also concerned with his own common-sense knowledge as a social scientist and the ways in which his social scientific work draws upon the common-sense knowledge of the members. For as we saw above, Becker makes use of his common-sense knowledge ('ordinarily thought of as deviant') but fails to analyse it, thus leading to confusion between the sociological model and the members' model.

Since the phenomenologist treats concepts used by labelling theorists as problematic, the concept of 'deviance' itself is problematic in the same way. He cannot accept the implicit position of the symbolic interactionist that 'all social scientists know what we mean by deviance'. The phenomenologist demands, in the words of Phillipson and Roche (1974) in their lucid and incisive essay,

> the clarification of the concept of social deviance itself.
> A clarification would require a statement of the interpretive rules according to which sociologists and the members they study designate an act, event, or member, as deviant. How do members and sociologists decide that an event falls in the category which sociologists call social deviance?

The implications of asking such a question are daunting.

> In fact a shared but tacit assumption among sociologists about what social deviance is allows discourse to proceed unhindered,

even though the rules for deciding on the conformity or non-conformity of an act are unknown. When the work of those authors writing under the deviance rubric is examined, no clarified, held-in-common observers' or members' rules for deciding the occurrence of deviance and control are found; observers' definitions and depiction of deviance rest on meanings which are presumed to be common-sense and known in common by sociologists. The concepts 'social deviance' and 'social control' then become sociological short-hand terms for grouping together 'what everyone knows' to be rule-breaking and rule-enforcement. But what is lacking is an attempt to specify the interpretive procedures used by members and sociologists in deciding what events are to be included and what are to be excluded from the field of investigation; there are no rules specifying how the sociological concepts relate to members' typifications of the events studied. Until we can describe how members typify some events as deviant and how sociologists jump from their own constructions, then we have no means of choosing between alternative descriptions of the same phenomenon. One account is as good as another as they all (members' and sociologists') rest on unclarified common-sense typifications. This requires the sociologist to inquire into members' and sociologists' rules for imputing deviance to an event.

On this view the dominant, symbolic interactionist version of labelling theory rests on unexamined and unexplicated foundations. They may be sand.

2 *Deviance and education*

The study of deviance in school has hitherto been the province of the psychologist rather than the sociologist. Educational psychologists, whether as officials employed by local authorities or as academics in universities and colleges, belong to a well-established and numerous profession against which the sociologists and social psychologists of education are a relatively small group of newcomers. The dominant perspective among educational psychologists has been clinical and psychometric, and it has also tended to dominate the thinking of the members of the profession of school counsellors, whose training has largely been in the hands of educational psychologists. This perspective has generated a vast body of theory and research as well as many preventive or ameliorative applications.[1] The fertility of the clinical and psychometric approach is revealed in the array of psychological tools (e.g. test batteries and test manuals) and in the popularity of certain conceptual categories (e.g. 'maladjustment' and 'school phobia').

In comparison, the sociological literature is very small. Here the major interest, which reflects only one of the interests of the psychologists, has been the relationship between school experience and juvenile delinquency (Johnson, 1942; Clegg, 1962; Gold, 1963; Stinchcombe, 1964; Webb, 1962; Downes, 1966; Hargreaves, 1967, 1971; Power, 1967; Schafter and Polk, 1967; Belson, 1968; McDonald, 1969; Cannon, 1971; Phillipson, 1971). The sociologists (like the psychologists) have tended to relate their work to the more mainstream literature of their own discipline, notably the theories of juvenile delinquency of Cohen (1955) and Cloward and Ohlin (1960), both of which referred to the role of school experience.

Neither the psychological nor the sociological literature is closely relevant to the research presented in this book which is concerned with the application of a particular perspective on deviance, labelling theory, to schools, but which is not concerned with the relationship between deviance in school and juvenile delinquency. To our knowledge there is no major empirical study which applies labelling theory to the study of deviance in school.[2] We shall not attempt to make a systematic examination of the relationship between our own work and the existing literature. To do so adequately within a short space would be impossible, especially since our own work is within the 'phenomenological' paradigm whereas most of the earlier literature is within the 'positivistic' paradigm. Instead we shall confine ourselves to the more limited task of examining a few of the writings which influenced us during the period in which we were formulating the plans for our research project. Most of the questions and problems for investigation that we framed were drawn from the mainstream literature mentioned in chapter 1; but we also took account of a small number of contributions which, in spite of not being directly concerned with labelling theory as such, appeared to be relevant to our project.

The first of these is a paper entitled 'The social organization of the high school and deviant adolescent careers' by Aaron Cicourel and John Kitsuse, first published in Rubington and Weinberg's (1968) collection of readings of interactionist approaches to deviance. Kitsuse (1962) had already, as we have noted, made a highly significant contribution to the emergence of labelling theory, and at the time when we began our research Cicourel was regarded as one of the leading exponents of phenomenological-ethnomethodological work. Together they had written a paper (1963a) on the use of official statistics which was to become a classic in its field. The 1968 paper on the high school was based on an earlier (1963b) investigation of the role of the school counsellor. The purpose, perhaps surprisingly, was not to make an explicit application of labelling theory to the study of deviant adolescent careers in school, but rather to draw on the phenomenology of Alfred Schutz, very much in the manner of Cicourel's pioneering study of juvenile delinquency published in the same year (1968).

The purpose of the paper was to analyse 'the range of adolescent behaviours observed and interpreted by the personnel of the school and other organizations, and the social processes whereby adolescents come to be defined and classified as social types'. The second task was to determine the consequences of such processes for any given adolescent's career within the specified organization. They showed that 'adolescent problems' identified in the vocabulary and syntax of teachers can be grouped into three headings: (1) academic activities (e.g. 'over-achievers' and 'slow-learners'); (2) infractions of rules of conduct (e.g. 'troublemakers' and 'delinquents'); (3) emotional problems (e.g. 'nervous' and 'withdrawn'). The typing of students in the three problem areas provides the basis for a variety of careers within school—the 'academic', 'delinquent' and 'clinical' careers respectively. The organizational actions which chart the course of these careers are then analysed, with special reference to the work of the school counsellor and the compilation and use of school records. Attention is also paid to the significance of contacts between school personnel and teachers and parents. They note that

The consequences of social typing for differential interpretation and treatment of the behaviour of individuals so typed are commonplace and quite obvious. What is not so obvious, and the central concern of this paper, are the interpretive rules utilized by the organizational personnel who decide what forms of behaviour and what kinds of evidence warrant actions which define individuals as deviant within the system. . . . In any investigation of how 'deviant' and 'non-deviant' populations are differentiated within a system, the rules of interpretation employed for evaluating the behavioural elements observed and classified in the day-to-day activities of the personnel must systematically be taken into account.

What Cicourel and Kitsuse took to be the central concern of their paper, we accepted as being an inevitable central concern in our own study. Their paper certainly documents, at both the theoretical and the empirical level, the importance of such an analysis; but the evidence they produce is extremely sketchy. Although they cite examples of vocabularies of teachers and pupils, they make no extensive quotations from members nor do they analyse in detail incidents in school which they have observed. In particular, they do not tell us how teachers routinely define pupils or pupil acts as deviant during lessons. So whilst we accepted this as a pioneering paper, which draws attention to the need for a theory of how teachers type pupils and come to define them and their acts as deviant, we felt that much empirical work needed to be done before we would have adequate answers to these questions. We were also alerted to possible differences in British schools, where there is normally no counsellor and no such extensive record-keeping, and where 'bureaucratization' may take a very different form from that in the American high school.

The second influential paper was Carl Werthman's (1963) study, entitled 'Delinquents in school: a test for the legitimacy of authority'. Without reference to any theoretical perspective, the paper begins with a bold statement of the problem: why is it that members of delinquent gangs create difficulties for, and get into trouble with, only some teachers, but not with others? The answer, suggests Werthman, lies in the pupils' acceptance of the teacher's authority. Whereas most pupils accept the legitimacy of the teacher's authority on a general basis, delinquents do not a priori accept the authority of any teacher in this way, but confer such legitimacy only when this authority is exercised on certain grounds and in certain ways by the teachers. It is these differences between teachers which can be used to account for the fact that delinquent pupils behave as 'delinquents' in one classroom but as 'ordinary pupils' in the classroom next door with a different teacher. Werthman suggests that these pupils will misbehave with those teachers who claim authority in the areas of race, dress and hair styles, where the delinquents believe that the teacher has no legitimate right to exercise any authority, and with those teachers who exercise their authority in an 'imperative' style which threatens and insults the status and autonomy of the pupils.

The main analysis, however, is devoted to another area, the assignment of grades to the pupils by the teachers, to which, of course, there is no precise equivalent in British schools. From his interviews with the pupils, Werthman is able to show that pupils impute to the teacher four rules for assigning grades: they can be assigned fairly, as a discriminatory weapon against students, as a means of bribery, or on a random basis. Where the delinquents believe that the teachers are assigning grades on any basis other than that of fairness, they regard the teachers as exercising their authority illegitimately and behave accordingly, that is, they avoid any conduct which suggests implicitly or explicitly that they recognize that authority. The brilliance of the research lies in the demonstration that delinquents do not behave badly with all teachers, or merely with the 'soft' as opposed to the 'strict' teachers. Rather, the 'trouble' these pupils create with selected teachers has a rational basis, that is, there are reasons for such conduct; to describe it as 'stupidity' or as 'sheer devilment', as some teachers do, is inadequate. Implicitly, Werthman's contribution is symbolic interactionist, emphasizing the pupils' definition of the situation, the pupils' interpretation of teachers' activities and the pupils' conduct as an organized, rational response to their situation. The article reinforced our view that the study of deviance in school demands careful attention to the pupils' perspective on events. Cicourel and Kitsuse scrutinized the teachers, and largely ignored the pupils; Werthman scrutinized the deviant pupils, and largely ignored the teachers. In our own study we would, ideally, need to consider both parties.

Two further studies appeared to be relevant to us although, once again, neither was directly concerned with an application of labelling theory. Robert Stebbins's article, 'The meaning of disorderly behaviour: teacher definitions of a classroom situation' (1970), is a highly explicit attempt to give a symbolic interactionist account of 'discipline problems' in the classroom and was therefore inevitably subject to the phenomenological criticisms we outlined in the previous chapter. Jacob Kounin's book (1970) represents a 'positivistic' approach to classroom deviance and is the only one of these four studies that is directed towards the provision of 'practical' help for teachers. We were impressed by the fact that when Kounin's early researches proved to be singularly fruitless he responded to this failure by changing the nature and direction of his research. The outcome was that Kounin was able to specify a number of general managerial techniques which, when used by teachers, served to reduce the amount of deviant conduct in classrooms. Kounin's work complements Werthman's in that both studies help to explain why there is more deviant conduct in the classrooms of some teachers than of other teachers, even though their researches were undertaken from very different theoretical and methodological positions. Since the work of Stebbins and Kounin will be discussed in greater detail later in the book, in chapters 8 and 9 respectively, we need say no more about them at this point.

In the autumn of 1972 our research project began. We had two years in which to plan the research, undertake the field work in schools, and write our final report. We had at our disposal the writings of the labelling theorists referred to in chapter 1—or at least those writings which were published and available to us at that time. We also had the four pieces by Cicourel and Kitsuse, Werthman, Stebbins and Kounin, which were impressive analyses of deviance in school, but none of which was directly related to labelling theory. One of us had written an article on the applicability of labelling theory to the analysis of deviance in school (Hargreaves, 1975), but this discussion was very general and did not report any new research. Our first task, therefore, was to bridge the gap between labelling theory and empirical research in school by formulating a list of research problems or questions which would draw on all this literature and guide our own research enterprise.

In re-reading the labelling theory literature with our own project in mind, we were struck by the fact that on the whole labelling theorists appear to treat *crime* as the archetypal form of deviance. This is perhaps not surprising, since it is criminal forms of deviance which have been the main, though not the exclusive, topic for research. In reading Becker's (1963) outline, we noted that in most cases where he uses the concept 'rules', which is one of the most basic concepts in labelling theory, one could substitute the word 'laws' without in any way impairing the sense of the text. So whilst the analysis can be applied to non-criminal deviance—which is why the more abstract concept of rules is to be preferred—it is this 'criminological model' of deviance which is heavily implicit in the literature. So we considered the differences between criminal deviance and deviance in school. On the one hand we did not want to 'force' or 'distort' own own data into the concepts and ideas developed by labelling theorists within the criminological model, even though we wished to make a substantive contribution to labelling theory by applying it to a hitherto neglected area. On the other hand, we wished to make a theoretical contribution to labelling theory, and again this suggested that we must be as sensitive and faithful as possible to the phenomena under investigation. In short, at both the substantive and theoretical levels, we must consider the differences between deviance in school and those forms of deviance to which labelling theory has been applied in the past.

We considered the case of juvenile delinquency as a comparison. It is usually fairly clear which rules the delinquent has broken, for they are laws which are normally written down and stated during arrest and trial. In school the rules do not normally have such a formal status. Rules in school seemed to be closer to the kind of rules examined by Goffman (1963, 1971) than to the laws of the criminological model. The deviant acts of delinquents are typically known to and discussed by a wide variety of persons, who may all be involved in the judicial process by which the delinquent becomes officially defined as deviant—the victim, the complainant, the police, the probation officer, the social worker, the solicitor or lawyer, the magistrate or judge, and so on. Yet in the school all these roles are often combined in the same person; the teacher can be the victim, the detective, the prosecutor, the judge, jury and executioner. The delinquent's offences are normally small in number and his appearance in court is a relatively rare event. In school the deviant pupil can commit several offences per lesson per day, and most of these will be known to the teacher who then reacts to them. In schools, it is the appearance before the headteacher which is analogous to a court appearance, for a teacher may send a deviant pupil to the headteacher when the misconduct is serious and may offer something in the nature of a formal charge, as well as asking the headteacher to 'take into consideration' numerous other misdemeanours. The sheer extent of multiple offences and multiple reactions from the teachers is, in classrooms, on a scale that is unimaginable in the juvenile court. Further, in courtrooms, the hearing or trial is relatively lengthy, since the reporting and the collating of the evidence as well as the explanation and justification of the final decision and the proposed treatment are relatively explicit. In classrooms it is often the case that almost none of this is explicit; the whole process from the detection of the rule-breaking to the teacher's judgment and treatment can be collapsed into an event of two or three seconds' duration. In courts the magistrates know relatively little about the delinquent, even when he has appeared before, whereas in classrooms teachers normally have considerable knowledge of their pupils which has been daily and cumulatively acquired over the years. In short, in classrooms we are often concerned with what we might term 'routine deviance'—the rapid 'processing' by the teacher of common and minor breaches of the rules. We were therefore on our guard against too ready an acceptance of labelling theory's concepts derived from the criminological model, for we might then be led to ignore, or to impose an inappropriate analytical scheme upon, the routine deviance of classrooms. Instead we should regard our work on classroom routine deviance as an opportunity for correcting the emphasis on the criminological model by labelling theorists who have paid far too little attention to the analysis of routine deviance in the everyday lives of members of our society.

Armed with the writings of the mainstream labelling theorists, with the differences between the symbolic interactionist and pheno-menological-ethnomethodological perspectives, with the four con-tributions to the study of deviance in school which we regarded as significant, and with our notion of routine deviance, we drew up a list of research problems or questions which, if we had unlimited time and resources, we would ideally like to pose and then answer. The list consists of an elaboration of Kitsuse's (1962) early formula-tion of labelling theory's task:

> deviance may be conceived as a process by which the members
> of a group, community, or society (1) interpret behaviour as
> deviant, (2) define persons who so behave as a certain kind of
> deviant, and (3) accord them the treatment considered
> appropriate to such deviants.

Applying this scheme to deviance in school we obtain the following list.

Rules.   What are the rules in schools and classrooms? Which rules are allegedly broken in imputations of deviance? Who makes the rules? Are the rules ever negotiated? How are the rules com-municated to members? What justifications are given for the rules, by whom, to whom, and on what occasions? Do teachers and pupils view the rules in the same way? Are some rules perceived as ille-gitimate by some teachers and some pupils? How do members know that certain rules are relevant to (i.e. are 'in play' in) a given situation? How do members classify the rules? What differences do members see between different rules? For example, do rules vary in importance?

Deviant acts.   How do members link an act to a rule to permit the imputation of deviance? How do teachers know that a pupil has

B

broken a rule? That is, what is the interpretive work undertaken by teachers to permit the categorization of an act as deviant? Similarly, how do pupils know that their acts are deviant? In what terms are deviant acts described? That is, how are deviant acts labelled? What is the relationship between different labels? Why is one label used rather than another? In what circumstances are acts labelled as deviant? What motives are imputed to the pupil who commits the act defined as deviant? How do pupils respond to the imputation that their acts are deviant? Are these deviance-imputations negotiable? Can deviance-imputations be 'neutralized' or 'normalized' by members?

Deviant persons. How do teachers link deviant acts to persons so that persons are defined as deviant? In what terms are persons labelled as deviant? What is the relationship between different labels? Why is one label used rather than another? In what circumstances are persons defined as deviant? How are these deviant labels communicated? What motives are imputed to deviant pupils? How are deviant pupils 'explained' by teachers? How do pupils respond to these imputations that they are deviant persons? Are such deviant identities negotiable? What are the consequences for the pupil in being defined as a deviant person?

Treatment. What treatments are made by teachers in relation to acts or persons defined as deviant? On what grounds and with what justifications do teachers decide on one treatment rather than another? What are the reactions of the pupils to these treatments? What are the teachers' reactions to the pupils' reactions to the treatment? What are the consequences of different treatments for teachers and pupils?

Career of the deviant. What is the structure of the career of the deviant pupil? What are the contingencies of such careers? How are such careers initiated and terminated?

Having posed our research questions, it would seem natural—at least to many social scientists—that we should now consider how we propose to answer them. In other words we should follow the common practice of social scientists of specifying our methodology, which serves as the bridge between our theoretical concerns and the presentation of our research findings. This scheme of presentation is traditional among social scientists working within the positivistic paradigm, because it is the scheme adopted by many natural scientists. This pattern reflects the structure of positivistic science, whereby a set of hypotheses is derived from a theory; these hypotheses are then stated in a falsifiable and operational form; an appropriate methodology by which the hypotheses can be tested is employed;

the research is then undertaken, and the results, which support or do not support the hypotheses, are related back to the original theory. In fact, in the social science version this scheme is rarely adhered to in any strict sense. For instance, hypotheses are frequently not derived from a theory in the strict sense at all, but take the form of 'hunches' which are only loosely related to any formal theory.[3]

We have made it clear that our study is not within the positivistic paradigm, but within the phenomenological paradigm, where there is no widespread consensus about the nature of social scientific theory, or methodology—at least at the present time. There is, however, consensus among the phenomenologists concerning the inappropriateness of the positivistic paradigm to the study of man. They are united in what they are against, but they are much less clear in the details of what they are for. Thus the collection of papers by Filmer et al. (1972) is more notable for its sustained polemic against positivists than for its detailed exposition of the proposed alternatives. These writers use the term 'directions' in the title advisedly, since what they offer is in the nature of sign-posts to new destinations, but they do not travel very far themselves. That is in the nature of the development of new paradigms. This book, like many others, expresses the belief of phenomenologists that social scientists should not treat human beings as 'objects' akin to the phenomena investigated by natural scientists. An adequate social science, it is argued, must take account of the 'subjective' aspect of man and the 'meaningful' nature of his experience. The repercussions of such a position are massive for the nature of theory and methodology in social science. It has to be conceded that there is a continuing debate among phenomenologists about the nature of theory and methodology, and especially about the relationship between the work of social scientists and the 'theories' and 'methodologies' of the persons whom social scientists study. One of the great strengths of the phenomenologists is that they have drawn attention to the problematic nature of this relationship. They have shown that social scientific work (e.g. theory construction, the implementation of methods) is not a 'separate' or 'independent' activity, but an activity which tacitly draws upon, and is underpinned by, a vast amount of 'common-sense knowledge' which is shared by scientist and member alike. Social scientific work rests upon this common-sense knowledge, which is treated as an unexplicated resource; that is, it is used but is not seen as problematic and in need of investigation. A good example of the advances made by phenomenologists in this area is Harold Garfinkel's (1962) demonstration that both social scientists and members make use of 'the documentary method of interpretation' in their work of assigning sense to their own and to others' activities.

It is clearly not possible within the space of this chapter to evaluate, or even to describe, the many contributions (and the implications of these contributions) to the rapidly expanding field which we have, perhaps imprecisely and injudiciously, typified as the phenomenological paradigm; there are many introductory books available to the interested reader.[4] Rather, we shall confine ourselves to a brief discussion of some writers who have been particularly influential upon us in regard to the theoretical and methodological orientations adopted in the research presented in this book.

Glaser and Strauss (1967) show that the dominance of positivism within the social sciences has led to a preoccupation with the verification of existing theory and a de-emphasis on the generation of theory. They do not reject the importance of the practice of testing and verifying theories; but they believe that researchers who restrict themselves to this goal are emasculating their potentialities for discovering new theory from their research. Their book seeks to put a new emphasis on *'theory as process*, that is, theory as an ever-developing entity, not as a perfected product'. They offer a useful distinction between what they call substantive theory and formal theory.

> By substantive theory, we mean that developed for a substantive, or empirical, area of sociological enquiry, such as patient care, race relations, professional education, delinquency, or research organizations. By formal theory, we mean that developed for a formal, or conceptual, area of sociological enquiry, such as stigma, deviant behaviour, formal organization, socialization, status congruency, authority and power, reward systems, or social mobility.

They advocate, and give detailed advice about, the development of substantive theories from which formal theories can be derived; and they are sceptical of the more traditional approach of merely applying a few ideas or concepts from an established formal theory to a hitherto unexplored substantive area. In terms of our own research, this means not merely applying some current conceptions from labelling theory to educational phenomena and showing that there is some kind of 'fit'; this has already been done on a wide scale in other substantive areas with the result that labelling theory has become tired, static and sterile. What it does mean is being sufficiently faithful to, and open minded towards, the substantive area of education, to make it possible to generate theory at the substantive level and from that to alter, qualify and extend labelling theory at the formal level. It was with this notion in mind that we made our earlier distinction between the 'criminological model' of deviance implicit at the formal level and 'routine deviance' which is characteristic of deviance at our selected substantive level. In other words, we must be ready to adapt labelling theory to our substantive area, and from our analysis of the substantive level propose adjustments and developments at the formal level.

The second influential writer is Alfred Schutz, who is the 'philosophical father' of social scientific phenomenology, just as George Herbert Mead is the 'philosophical father' of symbolic interactionism. In a famous and oft-quoted passage, Schutz (1954) outlines some of the main features of the phenomenological paradigm.

There is an essential difference in the structure of the thought objects or mental constructs formed by the social sciences and those formed by the natural sciences. It is up to the natural scientist and to him alone to define, in accordance with the procedural rules of his science, his observational field, and to determine the facts, data, and events within it which are relevant for his problem or scientific purpose at hand. Neither are those facts and events pre-selected, nor is the observational field pre-interpreted. The world of nature, as explored by the natural scientist, does not 'mean' anything to molecules, atoms, and electrons. But the observational field of the social scientist— social reality—has a specific meaning and relevance structure for the human beings living, acting, and thinking within it. By a series of common-sense constructs, they have pre-selected and pre-interpreted this world which they experience as the reality of their daily lives. It is these thought objects of theirs which determine their behaviour by motivating it. The thought objects constructed by the social scientist, in order to grasp this social reality, have to be founded upon the thought objects constructed by the common-sense thinking of men, living their life within their social world. Thus, the constructs of the social sciences are, so to speak, constructs of the second degree, that is, constructs of the constructs made by the actors on the social scene, whose behaviour the social scientist has to observe and to explain in accordance with the procedural rules of his science.

There are two basic problems for the social scientist: the discovery of the first-order constructs of the members that are relevant to the scientific problem, and the translation of these into the second-order constructs that comprise the scientific theory. In relation to the second problem Schutz (1953) offers three postulates which specify the requirements that must be fulfilled by scientific concepts.

a. The Postulate of Logical Consistency
The system of typical constructs designed by the scientist has to

be established with the highest degree of clarity and distinctness of the conceptual framework implied and must be fully compatible with the principles of formal logic. Fulfillment of this postulate warrants the objective validity of the thought objects constructed by the social scientist, and their strictly logical character is one of the most important features by which scientific thought objects are distinguished from the thought objects constructed by common-sense thinking in daily life which they have to supersede.

This postulate would be acceptable to all social scientists, but for the phenomenologists it poses the problem of the relationship between the scientist's second-order constructs which must have this logical character and the members' common-sense constructs which are typically grounded in a very different kind of logic. As Schutz points out elsewhere (1944), 'the knowledge of the man who acts and thinks within the world of his daily life is not homogeneous; it is (1) incoherent, (2) only partially clear, and (3) not at all free from contradictions'. There is, then, an inevitable disjunction of some kind between 'common-sense knowledge' and 'scientific knowledge'. The phenomenologist, unlike the positivist, is not willing to dismiss common-sense knowledge simply because it does not conform to scientific canons of logic. For the phenomenologist, common-sense knowledge which provides the source of his data, is something he draws upon in his own scientific work, and is to be respected as well as explicated. It is this which explains the preference for qualitative data in which common-sense knowledge is enshrined, whereas in quantitative data common-sense knowledge is overlooked or discarded because its character is filtered away in the imposition of the pre-coded measuring instrument. When phenomenologists make extensive quotations from members' own accounts, they are often accused by positivists of being mere journalists or of being merely descriptive. This is usually unjustified in that the phenomenologist is analysing the data rather than simply reporting it, and is striving to convey to the reader the source of his interpretive and analytical work. In other words, the reader has some kind of check on the extent to which the social scientist has distorted the character of common-sense thinking. There is, of course, a severe restriction on the reader's independence here, for the social scientist has already made a selection from the data. Nevertheless, in quantitative work the 'raw data' that might be available to the reader have already been processed on a massive scale since these typically consist of 'test-scores', etc., through which the common-sense thinking is simply not available at all.

b. The Postulate of Subjective Interpretation
In order to explain human actions the scientist has to ask what model of an individual mind can be constructed and what typical contents must be attributed to it in order to explain the observed facts as the result of the activity of such a mind in an understandable relation. The compliance with this postulate warrants the possibility of referring all kinds of human action or their result to the subjective meaning such action or result of an action had for the actor.

This postulate affirms the importance of the subjective meaning of social action and its place in the scientist's model. As Schutz explains more simply, 'scientific constructs on the second level, too, must include a reference to the subjective meaning an action has for the actor . . . all scientific explanations of the social world can, and for certain purposes must, refer to the subjective meaning of the actions of human beings from which social reality originates'.

c. The Postulate of Adequacy
Each term in a scientific model of human action must be constructed in such a way that a human act performed within the life-world by an individual actor in the way indicated by the typical construct would be understandable for the actor himself as well as for his fellow-men in terms of common-sense interpretation of everyday life. Compliance with this postulate warrants the consistency of the constructs of the social scientist with the constructs of common-sense experience of the social reality.

This postulate affirms that there must be a consistent relationship between the first-order and second-order constructs, whereby scientific knowledge can be translated back into the common-sense knowledge from which it was initially derived. It is through this translation process that the members can understand the scientific constructs in which their actions are represented. The implication is that the members should be able to comment upon and criticize the scientific formulations and assess their plausibility as well as their compatibility with their own common-sense constructs. (Obviously there are difficulties here, as when the members are small children or mentally deficient.) Few phenomenologists have taken this insistence on the understandability of scientific analysis to members at all seriously. Goldthorpe (1973) has claimed that their 'determinedly esoteric and often impenetrable language . . . created the impression that they were more interested in forming a cult than in effective communication [i.e. to other social scientists!], and also the suspicion that obscurity . . . [was] being deliberately used as protection against critics from without'. We accept Goldthorpe's charge—and challenge—though we do not necessarily accept the rest of his critique.[5]

The writings of Glaser and Strauss and of Schutz are concerned with the nature of the relationship between theory and methodology in the social sciences, a relationship which has hitherto been subject to insufficient attention. (This neglect is patently betrayed by the traditional separation between courses in 'theory' and in 'methods' in university departments.) At the same time, they naturally do not give any guidance about, or justification for, the selection of particular methods for a particular research project. Certainly it is true that, like all social scientists working within the phenomenological paradigm, they show a distinct preference for qualitative as opposed to quantitative methods. This is because, on the one hand, qualitative methods permit the investigator to get close to his subjects, and thus to witness, in an 'appreciative' manner, persons and events in their natural setting; and because, on the other hand, they inhibit the unguarded and potentially distortive imposition of pre-fabricated constructs developed on the basis of a (too frequently) tenuous contact with the world of the subjects. Yet there is still a range of qualitative methods[6] from which a selection must be made. Since our own study was of an exploratory nature, we opted for participant-observation and 'open-ended' interview, which would allow us to remain in sustained contact with the world of teachers and pupils.

Our choice of schools was not so easily decided. Our selection revolved around the number of schools and the type of schools in which to work. We preferred to work in two schools rather than one, since this would reduce the demands that we would inevitably make on a school and would prevent the collection of data which might be regarded as idiosyncratic to that institution. It then followed that we should find two schools of the same type, which meant that we had to work in either primary or secondary schools. We chose secondary schools on the grounds that we ourselves had more experience of such schools and it is here that deviance is held to be the greater problem. We also chose urban schools, partly because there are more of them than rural schools, and partly because of our greater ease of access to urban schools. In addition, we chose schools where the headteacher assured us that the school was a 'normal' school, without 'special problems' and without, in his view, unusual numbers of 'difficult' pupils. Both schools are 'unreorganized' secondary modern schools; the comprehensive schools to which we had possible access were either in the process of reorganization and/or were on multiple sites, factors which might undermine their 'normal' and 'stable' functioning.

School A is situated in an industrial area on the fringe of a major conurbation in the north of England. Its locality has seen the decline and contraction of traditional industries and their replacement by new, light industries. As such, it retains many of the characteristic features of the northern industrial region, but its location on the periphery of the conurbation gives it few of the problems of the inner city or 'slum' areas. Though scarred by its industrial heritage, it has little of the depressing squalor that still disfigures parts of similar industrial areas. The school itself, which is of post-war construction and has its own playing fields, is sited in one of the more open parts of the district on the edge of a council estate. The school population is about 650 pupils.

School B, situated in a residential suburb on the fringe of the same conurbation, is surrounded by privately owned detached and semi-detached houses. The small number of council houses are of a more modern variety than those in the vicinity of school A. Within the district there is an abundance of trees and grassy areas, which combined with the extensive gardens of the private houses gives a colour and freshness that is in marked contrast to the grey drabness of the area in which school A is situated. School B is of a similar age to school A and also has its own extensive playing fields. The school population is about 800 pupils.

School A is a co-educational school and school B is a boys' school. This helps to account for the relative infrequency with which girls are mentioned in this book. It must also be said that teachers very rarely talked to us about 'difficult' girls, perhaps because they did not think we were as interested in girls(!). Doubtless the presence of a female member on the research team would have made a difference in this as well as other respects.

Our research is reported in the next six chapters. From what we have said about the phenomenological paradigm in general and about those writers who have influenced us in particular, it will be obvious to the reader why, throughout our analysis, we shall make every effort to report in a very self-conscious way the relationship between our own investigative work and the phenomena that were the topic of the investigation. We are aware that in this respect we have not gone far enough, as was brought home to us in a report by Wieder (1974) which we read after most of this book was written. We have also tried to show how some questions developed in the light of our initial work, and how the pursuit of these meant abandoning other questions. Most of this will become apparent as the book proceeds. Here we need mention only one fundamental diversion from our original intentions. We planned to devote at least as much attention to pupils as to teachers. In the event, our analysis is devoted almost entirely to teachers. Many will regret this one-sidedness but we believe that it can be defended. Teachers have not on the whole fared well at the hands of researchers, who are so often, by implication, if not overtly, critical of them.[7] This bias would seem to be almost inherent in labelling theory, where it is traditional to treat the labelled person as the 'victim' and the labeller as the 'victimizer'. We hope our contribution will help to redress the balance in both labelling theory and in educational research by giving the teachers a more 'appreciative' treatment.

For reasons of space we have had to omit much about our own developing conceptualizations; the notes we kept are littered with rejected concepts. We regret being unable to include these, because so many books present research in such a 'polished' form that the young researcher frequently feels frustrated and disheartened when his own developing work does not have the clarity or neatness of the tailored product presented in books. Within our limitations of space we have sought to show that relatively experienced researchers have an equally troublesome journey into understanding our fellow-men.

3 *Rules in school*

The perspective of labelling theory draws special attention to two major concepts—the 'rules', and the 'labels' (social reaction) by which one person or group, the labeller, imputes deviant conduct or rule-breaking to another person, the offender. So a primary research task for us was to analyse in some depth the nature of rules in school. Without this, it would clearly be impossible to answer other important questions, such as: who makes the rules? in what circumstances are rules made? who communicates the rules to members of the school? on what occasions? what justifications (if any) are given by rule-makers or rule-communicators to others? in what terms and on what occasions are such justifications given? how do members learn the rules? how do members (teachers and pupils) regard the rules? are some rules regarded as illegitimate? are some rules seen as more important than others? and, most important of all perhaps, on what occasions and in what terms are the rules invoked in the imputation of deviance (rule-breaking)?

Unlike the rules in the criminological model, the rules in school are not for the most part written down in a carefully codified form.[1] A few rules, such as 'Pupils must not drop litter in the school', are sometimes written down in a formal way and a list of such rules may be posted on the notice board in each classroom. These rules may also be reaffirmed verbally by the headteacher during assembly when the rule is being broken on a wide scale by the pupils. But these lists of rules are very brief and evidently contain only a minute portion of the rules governing conduct in school. Since most of the rules are not written down, our obvious next step was to ask the members, both teachers and pupils, to tell us the rules.

When we asked members about the rules, they usually furnished us with a list of what they thought of as '*the* rules' or 'the *school* rules'; the two concepts being used synonymously. This was because in part the question was understood to be asking for the school rules: in part because these are the rules which have general applicability and a general question seemed to merit a general answer: and in part because these are the rules which members tend to formulate explicitly—in many schools it is common practice to publish formal, written lists of 'the school rules' on notice boards.

This list of rules which constituted the written code of rules excluded all those rules which were not written down, but which our common sense informed us were indeed regulating social relations and conduct within the school. It was clear the members tended to use the construct 'rules' to refer to a particular and limited set of rules: most of the rules that we as social scientists would wish to call rules were not so defined by members.

As researchers we were in an interesting difficulty, for what we saw as the rules were not often reported as such by the members. Was it that the members conceptualized as rules only a limited set of what we could call the rules? Or was it that the members simply interpreted our question 'What are the rules?' as a request for information about a limited range of rules? Or was it that so many of the rules were taken for granted by members that they were unused to reporting them as such? Perhaps, then, our best course would be to observe the conduct of teachers and pupils and to infer the rules in operation. We could then, following Schutz's postulate of adequacy, report these rules back to the teachers and pupils and ask them whether or not these were rules governing behaviour in school. If they assented to our formulation of such rules, then we could legitimately regard these as rules.

We thus embarked on a period of intensive observation directed at inferring the rules in operation in the school. In this we were like Schutz's stranger, who not being a member of the group 'has to place in question nearly everything that seems to be unquestionable to the members of the approached group'. We would have to suspend our own understanding of life in school, derived from our own experience as former pupils and teachers, in order to grasp what the members can take for granted.

Our initial observations suggested that, given the apparent absence of conceptual distinction in members' accounts of rules, it was possible for us to organize the rules in school in terms of a three-fold classification, which we shall call institutional, situational and personal rules. Some of the institutional rules appeared to be general rules covering aspects of pupil conduct in all parts of the school at all times. Examples would be the rule which stated that pupils should not drop litter; the rule which stated that pupils must be punctual (at school, at lessons, at lunch, etc.); the property rule which stated that pupils should treat school property with respect and not damage it beyond 'natural wear and tear'. Other institutional rules applied to most places in school but not to all. An example would be the rule about clothing and appearance, where special forms of this rule applied in the gymnasium and on the playing field. These institutional rules are predominantly rules about behaviour in public places, such as assembly, corridors, dining-room and playground. Many of these rules also applied in the classroom, though here they often appeared in an elaborated or modified form. There is a sense in which a classroom, including both the pupils within it and its more permanent physical accoutrements such as furniture and equipment, 'belong' to the teacher who is taking (i.e. in charge of) the class at a given time. Assembly, corridors, dining-room and playground are public places in the sense that they are not 'owned' by particular teachers. Thus teachers do not feel either the same degree of responsibility or personal autonomy in regard to the enactment or enforcement of these rules, that marks their attitude to rules in the classroom. Behaviour in these public places is regulated by general rules; teachers and pupils understood the universal quality of these rules. So it is not surprising that what we call the institutional rules were typically regarded by teachers as being *the* rules or the *school* rules.

It also became clear to us that each situation or setting within the school carried its own more specific set of rules, which operated in addition to (and sometimes as a replacement of) the institutional rules. Thus there were rules that were specific to assembly, to the dining-room, to corridors, to the playground, to the classroom. An example would be the corridor rules which proscribed running and prescribed walking on the left. These 'situational' rules were clearly numerous and complex. Since it was doubtful whether we would have the time and opportunity to examine all these varied situations in depth, we began to take a particular interest in the rules that were specific to a single situation, namely the classroom. In this report our analysis is almost exclusively confined to 'classroom' rules. We also became aware of a third set of rules, which were idiosyncratic to particular teachers and which did not share the generalized scope that is typical of institutional or situational rules. These we called 'personal' rules. An example would be the rule that pupils should stand when a visitor or the teacher enters the room, a rule which was operated by a single teacher in school A.

With this rough classification in mind, we began to analyse the rules in greater depth. For reasons of convenience, our observations became increasingly confined to classrooms, which we took to be the central arena for the process of schooling. It was obvious that these classroom rules were exceedingly complex. They were difficult for members (both teachers and pupils) and for us to formulate in any clear way. Our discussions with pupils suggested that some of these classroom rules might be generalized across classrooms.

(1) I.   Can you tell me what sort of things that you can't do in classrooms?
P.   Can't come in late, no chewing, no shouting out. If everybody is doing work then you can't even talk—let them get on with the work.
I.   What about moving around?
P.   Not so bad as long as you don't go too far.
I.   What do you mean 'don't go too far'?
P.   Just keep moving around all the time. You can go from place to place, but you can't go without asking.

(2) I.   Could you tell me about the things that you are not allowed to do in lessons?
P.   Messing about. Playing with other pupils and throwing things about and shouting and running about in the classroom. No talking when the teacher's talking to you.

By asking such general questions, we inevitably received general answers, which indicated that many areas of pupil conduct were subjected to rules in different classrooms. Our own observations of lessons indicated that the extent and nature of 'discipline problems' varied enormously from class to class, and from teacher to teacher.

Third year class—Geography
Mr ——— talks very quietly but clearly and achieves a quiet controlled classroom where much work is done. He confines himself to occasional asides in mid-sentence to check auto-involvements and achieves instant obedience with no questioning of his authority.

Third year class—History
There is general chaos at the beginning of the lesson. Teacher makes several attempts at securing silence, none of which is accepted. There is much shouting out by pupils. . . . There is a noisy little git who insists on shouting all the time. He is pulled up every now and again, but this has little effect. . . . At this point, 20 minutes after the beginning of the lesson, I'm struck by the pervasive noisiness and lack of involvement of the pupils in what they are supposed to be doing. This is in marked contrast to their behaviour in Woodwork this morning when they were all involved in the work and presented little or no discipline problem.

Third year class—English
Having enjoyed this very obstreperous lesson (noted above), the class are quite literally uncontrollable when they arrive for

English—certainly by this teacher who appears to lack any
vestige of control. All threats, pleadings and shoutings by the
teacher are ignored. Control finally achieved by telling them what
a bad impression they are creating on me. . . . It seems obvious
that anything the pupils do that does not make a noise is
acceptable. Three or four pupils are obviously not paying
attention to the reading but because they are quiet, their conduct
is acceptable.

(Early notes of one observer)

Given that the conduct of the same class varies enormously with
different teachers, any explanation of that variation which rests
exclusively at the pupil level must be deficient. Our problem was this:
should we conceptualize the variation as a product of individual
differences among teachers in their desire or capacity to enforce a
set of classroom rules that are common to all teachers, or should we
argue that under different teachers the classroom rules themselves
differ? In a sense the question is strictly an irrelevant one for us,
except in so far as the teachers or pupils themselves perceived this
to be a problem, for our main concern is to explicate the members'
conceptions of the rules. Our own conceptualization of the rules
must, following Schutz, have a statable relationship with the members' conceptions of the rules. Our impression is that neither of these
views was held in any clear way by the members. Our work suggests
that teachers and pupils see some common classroom rules but also
recognize important variations between teachers. Our distinction
between classroom and personal rules is by no means a sharp distinction. To the members, the distinction would be a very blurred
one. At the same time, the members do seem to recognize that
teachers vary enormously in their desire or ability to enforce those
rules which are more properly regarded as common rather than
personal. This becomes clear in pupil comments on classroom rules.

I. Are there times when you can talk in lessons?
P. Well, when she goes for some books in the stockroom, and
you can whisper when she turns her back and starts writing on
the board.

We must note here the ambiguity of the word 'can' both in the
interviewer's question and in the pupil's answer. He may mean that
he can whisper in the sense that he is allowed to, that is, there is no
rule proscribing whispering in such circumstances; or he may mean
that he can whisper in the sense that he can 'get away with' whispering, that is, he can break the rule with relative impunity in such
circumstances. There is always such an ambiguity in the word 'can'

which sometimes means 'may' and sometimes means 'is able to'. However, the same pupil does suggest that what he is allowed to do varies with different teachers, as is clearly indicated in his use of the word 'lets'.

He continues:

Mr —— doesn't like you to sort of shout or talk loud [suggesting weakly enforced proscription] but he lets you whisper [suggesting lack of proscription]. We can't talk when he's telling you the measurements or you might forget [suggesting proscription but can also be interpreted to mean 'we can't afford to' because of later consequences]. Mr —— lets you talk to people when you are sort of helping them out and when you are doing your work [suggesting lack of proscription]. You can't talk when he's talking [suggesting a proscription]: and sometimes he doesn't let us talk at all [suggesting rigidly enforced proscription in certain unstated circumstances]. Mr —— doesn't bother about me, he just lets me talk [suggesting that rules are applied differentially to this particular pupil]. Mrs —— only wants us to talk when you're helping your friends out [suggesting situationally enforced rule]. You can't talk when she's doing sums on the board or when she's moving around when we're working on our own [suggesting proscription in two different situations].

Most of the interviews with pupils bear similar massive problems of interpretation, which must be borne in mind by the reader. In the following four interviews it is clear that it is impossible for the pupils to say very much about classroom rules except by making comparisons between teachers. Only in the last of the four interviews is the pupil specifically guided towards making such comparisons by the interviewer.

(1) I. What sort of rules do you have in classrooms?
P. No talking, no moving about, no chewing and just get on with your work.
I. When you say no talking, is that all of the time?
P. Yes, well, sometimes you can talk in classes, then in other classes you can do what you want. In Art we can work if we want and if we don't want to we don't. With Mr —— we have to work all the time and if he sees anything wrong then he does one of his karate chops on you. Sometimes he lets you talk. He lets it go so far and then he tells you to shut up.
I. When are the times that you can't talk?
P. Well, if we're having a test or we're reading. Sometimes

we can talk amongst ourselves and to the teacher about
things, but when we are doing work we are not allowed to
talk. . . .
I.   You said that you're not allowed to move. Is that all
the time?
P.   Well, in some lessons. In Miss ——'s you're allowed to
move about and in Science, but not in English and Maths.
If you move about in Mr ——'s, he slaps you across the back.
You can only talk when he goes out of the room; we can talk
quietly then. You can only move if you're going out to see
him. . . . In Mr ——'s if you were chatting to your mates and
getting on with your work it's all right.
I.   What sort of talking would he not allow?
P.   Swearing and shouting.
I.   . . . Are there times in lessons when you can talk?
P.   Yes, when the teacher goes out of the room or when she
says, 'What were you doing at the weekend?' Or when we've
come back from holidays. . . . And when we're doing
projects or something like that we can talk, or we're doing a
display on the wall. We go and get ideas from other people.
I.   What about those times when you're definitely not
allowed to talk?
P.   When we're having a test or something or when we're
writing off the board.

(2) I.   What sort of rules are there in lessons?
P.   In all the other lessons with Mrs —— you're allowed to
get up but in French you have to put your hand up. I don't
know why that is. You can talk to a certain extent but if it
gets too loud you have to be quiet.
I.   Are there times when you definitely can talk and are
there others when you definitely cannot?
P.   You're not allowed to talk in tests. Mr —— makes us be
quiet when he's marking the register. You have to be dead
quiet when someone's getting the whack off Mrs —— 'cos if
you cheer you get the whack yourself. When she's doing
something with us, then we can't talk.
I.   How do you mean, 'doing something'?
P.   Well, if she's writing something on the blackboard or if
she is talking to us.
I.   When are you allowed to talk?
P.   When we're doing topic work in English, because some
people have got partners. When we're in groups in
Environmental Studies, PE, Science, when we're doing

experiments, but we can't talk when he's doing something or showing us what to do.

(3) I.   Do all teachers not allow you to run about?

P.   Mrs —— lets us sometimes when you're getting an atlas for crayoning something, and when you're getting a pencil or going for a rubber. You can walk about as many times as you want with Mr —— or Mr ——. Not with Mr ——, he stops you when he's talking and he'll shout at you.

I.   What about shouting? Do all teachers stop you shouting?

P.   I don't think any of the teachers like you shouting. If someone's working very hard, if you shout their name, just turn round like that and shout to them, well you might not know they're working and the teacher shouts at you 'cos you're stopping them working.

I.   How would teachers react to your throwing things or playing with other pupils?

P.   Mr ——'d tell you off. Mr —— would start throwing *you* about. Mr —— would leather you and Mrs —— would send you to [the headteacher].

(4) I.   What about Mr ——?

P.   He's not too bad, you can walk around every minute like, you know, as much as you want. And then talking, he doesn't bother about that, he's not so strict. If you do go out he'll say, 'Be back in a minute', and if you're not back he'll send you to [the headteacher], you know, to say where you've been. And walking around, you can't really, you know, but everyone does a lot of walking around for their rulers and equipment what they need, papers and stuff.

I.   Mr ——?

P.   You can go anywhere. A lot of us sneak out and come back in a bit and he says, 'Where have you been?' and we make some excuse up, you know. Like you say again, if you do classwork you can't shout out and walk around, but he does a lot of mending you know, TVs and Science stuff so we just do what we want while he's mending them.

I.   Mr ——?

P.   You can move around because you have to get all your tools and that. You can't go out. You can shout out sometimes but if everybody starts shouting out then it's a big noise and so he keeps you quiet then.

I.   Mr ——?

P.   You can go out, you know, you can sneak out but if he finds out that his class is going and there's hardly anybody in,

he'll lock his door and either locks you out or in. If he finds
out that you're out, he'll count his class up and see who's
missing and then he'll go to [the headteacher]. You can shout
out and walk around as much as you like.

From these interviews it appears that pupils, whilst being able to
some degree to give a general account of classroom rules, find it
easier to give an account by making comparisons between different
teachers, and by making comparisons between different activities in
the lessons conducted by the same teacher. This variation between
teachers was reflected in the commentaries provided by the teachers,
as the following two extracts from interviews reveal. In both cases
the discussion of rules arose out of situations in which the teachers
were asked to comment on their verbal deviance imputations which
were reported back by the researcher who had been observing the
lesson.

I.   And then you said to somebody, 'Get rid of that what
you've got in your mouth.'
T.   Yes, she was eating a sweet and she's not supposed to eat
sweets in school and she knows as well as I do.
I.   Eating, is that a school rule or what you might call one of
your rules?
T.   It's supposed to be a school rule. They got very lax last year
before [the previous headteacher] left. I don't think he bothered
to punish them. He didn't make any particular rule, he just used
to say, 'I don't want you eating when I'm speaking to you',
things like that, he never made a general rule. Now [the new
headteacher] gave it out [in assembly] and he said that there were
to be no more sweets eaten in the school because he was worried
about the litter for one thing. So I've clamped down. I was glad
of that because I'm sick of it and so I was glad when he made it a
school rule, but I do hear from one or two teachers that they do
allow the lower streams—well I don't. Perhaps that girl's got
away with it before but you see it's gradually creeping back and
I think it's a pity that it should creep back.
I.   Is it not allowed anywhere? What about in the school yard?
T.   Oh yes, that's all right, but they're supposed to watch the
litter.
I.   It's just inside the building?
T.   Yes.
I.   What we talked about last time, you made this distinction
between rules that applied to you and school rules. Is everything
that happens in the classroom decided by you?
T.   Yes, to a certain extent. You see when I first came to this

school they had the rule that if anyone came into the room the
children stood up, and I remember once I had a GCE form and
I noticed that it just wasn't the rule any more. I noticed other
forms didn't stand up when I walked in or any other teacher and
I still stuck to it with mine. Then one day I had a few GCE boys
and they were very nice boys but because of their prefect status
they got this idea that standing up was the sort of thing that only
the younger end did, and I remember on this particular occasion
I squirmed in my chair because [the headteacher] came in with an
HMI and I had to say, 'Will you please stand?' and they looked at
me as if they couldn't understand why so I apologized to [the
headteacher] after and he said, 'Oh never do it again. The HMI
doesn't approve', he said. 'He doesn't expect any child', he said.
'It didn't matter today but don't ever bother about it again
because he said he doesn't want them to stand up for him.' So I
thought it's not what I would like but this is what has gone by the
board, so after that no classes seemed to stand up. Well, when
[the headteacher] came in I insisted again, I started again at the
bottom right from the first form and I said, 'Now we stand up
when a teacher comes in', and I keep to that now. I wouldn't
like to say that any other teacher did. Mind you, they need a lot
of reminding. I think that other teachers probably don't
because I've often to say to the class I'm teaching, 'Will you
please stand up; Mr ——'s come in.' So I don't think that's a
school rule any longer, but it used to be.

I. Are there any others?

T. Well, I won't allow litter on my floor. Now some teachers
don't mind.

I. So it's not a school rule?

T. It should be because [the headteacher] is trying to stamp it
out and he says if litter is in desks he wants to know, so really
teachers ought to know but certainly in [the previous
headteacher's] time there was no rule. I remember once he came
in and found me sweeping up and said, 'I don't know why you're
doing this, this is what cleaners are for.' You see, so he didn't
mind. He didn't like a filthy room, but he wasn't as bothered
about the room being so spotless, you know, as I would, but I
think that's part of the training, so that's why I insist. But I don't
think it's a good rule to that extent.

I. You think it's pretty much up to the teacher how she runs
her own classroom?

T. Yes it is.

For this teacher, a 'school rule' or a 'general rule' acquires its status as such by being officially and publicly promulgated by the headteacher and then being enforced by him. It ceases to be a 'school rule' when it is no longer enforced by him on a general scale and when he declines to make it an official rule—even though he might enforce it on an ad hoc basis in his encounters with pupils. The teacher then turns from the rule about eating sweets to the rule that pupils should stand when a visitor enters the classroom. It appears that, at an earlier period, this was a rule with general applicability to classrooms—though it is not clear whether or not it was an officially promulgated rule—but that the previous headteacher rescinded the rule, perhaps in the light of the reaction of the HMI. Other teachers no longer enforce the rule. Thus this rule ceases to be a school rule or to be a general classroom rule, and instead becomes a personal classroom rule operated by this teacher alone. The third example taken by this teacher concerns litter in the classroom. Whilst at this school there was a school rule about litter, the question at stake here is the extent to which different teachers enforce the rule in one particular situation, namely the classroom. The teacher indicates that she enforces this rule quite rigidly, whilst other teachers do not. She seems to believe that logically it ought to be made an official school rule by the present headteacher since he is waging a campaign against litter in the school. Yet we are left with the feeling that this teacher sees an area for teacher discretion in interpreting these rules, whether official or not.

I. Then he threw something and you said, 'Who threw that?' and he owned up and you said, 'What was it?' You didn't punish him.
T. No. I made him pick it up and put it in the wastepaper basket. That's all I required. I don't let them throw things in my room, you know. They have a tendency to throw books when they're giving them out. They stand at one side from the person sitting at the other side to fling it across. Well, it's one of the rules they have to remember in my room that they don't throw things.
I. Is that a general school rule?
T. No, it's a class rule.
I. Is it a general class rule?
T. I shouldn't think that many people would allow it. I can't really say why I dislike it so much, but it is one of the things that annoys me, possibly because I don't like to see anything knocked about, books, exercise books, anything like that; and you see if they throw pencils about, the lead breaks. And if they throw the rulers we're using at present—they break. You've only to

drop them on the floor. I think it's a question of looking after property really; and I won't have my floor littered either, which was really what Harris was doing this morning. It wasn't that he was throwing property about because it was a bit of candle wasn't it?—so that was really the rule I was enforcing, that they don't throw things about my floor.

I.   Would you make a distinction between school rules and the classroom rules?

T.   Oh yes, I think there is a difference probably in every room they go into. They learn to accept it. Depending on the teacher, what the teacher will have.

I.   Are there some rules that apply right across the board?

T.   Well, I don't think there are any school rules that would come under that heading in the classroom because obviously if somebody gets up and belts somebody else across the head, it's not a school rule that they mustn't but nobody would stand for it, no teacher would stand for it. But apart from things like that which obviously have to be stamped on straight away I think that it's a question of what individual teachers will tolerate. In the way of talking, for example, or moving about the room or things like this morning. Didn't I have two people rubbing out on my blackboard with fingers?

I.   If you did I didn't notice.

T.   You didn't notice? Well, that sort of thing I expect them to remember in my room because it makes the surface of the board greasy and they quite like drawing on the board.

I.   When you came to the school were there ever any discussions with other members of staff about rules?

T.   No, no. I think you've got to decide what you're having in your classroom, and that's it. Some people can put up with a great deal of noise and other people can't stand any at all. There are some teachers who want absolute silence in every lesson all the time. I think the children learn, they know what sort of atmosphere they're coming into. They have to put up with your idiosyncrasies as well as you put up with theirs.

I.   Is there any difference between moving about the classroom and moving about the school? On the corridor, for example? Would that be a school rule?

T.   Yes, about keeping to the left in the corridor, for example, well that's a school rule. There is no written school rule about whether they line up outside the door, for example. I think it is generally accepted that we ought to do this but it isn't down as a school rule.

This teacher explains her action against a pupil by reporting that she has a rule which forbids the throwing of objects in the classroom. She denies that it is a school rule, and says that it is a classroom rule. In this she may be saying that it is not part of the written code of rules; or she may be saying that it is a rule applying to a single situation, the classroom; or she may be saying both. She appears to concede that it is a general classroom rule since she believes that it would be enforced by most teachers. She then elaborates on her personal feelings about the rule and explains that she was enforcing this rule about throwing objects rather than one of the rules about property. Later this teacher makes a distinction between school rules and classroom rules. She reports that there is no school rule which forbids pupils to strike one another across the head; in this she appears to be saying that this is not one of the official rules promulgated by the headteacher or written down in the list of school rules. For her, a rule becomes a school rule when it is written. At the same time there are some general rules that are 'generally accepted' even though they are not written down. But these fuse into the individual preferences and judgments of teachers, who vary in what they will 'have' or 'stand for' or 'tolerate' within their classroom over which they exercise a legitimate autonomy.

We had narrowed the scope of our enquiry from the study of the school and its rules to the rules operating in one particular setting, namely the classroom. In giving accounts of these rules, the members did not possess a coherent and consistent framework in which they were able to talk about rules. Rough categories such as 'school rules', 'general rules', 'class rules', 'my own rules' were used in a loose way to describe the rules at work in classrooms. For us to create, rather than to discover, a neat, clear and coherent classification of rules would be to be unfaithful to the members' common-sense knowledge of these rules, which like most common-sense knowledge is, in Schutz's famous words, 'incoherent, only partially clear and not at all free from contradiction'. Such knowledge is for members perfectly adequate 'for all practical purposes' in their daily lives. In this sense our questions, designed to uncover the nature, pattern and logic of this common-sense, were themselves 'non-normal' or 'troublesome', for they were questions which would hardly arise naturally in the lives of teachers and pupils in the absence of researchers. In searching for the structure of common-sense thinking we had to guard against imposing a structure that would misrepresent and distort it rather than explicate it.

A research enterprise rarely takes a single approach to the study of a phenomenon and then follows this resolutely to its ultimate conclusion. More commonly, observational research which involves lengthy participation is more likely to follow several different avenues simultaneously. This was certainly the case in our own work. Whilst we were asking teachers and pupils about rules, we were also observing extensively. One strand, the verbal statements made by teachers in imputing deviance (and thus in invoking rules), will be dealt with shortly. As matters stood at this period we were in danger of becoming depressed by the sheer quantity and complexity of what to us appeared to be the rules at work in classrooms. Rarely were these rules stated in any explicit form. How, then, were we to make sense of the data in which we were steadily beginning to drown? The straw at which we clutched was a self-conscious attempt on our part to introduce some sort of imposed order on this chaos. We attempted to create, as it were, an artificial floating platform from which we could work, but which we would happily discard when we began to feel less at sea in the data. We were very aware of the danger of making this platform our permanent base. The temporary platform consisted of an imposed classification of the rules. Initially we thought in terms of two kinds of classroom rules, those concerned with 'work' and then the others. This proved to be as confusing as it was crude. We seemed to capture the flavour of life in the classroom more adequately by grouping the rules into five themes:

1. The talk theme. Many of the rules related to the area of pupil talk. One of the most frequent teacher statements was 'stop talking'. We included in this theme all talk-related conduct, such as noise and laughter.

2. The movement theme. The many rules about standing and sitting, entering and leaving the room, moving around the classroom, seemed to bear a common movement theme.

3. The time theme. This theme included the rules about arriving late, about 'wasting time', and about the time taken by pupils to complete tasks assigned to them.

4. The teacher-pupil relationship theme. The ways in which pupils were expected to treat the teachers were a common focus for a variety of rules. The most obvious rules covered obedience, manners and insolence.

5. The pupil-pupil relationship theme. This theme included all the rules about how the pupils were expected to treat one another. Examples would be rules about fighting, name-calling and the various forms of interfering with another pupil and his work.

Each of these themes covers a wide range of rules. To illustrate this, we shall examine the talk theme in great depth. Talk within the classroom is of two types: pupil-pupil talk and pupil-teacher talk.

1. *Pupil-pupil talk*

(a) All talk by pupils is illegitimate ('No talking'): e.g. Assembly (Here the proscribed talk is informal pupil-pupil talk. Failure to indulge in certain prescribed talk, e.g. saying prayers, is defined as deviant); when teacher is addressing the class; when teacher specifically forbids talk in a given situation, such as 'tests'. All these talk rules can be broken in situations which constitute 'emergencies'.

Pupil-pupil talk can be legitimated before its occurrence by seeking the teacher's permission ('Can I ask him for his rubber, Miss?'). Pupil-pupil talk can sometimes be legitimated after its occurrence by a negotiation of the motives ('But, Miss, I was only asking him for his rubber').

(b) Some talk is legitimate: e.g. Group work. On such occasions talk by pupils must meet the criteria of: (i) volume ('Don't shout'); (ii) amount ('There's too much talking'); (iii) content—talk must be task-related ('You're not discussing the project at all, Jones').

(c) Almost all talk is legitimate: e.g. Playground. But note that even here some kinds of content are proscribed, e.g. swearing.

2. *Pupil-teacher talk*

(a) Rules affecting talk initiated by pupils:

(i) Do not talk whilst the teacher is addressing the class ('Don't interrupt').

(ii) Do not talk whilst the teacher is talking to another pupil or whilst another pupil is talking to the teacher ('Don't interrupt')

(iii) Do not talk without permission ('Don't shout out'). This draws our attention to the rules of seeking permission to talk: (a) If the teacher is engaged elsewhere, signal by handraising, and wait for teacher to notice and give permission to speak; (b) If teacher for some reason is unlikely to notice the raised hand, say 'Sir' and wait for permission to speak.

(iv) To inform the teacher if serious problems are being encountered in making progress with the work. The pupil talk must consist of an appeal for help or of a statement of the difficulty or the asking of a relevant question. This rule counts as an exception to rule (i) above but must not contravene rules (ii) and (iii) above.

(b) Rules affecting pupil talk after initiation by the teacher: e.g. When the teacher asks a question.

(i) All questions must be answered. Silence is permitted when the question is rhetorical or when 'I don't know' would be an appropriate form of talk.

(ii) All questions must be treated seriously—that is, given an answer whose content is serious or non-flippant.

(iii) Answers must be couched in the right style, in conformity to teacher-pupil relational rules.

(iv) Do make contributions to a discussion session initiated by the teacher. All contributions must be relevant to the topic under discussion, and must conform to rules (a)(i) and (ii) above. Normally in a discussion session rule (a)(iii) will be suspended.

It is obvious that these rules presuppose many other rules. For instance, the rule about volume in pupil-pupil talk indicates that teachers have some rule by which such talk can be defined as 'too loud' or 'too noisy'. The rules of asking questions (in 2(a)(iv) above) suggest that teachers and pupils have rules by which pupil-initiated questions can be defined as 'stupid' or 'silly'. If the answer is quite 'obvious', i.e. known by everyone, or if the question is utterly irrelevant to what the teacher is saying, or if the answer has already been clearly stated by the teacher, then a question will be given the deviant definition of 'stupid'. In these ways, the list of rules under the theme of talk is fairly superficial.

Our examination of the rules in terms of the five themes had the effect of sensitizing us to several very important ideas. First, it made us realize the enormity and complexity of our aim to explicate the classroom rules. One ideal would be to provide some kind of hand-book of rules, a knowledge of which would allow a complete stranger to the classroom (that legendary Martian) to 'pass' as a pupil in a classroom.[2] By this criterion, our list of talk rules was very in-adequate. Second, we were again alerted to a feature which had emerged in the interview material, namely the changes in the rules in different contexts. It is clear that there are different talk rules in operation when 'the teacher is addressing the class' as against when the class is 'doing a test' or 'carrying out group work'. Third, we realized that our themes overlapped very heavily. It was impossible to say much about talk rules without mentioning teacher-pupil relationship rules for instance.

Fortunately for us, we had little interest in producing a systematic classificatory scheme of rules with mutually exclusive categories. The themes were, for us, no more than a loose heuristic device to sensitize us to the nature and content of the classroom rules. It was our attempt to match observed events, especially teacher imputations of deviance, against the themes which proved to be valuable. For instance, teachers commonly rebuked pupils for 'turning round' in their seats towards the pupil in the desk immediately behind. What kind of rule is being invoked on such an occasion? It might be regarded as a movement rule (rule = pupil must face the front); a talk rule (rule = pupils must not talk to one another), since turning round normally results in a pupil-pupil conversation; a time rule (rule = pupils must get on with their work and not waste time); a teacher-pupil relational rule (rule = it is rude to turn one's back to the teacher when he is talking); or a pupil-pupil relational rule (rule = pupils must not interrupt another pupil when he is working). Very sharply we were forced to recognize that a given act can be defined as deviant either because it breaks several classroom rules simultaneously, and/or, what in one sense is the same act ('turning round') breaks different rules on different occasions, depending on what rule is in fact being invoked. A group of acts can be given the collective deviant label such as 'turning round' even though they are different kinds of deviance because they are breaking different rules.

Before developing this argument more fully, we must consider another aspect of our analysis which was being used at the same time as our development of the five themes. This consisted of a close examination of teacher talk. Our concern was to examine all the verbal utterances by teachers in which they were making imputations of deviance. If the imputation of deviance is the same as the imputation of rule-breaking, as the theoretical perspective we were using claimed, then we might be able to infer the classroom rules from these imputations of deviance.

Most of the imputations were made in a single sentence. It is this which makes the 'routine deviance' of the classroom such a far cry from the processing of deviance in the criminological model. At the simplest level, the imputation could consist of a single word— 'Smith!' or 'Girls!' or 'Oi!'. Or the teacher might use a simple sentence, in the form of an order ('Be quiet'), a prohibition ('Stop that') or a question ('Have you finished?'). Sometimes the imputation would be in a compound or complex form, involving two or more of the above elements ('What do you want? Just sit down for a minute' or 'Stop talking, and get on with your work, instead of wasting time'). On occasions, the imputations could be non-verbal, as when the teacher stares at a child and shakes his head slowly until the pupil refrains from the deviant activity.

When we examined several hundred of these imputations, we found that they could be classified into eleven categories. We hasten to add that we do not offer these categories as clear and mutually exclusive. They are presented merely as a useful way of indicating to the reader the variety and range of imputations of deviance in their explicit verbal form. As we shall see later, each category presents different problems for the pupil in recognizing the teacher's statement as an imputation of deviance.

1. Descriptive statement of the deviant conduct
John Patterson, you're not working.
You're getting noisy again down there.
You're taking a long time to settle down today.
I see you're sitting there with no folder in front of you.
Why is it that whenever I turn round you're always chattering and messing about?

2. Statement of the rule which is being invoked
When I'm talking nobody else talks.
Rulers are not for fighting with, they're for measuring with.
I'm not having this shouting across the room.

3. Appeal to pupil's knowledge of the rules
How many times do I have to tell you?
I told you yesterday about this hubbub when I ask you to do something.
I've told you time and time again. I want it in your book.
Do I have to tell you two again?

4. Command/request for conformity to the rule
Shut up.
Turn round.
Sit down and keep quiet.
Put up your hand.
Put that away.
Keep your mouth shut.
Get your eyes on the book.

5. Prohibitions
Don't.
Stop that.
That will do.
Stop the natter.
Stop playing with your money.
Don't shout out.

6. Questions
Are you listening?
Have you finished?
Are you doing it, Harrison?
What is going on over there?
What are you talking about?
What's wrong with you?

7. Statement of the consequences of the deviant conduct
Andrew, do you expect to get through CSE with one paragraph?

I'm not going to waste my voice reading to you if you go on like this.
What are these doing on the floor? Somebody's going to get hurt.
Jennifer, these chairs make an awful noise when they're pushed back.

8. Warnings and threats
I hope that chat is constructive and has something to do with the lesson, but I don't think it has.
I'm going to lose my temper with you.
You're going to be detained if you don't stop the noise.
I'll have no more of that or I'm going to send you to the Head.
I'll take you out of the room in a minute if you don't do as I tell you.
You'll be out of that door in a sorry state if you don't do what I tell you, girl.
Stop rattling your pencils or I'll rattle your ears.
Mr Howarth and Mr Jefferson will be with us until five o'clock if they're not careful.

9. Evaluative labelling of the pupil and his conduct
Fritz, you're being foolish.
Stop misbehaving, you two.
Will you keep quiet. You're talking to yourselves. This is bad. It is something peculiar.
Stop behaving like a baby.

10. Sarcasm
We can do without the singing.
Have you retired?
That's the way! Throw them on the floor!
Do I have to screw you on the seat?
Brendan, you've a voice like a foghorn even when you talk quietly.

11. Attention-drawers
Girls!
3B!
Billington!
Sandra!

Our original purpose in collecting these teacher statements was a dual one. On the one hand, we wished to examine the ways in which teachers imputed deviance. On the other hand, and of more immediate relevance, we wished to use them as a source for inferring the rule(s) that the teacher was invoking. We hoped that this approach to the nature of rules would be more fruitful than our attempts to obtain direct statements of the rules through interviews. Yet there is a very important presupposition here, namely that we are able, in collecting these statements, to recognize these statements as imputations of deviance, i.e. as attempts at social control through defining an act as deviant by invoking a relevant rule. Although we did not find this coding 'troublesome', it was nevertheless an important accomplishment for us as researchers. Clearly we were not drawing on sociological reasoning as such; that reasoning simply suggested that a deviance-imputation must involve a rule invocation. In labelling theory a deviance-imputation must by definition rest on the imputation that the deviant person has broken a rule. But that reasoning does not explain how we are able to recognize the deviance-imputation in the first place, especially since the majority of the deviance-imputations in our list do not contain any explicit reference to a rule. To make the coding at all, we were drawing on our common-sense knowledge that certain teacher statements are 'obviously' deviance-imputations. In this we were probably using the same common-sense as that exercised by the members, by which all of us were able to make sense of the teacher statements. We, as researchers, were additionally performing a translation process by which, after using common-sense knowledge to make the teacher statements meaningful, we were able to code them in social scientific terminology (deviance-imputation). In other words, we were using the same common-sense as members as an unexplicated resource in our own work, rather than as a topic itself in need of explication.[3] This explication was essential both to the analysis of the members' activities and to the documentation of our own research practices.

Our close examination of these teacher statements led to a number of important conclusions which affected our subsequent research. One conclusion was that it was not possible, on the basis of the verbal statements alone, to infer the rule that the teacher might reasonably be held to be invoking. Only the researcher who had made the original observation was able to do this, because only he was familiar with the context from which the statement had been extracted and it was this context which was essential in understanding the rule that had been invoked. Thus when we debated among ourselves the meaning of a deviance-imputation or the rule we inferred was being invoked, the original observer argued for his interpretation, against other possible interpretations suggested by researchers who had not witnessed the event, by explaining in detail the situation in which the statement had been uttered and the events that had immediately preceded it. In so doing, of course, the observer was making explicit some of the common-sense knowledge that he had used to make the original coding—and this might well reflect the common-sense knowledge used by the members in their own attempts to give meaning to these utterances. To decontextualize these statements, we learned, was to discard the most significant data, namely the basis of our own as well as the members' ability to apprehend the meaning of the statements.

A second conclusion also derived from our debates about the meaning of these statements, for sometimes one of the researchers who had not observed the event would question whether or not a statement was indeed an imputation of deviance. In resolving these differences about the correctness of the coding by recontextualizing the statements, we learned that many statements which in certain circumstances can be an imputation of deviance can in other circumstances be merely an instruction to the pupil or to the class. A 'deviance-imputation' typically involves an explicit teacher statement which indicates that a pupil has broken or is breaking a rule with the implication that this conduct must cease and be replaced with conduct which conforms to the rules. An 'instruction' is a kind of rule in that the pupils are expected to follow the instruction. It is quite distinct from a deviance-imputation in that there is no suggestion that present conduct is rule-breaking. Instructions have a future reference and lack that retrospective orientation of deviance-imputations by which past/present conduct is interpreted in the light of the rule.

We can exemplify the difference between a deviance-imputation and an instruction, by examining a number of teacher statements which, according to context, can be either an instruction or a deviance-imputation.

1. Teacher statement—'Pay attention.' Deviance-imputation: the meaning is that the teacher is talking and the pupils should be listening rather than talking or fidgeting. Instruction: the meaning is that the pupils are working in their books as required, but they must stop that for a moment as the teacher has some further instruction/ information to give.

2. Teacher statement—'Sit down.' Deviance-imputation: the meaning is that the pupil ought to be sitting down rather than wandering about the room without just cause. Instruction: the meaning is that the pupils were right to stand when the teacher entered the room, but now they are being given permission to sit down.

3. Teacher statement—'Have you finished?' Deviance-imputation: the meaning is that if the pupil has not finished the assignment then he has no justification for talking to his neighbour. Instruction: the meaning is that the teacher is seeking information on the extent of pupil progress before he moves on to the next part of the lesson.

Occasionally, the two can appear in a single statement, as in 'Listen a moment, 3B. Listen, I said, listen!' The first request for silence and attention to the teacher is an instruction; the second order is a deviance-imputation in that the pupils are not listening as required and are being defined as deviant, breaking the rule of listening. For the most part, we found that within its context almost every teacher statement can be seen as either a deviance-imputation or an instruction. But we did find occasions when it was difficult to be sure. Examples would be 'Are you ready?' and 'One at a time'.

Any readers who have a preference for quantification may have been wondering why it is that we made no attempt to quantify these events by assigning them to one of the categories in one of our classificatory schemes. Would it not be of interest, it might be argued, to code what we observed or heard and so be able to report on the relative frequency of such events in different classes and with different teachers? Our main, though not our only, reason for rejecting such an approach is perhaps now clear. To code the statement 'turn round' as a movement rule within our classification of themes would be to concentrate on the explicit word content of the statement and thus to decontextualize it. In doing so, we would distort the meaning of the statement to the actors, and that meaning is decided by the actors, not by the explicit content as such, but by that content within the context of its utterance. To extract it from its context would be to denude it of its meaning to the actors and to assign to it instead the arbitrary meaning of the researchers as given by the themes. In addition, in carrying out such an expensive (in terms of time) enterprise, we would be diverted from an analysis of the context in which the words derived their meaning. Similarly, were we to code 'turn round' as a command, as opposed to a prohibition, or a question or a warning, etc., in our second classificatory system, then we would necessarily be distracted from the analysis of the meaning of the statement in its context. Its status as a command as such is, in our judgment, far less important than its meaning as an instruction or as a deviance-imputation. And its meaning for the actors hinges upon their recognition that the same statement—same in the sense of using the same words—can have quite different meanings according to the context of utterance. The coding of decontextualized teacher statements into the common conceptual category 'commands' is to employ a researcher's practice which imposes a sameness on verbal events as a substitute for—and thus as a distortion of—the members' own practices for coding verbal statements which rest on deciding from the context of utterance that the statement either involves a deviance-imputation or an instruction.

It is clear that our early approaches to the analysis of rules, namely, our conceptions of themes, our examination of the verbal imputations of deviance and our interview data, all pointed in the same direction—the close and careful analysis of the changing contexts of lessons, with their different rules. What constituted an imputation of deviance, and what constituted the meaning of the imputation, including the meaning of the description of the pupils' actions, depended on our understanding—and on the teacher's and pupils' understanding—of the rules in operation during that context and of the events that immediately preceded the teacher's imputation. The next two chapters will be concerned with the development of this analysis. It was a direction we had not anticipated at the beginning of the research. It was in some ways a direction in which we did not want to go, because it appeared that it might well force us to neglect many of the fascinating questions we had hoped to pursue. Some of these questions had a distinctly dramatic quality to them, and we were eager to enlarge on them. Now we were moving in a direction that seemed much more mundane—a detailed analysis of the structure of lessons and the 'contexts' of classroom conduct. However, we were of the view that we had to move in this direction, because that is where the data pointed. Hopefully, we would still have the opportunity to return to those of our original questions which had a more obvious 'labelling theory' source. For the moment, we consoled ourselves that we might be laying the foundations for the study of classroom deviance, even though we ourselves might fall short of our original research aspirations.

Before embarking on this analysis, one final element in our early thinking must be reported. We have seen that teachers make imputations of deviance in a variety of ways. In seeking to recognize and understand them ourselves, we were making explicit knowledge which must be possessed-and-taken-for-granted by the pupils who appeared to have no difficulty in recognizing what was being communicated in the teachers' verbal deviance-imputations. For both researchers and pupils to make sense of these statements, they must understand (1) the target of the communication, (2) the rule that is being invoked, (3) the action which is being held to constitute a breach of that rule, and (4) the conduct which constitutes conformity to the rule and which must be substituted for the deviant conduct. Only on very rare occasions were all four elements explicitly stated by the teacher (e.g. 'Jones, you know you're not supposed to be talking, so stop it and get on with your work'). More typically just one or two of the elements would be stated and the pupil was assumed by the teacher to be able to 'fill in', from his common-sense knowledge, the unstated elements.

Sometimes, the target alone was stated. This might be an individual ('Jones!'), a group ('Hey, you lot in the corner!'), or the class as a whole ('3B!'). On such occasions, the pupil(s) had to fill in the rule, the nature of the deviance, and the conformist behaviour being demanded. Occasionally, even the target could be unclear (e.g. 'You'). In this situation the pupil(s) can usually infer the target by checking on the person(s) the teacher is looking at. Sometimes, it is the deviant conduct which is indicated ('Stop talking'), where the members of the class have to fill in the target, the rule and the conformist conduct. Finally, it may be that the conformist conduct is explicitly stated ('Get on') and the pupils have to fill in both the identity of the target, the rule, and the deviant behaviour which is being proscribed.

On occasions all four elements are highly unclear, for example, 'I am waiting!' There is no explicit indication here of the target, the rule, the deviant conduct or the conformist conduct. This example draws our attention to a feature of all the deviance-imputations, namely that the filling in by the pupils can be accomplished only within the context of its utterance. Thus if we know that this teacher is giving a demonstration at the blackboard, that one pupil is talking, and that the teacher has paused for a moment, we—and the pupils—can appreciate that the teacher is saying, 'I am not going to proceed until Jones stops talking and until I am confident that the whole of the class is paying attention to what I am doing.' Similarly, even when one of the elements seems to be stated quite explicitly (e.g. 'Settle down'), both what is by implication deviant and what conduct is being enjoined can be understood only in reference to the context of its utterance. 'Settling down' can, according to the context, mean 'sit down and get ready for the lesson', or 'stop talking', or 'talk more quietly' or 'get on with your work' and so on. Since the teacher's talk in itself—'Settle down'—does not give its meaning to the pupils, then it must be from the talk-as-situated-within-a-context that the meaning is derived. Thus it is that the same teacher statement can have quite different meanings when the context in which it is uttered is different. At the same time different teacher statements can have the same meaning, that is they become functionally equivalent, provided that the context is the same. 'Shut up', 'Jones!', 'Get on' all have the same meaning in a context in which Jones is being asked to refrain from deviant talk and to carry out a prescribed task.

One of our common research techniques was to ask teachers to make a commentary on events or verbal statements that had occurred during the lesson. As we shall see in later chapters, the teachers provided us with extremely elaborate rationales for making the deviance-imputation in a particular verbal form, but they also reported that on some occasions it was merely a matter of chance or accident why one form rather than another form was used. A deviance-imputation could have been made in a different form, provided that it bore the same meaning. The teachers were aware that they had chosen a particular verbal form, but they could not account for their actual use of one form against an alternative and equivalent form. As we shall see later, they found it very much easier to explain why they had taken action at all.

(1) I. You then made a simple statement quite loudly. Can you remember why you said it at that time? Why just the word 'Jones'?

T. I don't know. I honestly can't say why. Jones is a talker, he's a gabbler in class and I suppose to try and be stern with him hoping that he won't talk as often and get on with his work.

I. The object was just to stop him?

T. Just to stop him yes, that was the only object.

(2) I. The next incident is when Nicholas wandered out to the front and was heading for your table then went over to a girl's desk. Again in question you said, 'Nicholas, what are you doing there?'

T. Yes, he was out of his original place, he had gone to get a pencil and then he made some comment to [two girls] I think. Instead of me saying, 'Get back to your own table!' I put this in the form of a question. For what reason I don't know.

I. This is what I would really like to get down to, you know, if it is a conscious thing at all. Why in fact this is said like this, 'Nicholas, what are you doing there?' rather than 'Stop interfering with Mary and get back to your seat'.

T. I think it's change, communication within the classroom situation. I don't think there is anything different about it. Rather than say 'Stop talking to Mary and get back to your own table!' I said 'What are you doing, Nicholas?'—that kind of thing. It would seem to be not consciously—maybe subconsciously—I don't know—obviously I don't know.

Whatever the form of the verbal deviance-imputation, the teachers assumed that the pupils could understand the meaning of the statement. Given this, in response to our interview requests for commentaries the teachers assumed that we also understood the meaning and that we understood that the pupils understood the meaning. Occasionally, however, the teacher's appeal to the pupil's understanding was made explicit.

(1) I. The first thing you said to somebody sitting at that table there, 'I think you will work better if you go somewhere else.'

T.   Well, he knew what I meant. It was just that they were
mucking about, distracting each other. They always sit
together and if they are apart there is a possibility they might
work.
I.   Then you said, 'There is not enough room for you all
there.'
T.   Yes, that is rather another way of saying, 'I don't want
you to go there.' Trying to convince them. They never work
well together.

(2) I.   'You will have to go to [headteacher] if you can't do any
better.'
T.   Well, I assume I am talking about effort rather than
standard, and I think they know this. I'm not quite sure
what I was talking about when I said 'better'.
I.   You could have been talking about their behaviour as
well?
T.   Well, this all ties in with it anyway and I think the way
you try to control their behaviour is by making them do
some work.

It is now evident that the rules are rarely stated in an explicit form
by the teachers, either in the deviance-imputations themselves or the
teacher's commentaries upon them. Normally the deviance-imputation appears in a highly condensed form; there is no direct reference
to the rule, but rather there is a direct reference to persons and to
acts. Sometimes there appears the fuller form: target-person +
deviant act + conformist act; more typically only one or two of these
elements appears. The other elements have to be filled in by the
pupils, and the teacher assumes that the pupils have no difficulty in
doing this. Indeed, when a pupil claims to be unable to fill in the
teacher will interpret the ignorance as feigned. Thus the following
teacher-pupil interaction occurs.

T.   Jones!
P.   What, sir?
T.   You know, laddie.

That the teachers assume that the pupils can fill in; that the pupils
can in fact fill in and find the teacher's statements meaningful; that
we as researchers were also able to fill in and find events meaningful—
none of these facts explains how the filling in is accomplished by
either pupils or by ourselves. Without an explication of this accomplishment it is impossible to explain how it is that the researchers and
the members (pupils) were able to recognize a deviance-imputation

and distinguish it from an instruction, since these can have an identical verbal form but have different meanings according to the context of their utterance. Just as teachers find it difficult to state the rules in a coherent, explicit formulation, so also they find it difficult to give such an account of contexts. Both the rules and the contexts in which they are embedded are background features of their utterances and actions, which at the explicit level deal with persons and acts. Our research task was clear. We needed to provide a detailed analysis of the structure of these contexts and the rules that are in operation in particular contexts. Further, it would be necessary to discover how members know that they are acting within a particular context and its associated rules.

This will provide the main topic for chapter 4. As a conclusion to this chapter, we wish to demonstrate how a study of the process of filling in requires such an analysis. It was shown earlier that deviance-imputations could take a wide variety of forms, most of which explicitly mention only one or two of the four elements that are involved in an imputation. For the sake of simplicity, we shall examine those cases where only one of the four elements is stated, and try to throw light on the 'interpretive rules'[4] that pupils and researchers must follow to recognize a deviance-imputation as such.

1. The explicit reference is to the deviant conduct that is taking place. Common examples in this category are descriptive statements and prohibitions. Sometimes the term used by the teacher is one that clearly expresses a negative evaluation of the pupil's conduct, e.g. 'misbehaving' which gives strong indications that the conduct is being disapproved. The interpretive work needed by the pupil is still lower when such terms appear in the form of a prohibition, e.g. 'stop misbehaving'. Although the statement 'stop misbehaving' could be nothing but a deviance-imputation, the pupil has to undertake much interpretive work to give the utterance its full meaning. He must (1) decide that he is the target of the utterance; (2) discover which of his own current acts constitutes a 'misbehaviour'; (3) discover the rule 'in play' against which his act(s) can be held to be deviant; (4) from that rule discover the conduct which the teacher requires him to display.

If the teacher does not use an evaluative term like 'misbehave' but instead uses a descriptive word like 'talk', then more basic interpretive work by the pupil is required. The statement 'stop talking' need not be a deviance-imputation at all, but may be an instruction to cease an activity which hitherto has constituted conformity to the rules in play. In the latter case 'stop talking' effectively changes the rules in play, suspending the rule that up to this point has permitted talking and introducing a rule that forbids talking from now on. Thus the pupil can interpret 'stop talking' as a deviance-imputation only when he understands that there is a rule against talk in play at the time. Typically the pupil is provided with additional clues that help in the determination of the status of the utterance. The most important of these is the teacher's tone of voice, for deviance-imputations are often spoken in a hard, sharp, disapproving manner which contrasts with the relatively neutral tone used for instructions. Given the tone of the utterance and the existence of the rule in play, then the pupil can fill in the rest of the deviance-imputation as outlined above.

2. The explicit reference is to the conformist behaviour that is being demanded. Common examples here would be 'get on', 'keep still' and 'listen to me'. These can be interpreted as deviance-imputations rather than as instructions only when the pupil can fill in (1) a rule in play which prescribes such conduct, and (2) some conduct of his own that is breaking this rule. If there is no such rule in play, then the pupil must interpret the statement as an instruction, not as a deviance-imputation.

3. The teacher's statement consists of a statement of a rule. An example would be, 'When I'm talking, nobody else talks.' If the rule is not in play at that time—that is, if the teacher was not talking, or no pupil was talking whilst the teacher was talking—then the pupil would interpret the statement as an anticipatory or explanatory exposition of a rule. On the other hand, if a pupil was talking simultaneously with the teacher, then the pupil would interpret the statement as a deviance-imputation. In this case the pupil has relatively little filling in to do, apart from the intended target, since a statement of a rule makes explicit mention of what constitutes deviance and conformity.

4. The teacher's statement consists of an indication of the target. There are three main forms of target: named individuals ('Jones!'), named collectivities ('3B!') and unspecified targets ('You!', 'You lot!'). When the target is not clearly specified, the pupil has to fill in that he is the target. This is typically achieved by looking at the teacher to check the direction of the teacher's gaze. This is not always an adequate check, for the teacher may be demonstrating that he 'has eyes in the back of his head' and may be intentionally not looking at the target. In this case, the pupil must define some aspect of his conduct as deviant in relation to the rules in play, and from that infer that the teacher is aware of it and is taking action against him. The statement of a target, whether specified or not, is not automatically a deviance-imputation. Again, the context of the utterance is of crucial significance. If, for instance, the teacher is marking the

work of individual pupils at his desk and is summoning pupils in rotation, then the statement 'Jones' will be interpreted by that pupil (and by pupil witnesses) in the light of the teacher's rule that he calls out names when he is ready for a pupil and that the pupil must, on hearing his name, approach the teacher's desk. Of course, it could be a deviance-imputation even in such a situation, and it is probably the tone of voice which would indicate this. Thus the teacher may repeat the name if the pupil does not come to the front on the first call. The second 'Jones' becomes a deviance-imputation, typically uttered in a louder and sharper tone, since it indicates that Jones is failing to follow the rule of turn-taking in play.

Even when the naming of a target comes 'out of the blue' it need not be a deviance-imputation. It is frequently a preliminary to initiating another kind of interaction between teacher and pupil. The following situation is a common occurrence in classrooms.

Teacher: Jones!
(Pause until pupil looks at teacher to show he has heard.)
Teacher: Will you take a message for me?

The meaning of such naming of a target can be interpreted by a pupil only in the light of subsequent events. It is the teacher's subsequent statement which will clarify why the pupil is being targeted. When no subsequent statement follows, then the pupil will interpret that a deviance-imputation is being made. The absence of the subsequent request or order, etc., is interpreted by the pupil as an indication that he must fill in appropriately for a deviance-imputation, namely, the rule in play, his conduct which is breaking that rule, and the conduct he must now display to conform to the rule.

It is clear that statements of targets are very high in ambiguity for pupils. When an unspecific target is made, most pupils will make attempts to check whether they or some other pupil(s) are being targeted, and frequently they will refrain from certain deviant conduct and display conformist conduct, even when it seems fairly clear that they are not being targeted for a deviance-imputation[5] or when subsequent events reveal that an instruction rather than a deviance-imputation is taking place. It is as if the high degree of ambiguity in the situation suggests to pupils that they would be wise to 'play on the safe side'.

The basic case has now been made. It is impossible to give an adequate account of deviance-imputations, as they are issued by teachers, understood by pupils and recognized by researchers, until we have a much clearer appreciation of rules-in-contexts. For us researchers, with our own earlier experience as former teachers and former pupils, this meant suspending our usage of this background feature of the common-sense knowledge of the classroom. What we, like the pupils and teachers in our study, had so successfully learned could no longer be taken for granted by us as researchers; instead we had to treat it as problematic and in need of explication.

4 *Rules in context*

The definition of problems and the first tentative steps towards solutions, as reported in chapter 3, were the product of our first few weeks' work in school A. Naturally, at the time the issues were not so sharply defined as they have been presented in chapter 3, which was written much later after we had made considerable empirical and theoretical advances. The orderly way in which they have been presented and the details that have been added constitute something of a distortion of our thinking at that time. Our next step, the study of 'contexts', lasted for many months. As the data will betray, the problem occupied us in school B as well as in school A. It is much more difficult, therefore, to present the history of our thinking, our data-collection and our theorizing in any detail. It would take too much space to report the concepts we developed, sometimes refining them and sometimes abandoning them. So we shall have to confine ourselves to giving a simple outline of our basic thinking, leaving the reader to imagine the problems we experienced in matching our conceptualizations against the data which we were collecting. Our general principle was to collect data in the form of observation notes and interview material; to conceptualize the data; and then to test out our conceptualizations against new data, which sometimes fitted in with our concepts and which sometimes forced us to make changes. This is clearly in line with the methodological approach of Glaser and Strauss (1967). Some of the interview material given in this chapter shows how our developing thinking shaped the questions we asked in interviews with teachers, and at times the questions get close to presenting the teachers with our current conceptualizations.

We showed in chapter 3 that for us and for pupils to grasp the meaning of certain teacher utterances, especially the ones which we as social scientists would refer to as deviance-imputations, presupposed an understanding that certain rules were in play in the context of utterance. It is the pupils' and researchers' understanding of these contexts and their rules which is drawn upon in deciding 'what is going on' and 'what the teacher means'. Thus we could interpret all the following statements

c*

'Stop talking.'
'Turn around.'
'Listen to me.'
'Look this way.'
'Stop that.'
'Have you finished?'
'You're daydreaming again.'
'Jones!'

as having the same meaning, namely 'pay attention to me', because they were all uttered in the same kind of context. Similarly, we were able to interpret the same statement, 'stop talking', as having different meanings because the context of its utterance was different, and this was true even when each example was coded as a deviance-imputation. To understand the different meanings of the same words required us to make explicit the differences in the contexts of utterance. Hopefully, such a procedure would enable us both to refine what we meant by context and to formulate the rules that were in play in different contexts. Let us illustrate this approach in the case of the very common utterance 'stop talking'.

1. Stop talking = no cheating. We knew it meant this from our knowledge that the context was a test or examination.
2. Stop talking = don't interrupt. We understood this from our knowledge that the context was one in which all the pupils were meant to be listening to another person, usually the teacher.
3. Stop talking = get on with your work. We knew this from our knowledge that the context was one in which the pupils were meant to be reading from their books.
4. Stop talking = don't be impolite. We knew this from our knowledge that the teacher was talking and that pupils were supposed to listen to the teacher's talk and not to talk with another pupil at this time.
5. Stop talking = don't disturb other pupils. We knew this from our knowledge that in this context pupils were allowed to talk to one another but not in a form which constituted preventing another pupil from getting on with his own work.

On the basis of such thinking, and given our interest in making a phenomenological analysis, we developed a set of questions to define our problem. Precisely what are these contexts which we invoke? How are they to be described and analysed by us? How are they described by members in their everyday lives? If they are merely part of the members' common-sense knowledge, and so taken for granted, how could they describe them to us? How are these contexts brought into existence? How are they changed, i.e. how does one context come to replace another? What rules are in play in a given context? How do members know that a given context (and its rules) is in operation at a particular time?

Our own first descriptions of contexts consisted of descriptions of the 'tasks' or activities being pursued by members at a given time. In the 'stop talking' illustration above, we described the context in which the meaning is 'don't cheat' by reporting that 'the members were doing a test'. Similarly, the members would say, 'we were having a test'. Sometimes in response to our asking teachers for commentaries on their utterances after a lesson, the teachers would themselves have forgotten the context of what they had said, and would ask us, 'What were we doing at the time?' Thus the context is most easily described in terms of the tasks being undertaken by members. In these terms, we could conceive of the school day as a sequence of tasks being undertaken by members at different times and in different places. With respect to the classroom, we could conceive of a lesson as a sequence of tasks. In saying this we were conceptualizing a lesson as a structured series of tasks over time, so we abandoned the loose concept context with its very broad connotations and substituted the term 'task-phase', which more accurately reflected the restricted sense in which we were using the concept context. We soon dropped the term 'task' and spoke in terms of the 'phases' of the lesson. Our observations from this point were directed towards detecting these phases, the ways in which they followed one another, and the ways in which members knew that a phase had changed. These three questions were being asked simultaneously, and the analysis being presented here was collated slowly and somewhat unsystematically. At a very early stage in our observations we detected what seemed to be the 'obvious' task-phases, such as 'tests', 'demonstrations by the teacher' and 'group work'. We then tried to delineate other task-phases and simultaneously we made careful observations of what teachers said and did at transition points between what we conceptualized as one task-phase and its successor. On the basis of these observations we developed the concept of the 'switch-signal', and we shall illustrate this concept before giving a systematic account of the sequence of task-phases and switch-signals that occur in typical lessons.

A switch-signal refers to the action taken by the teacher, typically in the form of a verbal statement, which puts an end to one task (or phase) and initiates a subsequent task. As the task being pursued by teacher and pupils changes, so also are the rules governing those tasks changed. This means that the switch-signal switches off the rules related to the first task and switches on the rules relating to the subsequent task. Tasks and rules are changed simultaneously and by the same procedure. The members themselves talk about the tasks or activities but not about the rules, which constitute a background taken-for-granted feature of the tasks.

Typically, a switch-signal has three components: an attention-drawer, a linking instruction and a task indicator. For the most part, the attention-drawer consists of the word 'Right' or one of its variant forms such as 'Right now, 3B'. The attention-drawer brings into play the 'pay attention' rule, which requires that the pupils look at and listen to the teacher. All activity which conflicts with this must cease, which in effect means that the pupil must stop the activities connected with the previous on-going task. The attention-drawer has a 'wait-and-see' quality, indicating to the pupils that the teacher is about to make an announcement. If the 'pay attention' rule is already in play, for example if the teacher has been giving a demonstration or explanation to the whole class from the front, then the switch-signal component involves no change in pupil activity but warns the pupils that 'something is going to happen'.

Whilst there is usually a brief pause after the attention-drawer during which the teacher checks that the pupils are conforming to the pay attention rule, the linking instruction follows almost immediately. It may consist of a statement which ends the previous task (e.g. 'Put your pens down'), or which prepares the pupils for the new task (e.g. 'Go back to your benches'), or both (e.g. 'Put your maths books away and get out your exercise books'). There are considerable variations in the explicitness with which one task is terminated and another task initiated.

With the task indicator, the teacher specifies the precise nature of the new task, thus resolving the wait-and-see aspect of the attention-drawer and linking instruction. Examples are 'Do exercises one to ten' or 'Copy the notes off the blackboard'. In this way the next task or phase is set in motion, according to the rules which the pupils have learned are associated with that task.

We shall see that many switch-signals appear in a very brief condensed form. The illustrations given here are in the 'full' form, with an explicit verbal reference to each of the three components.

1. 1st task-phase: question-and-answer session.
   2nd task-phase: written work.
   'Right now (attention-drawer), get out your exercise books (linking instruction) and do the first three problems (task indicator).'
2. 1st task-phase: demonstration by science teacher, with pupils round the teacher's desk.

2nd task-phase: pupils conduct the experiment themselves.
'Right (attention-drawer), go back to your benches (linking instruction) and begin the experiment (task indicator).'
3. 1st task-phase: teacher explanation to whole class.
2nd task-phase: question-and-answer session.
'OK now (attention-drawer), let's see how much you've understood (linking instruction). Who can tell me. . . ? (task indicator).'

There are five principal phases which are common to virtually all lessons. These phases are:

1. The 'entry' phase.
2. The 'settling down' or preparation phase.
3. The 'lesson proper' phase.
4. The 'clearing up' phase.
5. The 'exit' phase.

What we have called the lesson proper is regarded by teachers as the main activity of a lesson. Typically it occupies most of the time, being sandwiched between the first two phases ('getting started') and the last two phases ('finishing up'), though with some teachers these initiatory and terminatory phases were sometimes fairly lengthy.

The first two phases tend to fuse into one another and so will be analysed together. Our early observation notes suggest how we developed the concepts of phases and switch-signals and also reflect the great variations between teachers in the rules that govern these phases.

(1) As the class comes in there is much noise. 'Quiet please,' says teacher. The talking continues. 'I want everybody quiet,' he says.

(2) When I enter the class the teacher points out to me, 'They're only reading.' I reply, 'That's OK.' 'Right now, shall we settle down and read?' says teacher to the class as a whole, who up to now have been sitting and standing, talking amongst themselves, whilst the teacher has been talking to one or two pupils at her table. As a result of this remark the pupils stop talking and begin reading.

(3) I enter as the class is seated and the teacher is saying to the class, 'I want this finishing today.' The class talks as the books are being given out. As the teacher gets things together she says, 'Shut up' to the class. No result. 'Shut up,' she repeats, though still in a quiet voice. Class quietens and teacher goes on, 'Now just be quiet now,' and the class is quiet and the books given out. 'Turn round, Barker,' teacher says to a pupil who persists in his talking. When all the books have been given out—time finally run out for the pupils?—pupils get into work.

(4) Books given out. Chatter. One boy moves from his seat and is

67

told to sit down. 'Right 2D, quiet now,' says teacher. Teacher then slams door shut. 'Right 2D, sit quietly, sit down.'

(5) The lesson begins with the giving out of rulers, tools, etc., the teacher says, 'Right, pay attention now.' The noise continues. 'Dodgson, how many more times do I have to tell you?' he says. 'None, sir.' 'Right, sit down then.' The boys sit down and it is quiet and the books are given out. Teacher then says, 'Turn to page 42.'

(6) Talking in class as pencils and other equipment given out. Laughing. Movement. 'Right, let's have you quiet,' says teacher after a few minutes. 'Mary, have you finished?' Teacher notices that some pupils are missing and one boy calls out, 'They're wagging it.' 'Right, I'm not waiting all day for you lot,' says teacher. They quieten down and teacher talks to class as a whole, sitting on the table at the front of the class.

The entry phase—which is somewhat neglected in the above notes—is concerned with the task of ensuring that the teacher and pupils are assembled in the physical boundaries of the classroom. Accordingly, there exists a set of rules for accomplishing this task of entering the room. Because the precise rules of entry are at the teacher's discretion, there is considerable variation between teachers in the nature of these rules and the emphasis placed upon conformity to them. Typically there are three rules in play in this phase: (1) Pupils must line up outside the room in the corridor. (2) Pupils must not enter the room until the teacher gives them permission to do so. (3) Pupils must enter the room 'in an orderly fashion', i.e. without running or pushing.

(1) I.   They were lining up outside, then you said, 'Come in', and then you had to repeat it, 'I said come in', because they didn't come. Is that a kind of school rule that the pupils don't come in unless you give instructions?

T.   Well, I don't know whether it's a general school rule but it applies to me because often I'm not quite ready and perhaps I'm speaking to my own form, but it may not be the same with every teacher, but I do it. Often I'm not quite ready for them to come in or I'm speaking to someone and I don't want an interruption. But normally I call, 'Come in' regularly and they don't hear me and I have got to say again, 'Come in', you see. Often they don't hear me but I do say it and have to repeat it.

I.   Do you expect all forms to wait?

T.   Yes.

(2) I.   Sorry, can I just take you to a bit earlier, are there any rules of procedure for actually entering the room?

T. I require them to enter quietly. On occasions they barge in in a disorderly rabble and in that case I sometimes send them out and ask them to return in a proper manner. They go to their places—depending on the class. If it's a junior class, they know to sit down and look towards the board.

Many teachers did not apply these rules in the case of senior pupils, or small classes, or in other special situations. The pupils soon learn what each teacher expects of them in the entry phase.

(1) I. Yes, well, they all come along, this one girl came along, she waited outside the door. . . .
T. Christine, that's right.
I. And you said, 'Right, come on, Christine, come in.'
I mean is this a general sort of thing? Is it a rule that they have to wait?
T. Generally speaking yes. But I don't enforce it with 3E because they are such a small group and it doesn't matter to me whether they wait or not, and in fact it's rather awkward waiting outside my door because Mr —— and I are right next door to each other and if he gets a form lining up, girls on one side, boys another, well one of us is a space short for one line, so with small forms I tend to let them in as soon as they come.
I. It was as if Christine expected to wait—
T. That's right.
I. Now, with other forms then, is this with other forms you take—you take the fifth form and you take some fourth years—
T. Yes, I don't make them line up ever.
I. Is it the same with all forms you take?
T. No, any others, especially the large forms, they do need, you know 2A and 3A, do need to be made to come in in an orderly fashion.
I. So they have to line up outside?
T. Yes, because they tend to push you see, and crowd through the doorway and there are so many of them that you have to have some sort of rule.

(2) I. I'm sorry, shall we presume that you are sitting there or you're standing there perhaps and the pupils come in. Do you expect them to be, do you tolerate in fact a certain amount of behaviour at that time or perhaps misbehaviour, noise and disturbance, this sort of thing? Do you think it is a common characteristic of the start of the lesson?

T.   Yes, I think it is to some extent, unfortunately. I don't
agree that it is a good thing. Well, I think it is a very bad
thing but I think there often is—the more you are prepared
then the less you get this, if you like, this upset at the
beginning because the quicker you get them started. On the
other hand, I don't like them to come in in a too regimented
fashion because for me it doesn't create the right
atmosphere at the beginning of the lesson to have to come in
and stand there like zombies. It rather takes me back to
sitting with your hands on your head, that sort of attitude
and I think it differs with the age of the child. I mean, I don't
like the fourth years, particularly a fourth year group, I don't
want them to line up outside because this would create again,
for me anyway, the wrong atmosphere, the wrong
atmosphere between us.

I.   So you make a distinction on that? On lining up outside
you make a distinction on a sort of age basis?

T.   Yes, I think I would, I think at that point there ought
to be enough self-discipline. I know it isn't always there but I
suppose it's a form of trust and respect between teacher and
pupil because they're older. When all's said and done, they
ought to be able to come into a classroom. There would be
at least a semi-relaxed atmosphere.

(3) I.   In all these things, the rules you have at the start of the
lesson, does the age of the pupil have any influence on this,
whether it's a first form or fourth?

T.   Yes, with fourth years if I were not here, say this form
now, 4A, 4B that I take for commercial. They know I was
doing typing with them and not shorthand, like I am at the
moment. So now I walk in—if I were delayed anywhere I
would not expect them to be sitting there waiting for me to
come and tell them what to do. I would have expected them
to sit down and get a piece of paper in their typewriter and
be doing some straightforward copying. When I was at my
previous school, girls used to be sitting in desks and
immediately I walked in they used to stand up. Now this is
all right for perhaps first, second, even third years, but, by
the time they get to the fourth and fifth year I expect them
to be working when I arrive and not sitting waiting for me to
arrive in the classroom. More often than not I'm there
already anyway as they come to me and I'm not going to
them. .... Now, of course, the lower down the school you
are they don't know what you're going to start doing, but I

wouldn't expect them to be romping all over the classroom and of course 2C are not, but 3D often are because they just don't know how to behave.

For most teachers, the entry phase ends as the pupils enter the room and move towards their seats. In rare cases, there is an additional rule that pupils must proceed to their seats and wait for the teacher to tell them to sit down.

I.   When they came in you said, as they were standing about in the class, 'Good morning, 3C', and they said, 'Morning, Miss', and they all sat down. Would they not have sat down if you did not say, 'Good morning, 3C'?
T.   They are supposed to stand until I have said, 'Good morning' to them and if they forget they soon get to realize they have got to stand up. It is one of my rules.

In these cases it is the teacher's statement of 'Good morning' or 'Sit down' which serves as a switch-signal to end the entry phase and usher in the preparation phase.

During this settling down or preparation phase, the following rules are typically in play: (1) Pupils must go to their seats and sit down or remain in close proximity to the seat. (2) Pupils are free to talk to other pupils on any matter, but they must not shout or scream. (3) Pupils must co-operate in the distribution of equipment, if this takes place. There are, of course, considerable variations in the noise-level of the talk permitted under the second rule.

(1) I.   When the kids come into the lesson, do you expect them to come in and sit down straight away and stop talking?
T.   I don't expect them to. As a teacher I ought to, I could make it so. I could keep sending them out until they came in—the only thing is, I remember at school it was a good thing because it meant wasting a bit more time of the lesson to keep charging out and coming back in again. I don't think they get bored with doing it. The thing is I don't insist on it because most of them come in and they make a noise and then eventually I say 'Quiet' and then I talk. These lot are the worst I have in that respect because this morning they just did not keep quiet any of the time. I could not really explain anything or do anything.

(2) I.   Once they came in there were various acts going on—talking, shouting out, and moving about, and even some whistling; now, during this warm-up period, you might say, you are prepared to accept this sort of—

T.   Oh yes, I don't expect them to be quiet until I tell them
to, it's just too much to expect with 3E that they will come
in and say, 'What are we doing? Can we get anything ready?'
which an A form might do, you know, 2A might do that
but not 3E.

(3) I.   Right, now we have noticed, or we think we have noticed
anyway, that there seems to be a very indeterminate period
between pupils entering the room and the lesson starting,
in a lot of cases. How do you start your lessons?
T.   Well, if the equipment isn't out that's the first job. And
then I'll say, 'The board boy, will you please give out the
boards', which he does and while that is on I ask the
T-square boy to get those out. I then ask all the other
monitors to give the equipment out. Now this equipment
consists of clips, pencils, rulers, rubbers and set squares
and then if new paper is required I ask a boy, he knows who
he is, to get out the new sheet of paper for each boy and give
it out. If the work is a continued lesson the same boy will
come to me, into my cupboard, and find the folder that has
their incomplete work and he'll distribute it.

The preparation phase is terminated and the lesson proper phase
is initiated by a verbal switch-signal. Although occasionally non-
verbal switch-signals are used, such as banging on the desk with a
blackboard duster or standing silently at the front of the class with
arms akimbo, the verbal form is much more common. Sometimes
the switch-signal is a statement of the teacher's readiness to begin
the lesson, i.e. the lesson proper.

'Right, I'm ready, 3B.'
'Right, are we ready to begin?'

If equipment has been distributed, the switch-signal can take the
form of a check that this task of the preparation phase has been
completed.

'Right, have we got everything out now?'
'Right, have we all got what we're supposed to have?'

Alternatively, the teacher may indicate that silence is required.

'Right, quiet now.'
'Right, let's have quiet now.'
'Right, pay attention now.'

The switch-signal terminates the preparation phase, and its rules
are no longer in play. Instead, the pay attention rule is brought into

play: pupils must stop talking, listen to and look at the teacher. On most occasions, it is also understood that pupils will be sitting at their desks unless other spatial locations are required for pupils.

(1) I.   When they come into lessons, at the start of the lesson, do you expect them to come in and sit down and be quiet?

T.   Oh, no, I don't expect 3E to be quiet. I know whether they are making more noise than I want or not. I'm going to have to say something but if they haven't been making such a terrific row as they were this morning I would simply say, 'Right are we ready to begin?' or something like that.

(2) I.   In this period, when you were writing on the blackboard and giving the books out, are you prepared to tolerate the chatter and noise?

T.   Yes, provided it keeps at a decent level and provided it doesn't interrupt me at the blackboard because I'm very susceptible to noise. I cannot do with a great amount and they know that. I don't mind them talking quietly because after all I'm not giving them anything to do at that moment only get ready, so I feel I can't impose on them a great restriction. But when I'm ready, that is when I start to put my foot down.

I.   When you say that you're ready, do you mean by that that at the same time it's time to start work?

T.   Yes, I'm ready as soon as I've completed the blackboard. I'm ready for them to start and they know they have not to talk.

I.   Later on you said, 'Right, no talking now.'

T.   Exactly, that's the reason.

(3) T.   I don't expect everybody to sit there absolutely dead silent and rigid while everybody's giving books and pencils out. This little bit of natter I don't mind, because it's sort of— it gets a lot of it over there and then at the beginning of the lesson. Then I'll say, 'Right, have we all got what we're supposed to have?' and then we're off. This is the signal of 'Let's cut the cackle' and we're off.

I.   Soon after that you said, 'Right, can I have everybody's attention', and there was hush. So I mean generally speaking, what do you mean by attention?

T.   I want everybody listening because I don't want to have to repeat things unnecessarily. It is necessary with 3E to a certain extent, but I object to doing it if they don't know because they haven't listened, so I always give them this warning and expect them to listen to the instructions about what they are doing.

I.   Do you expect them to be silent at this point?

T.   Yes, when they are listening to me.

From this point any pupil talk is defined as deviant, since it breaches the pay attention rule which is now in play. Often the pupil talk does not cease immediately or pupils do not look at the teacher, so the teacher reiterates the switch-signal, which now has the force of a deviance-imputation, or gives a specific instruction about paying attention, or makes a deviance-imputation against a target pupil.

(1) I.   Can I ask you a more specific thing about the beginning of your lesson with 3E? You said, 'Right, the lesson has started.'

T.   Because they were talking. Sheila was nattering and Andrew never shut his mouth for the last three months. I don't know what's wrong with him. They all just carried on talking. Sheila was talking with Andrew, and I was trying— well, I was just waiting to tell them what we were going to do. Actually, I explained that and just let them talk and see if they would all talk for the whole lesson.

(2) I.   'This is the third time I've said "right". You know that when I say "right" you are to be quiet.'

T.   I'm ready to start. That's an understood thing, at least I hope it is. It's something I know I say, I say it all the time. When they come in and they have got their books out, I say, 'Right 3D' or 'Right 1N', and usually they are quiet because they know I want to start the lesson and they quieten down.

I.   Yes, at that point I asked the boy I was sitting next to at the back what he thought you meant by that and he said, 'Pay attention' and sat up.

(3) I.   Second thing I've got down here, 'Bobby, come on, wakey wakey.'

T.   Yes, obviously sat there not ready to start the lesson, occupied by looking at the desk and looking away. I didn't wish to begin until he was obviously paying attention.

Occasionally, it is the pupils themselves who initiate the lesson proper.

T.   They usually ask me. They come in and tell me what they feel like doing very often. 'Can we write today, Miss?' And they want to do some writing and if I can see that they are in that mood then I abandon whatever I have prepared, because you have to catch them in the right mood. . . .

Once the pupils are paying attention, the lesson proper can commence. For the most part it is more adequate to conceive of the lesson proper not as a single phase but as a sequence of subphases, each of which is concerned with one dominant task. There is considerable variation between lessons in the number of subphases in the lesson proper as well as in the order in which they occur. We shall try to simplify this complexity by referring to three types of subphase.

The first type of subphase is one in which the teacher is highly active, usually in the form of talking, whilst the pupils are relatively passive. He is working examples on the blackboard; giving a verbal exposition or explanation; demonstrating at the front (especially in science, handicraft and domestic science); reading to the class. In all these subphases, the dominant rule in play is the pay attention rule, i.e. pupils must sit quietly, watching and listening to the teacher. Any pupil activity which conflicts with conformity to this rule is defined as deviant, especially talk, movement and auto-involvements.[1]

(1) I.   During the lesson—like, you can use this lesson's example
if you like—where you identified two kinds of phases, this
blackboard demonstration and then copying from the
blackboard. Let's call it A, the blackboard demonstration.
Now during that, what sort of things do you expect the pupils
to do whilst you're giving the blackboard demonstration?
T.   Well, I expect them obviously to be observing what I'm
doing, the writing I'm doing on the board and also I would
hope—I don't say this is always the case because one can't
be writing on the board and watching the class at the same
time—but I would hope that they would be following
everything I was doing on the board, and take, for example,
the rough working I did on the side of the board to support
the general run of the solution, I would hope they would be
following those details. Now I don't say they always do.
I don't say everyone does that, but I would hope that.
I.   Can I look from the other side now? What shouldn't
they do whilst you're demonstrating at the blackboard?
T.   Well, for example, talking to their next-door neighbour,
that's an obvious one, or if I caught anyone drawing the
image of a football or something like that when he's supposed
to be watching. To my mind I can't say that they can be
taking sufficient interest if they're fiddling about with other
things that are outside the classroom, thoughts which take
them outside the classroom. I think whilst a lesson is on,
concentration is necessary. . . . I do think that anything that
is detrimental to concentrating should be stopped.

(2) I.   Next one. 'Aitken, will you stop playing with your
money.'
T.   Well, again it's inattention if he is playing with his
money. He's not listening to me.

(3) I.   Whilst you're talking about this book, at the front
talking to them about it, explaining what you're going to do,
how do you expect them to behave and what do you expect
them not to do?
T.   I expect them to be quiet generally. I don't mind if they
are slouched on the desk, but I don't want them to put their
feet up on the desk. Generally I expect them to be quiet.
By the way, I don't stand in front and talk to them. I usually
walk around reading the book so that I'm sometimes in the
centre of the room so that my voice can reverberate around—
and that's generally what I do.
I.   What about movement while you're wandering about?
T.   I expect the kids not to walk about in the class, but
moving about on the chair, I don't mind that so much. When
we go in Mrs ——'s room which is the commercial room
where they have a typist's chair, they are on a swivel top and
these screech at times. Now this tends to annoy me and in
that particular room I do tend to get annoyed. I stop reading
and shout at the kid concerned. . . . But I don't want them to
move around generally when I'm reading.
I.   When you get on to the next bit then, when you're actually
reading the story, what do you expect them not to do?
T.   It's the same thing really. . . . All I expect of them is for
them to listen and if they're slumped on the desk then I don't
mind that so much, I don't mind not sitting up straight. But I
don't want them to move about. If they don't like it, very
often I say, 'Well, if you're so bored then just go to sleep
and let others listen to this'—kind of thing—'but for
goodness' sake shut up or stop moving', or whatever they're
doing.

A second important rule in play in this first type of subphase is
that pupils must not interrupt the teacher with superfluous or
irrelevant comments or questions. The teacher should not be
interrupted 'in mid-flight', unless the situation is urgent, for instance
when the pupil cannot see the teacher's demonstration. Otherwise,
comments and questions should be left until the end of the teacher's
exposition, explanation or demonstration.

(1) I.   You said after a while, 'Will you let me get my words out!'

T. Yes, that's a typical 3E trick. You get half of what you are saying out and the others start asking questions or tell you they can't do it, or 'I haven't got a pen', you know, in the middle of explaining what to do and then hearing half the story, 'We can't do that because . . .', and they will give you a list of reasons and you have not finished telling them how you are going to do it or why or anything and it is very irritating sometimes, but it is a thing I accept. They can't help it. They can't wait, I think that's the thing, they are impatient.

(2) I. 'A' is really when you're talking, explaining something to the class. . . .
T. Well, they know that when I'm speaking to the class that nobody is supposed to interrupt. I don't always get this but they know about it. They will shout out when they want to know something even though I'm in the middle of a lesson. I ask them to wait until the end and then ask when I've gone through but I do get interrupted. I have known cases of boys walking out to sharpen their pencils when I have been teaching at the blackboard. Now, whether these boys are being forgetful, arrogant, or disinterested in what I was telling them I don't know. I put it down to something missing in their upbringing perhaps, but only on odd occasions does this happen. They are expected to stop their work but it is such a temptation to carry on to them and I have many times, I have a job in getting them to stop. Some will stop and still hold their pencil and when my back is turned they'll be drawing again, especially if they are a little behind. So I do expect full attention, although I don't always get it. I've had boys call out to me while I have been teaching on something entirely different from what I've been talking about and one, of course, is a little shocked over this and wonders why, why should this youth not be listening to me?

(3) I. 'We don't need any comments, thank you.'
T. It's just that every time you're trying to explain something you say the first half of the sentence and immediately they are sort of shouting things out. I think this is more to do with their minds than in the discipline thing. I don't think it's intentional misbehaviour. It's immaturity that they can't sit and listen and concentrate, they have to shout something out as a reaction. I just have to keep saying, 'Wait until I have finished speaking.' You get a few there who were saying, 'Be quiet', because I had started and

they wanted to listen even if they weren't going to do it.

I. You said, 'Will you please let me finish', at the same time.

T. There was someone who was going to ask me about what they were going to do. I think that they are so sort of self-centred they don't see it as a sort of thing you are directing at people and they should wait and ask afterwards. They think of it immediately and shout it out.

In the second type of subphase in the lesson proper, it is the pupils who take the active role and the teacher no longer plays such a dominant verbal part in activities. Typically, pupils are assigned to a piece of work which does not involve directing their attention to the teacher. Common examples are: writing an essay; solving written problems; copying from the blackboard; reading on one's own; conducting experiments; doing practical work; group work; project work. The dominant rule in play in this type of subphase is that the pupils should involve themselves in the set task and carry it out according to the teacher's instructions. In contrast to the first type of subphase, pupil-pupil talk is permitted, provided that (1) there is no loud talking or shouting, (2) the talk is work-related or relevant to the task, except for the occasional irrelevant talk. Further, pupils must not interfere with, distract, or disturb other pupils in their work by excessive irrelevant talk or by any other kind of action. On some occasions movement is permitted (e.g. project work), when a certain amount of movement between groups or the collection of needed equipment is necessary to the accomplishment of the task. In other situations (e.g. reading alone) movement is forbidden.

(1) I. And if they're working in groups you're prepared to accept that then there is a bit of nattering?

T. Oh yes. The thing is I say to them, 'Look, I'm not having this nattering. If it's constructive natter I don't care. If it's got something to do with the lesson, yes, but I'm not having nattering about United's chances on Saturday.'

(2) I. What would you permit that you wouldn't permit when you were talking?

T. In behaviour? I don't expect them to speak too loudly. I've told them I don't mind them whispering amongst themselves.

(3) I. When you change from working at the blackboard to where they're working by themselves, what do you permit then that you wouldn't permit when you were talking at the blackboard?

T. Well, if they're working, I don't mind them sort of saying,

'What are nine times seven?' and the answer will come back
from somebody else because they pick one another's brains,
you know. It doesn't matter if they are nattering about
something else and it doesn't go on for long and they don't
raise their voices to disturb anybody else, so this is the thing.
I don't mind when a child's finished or in the middle of
something, something might cross his mind about—you know,
house matches or something that's going on—it might
suddenly dawn on him, something that he should have done
or wants somebody else to know. I don't mind as long as they
get the work done, this is the thing. I don't want a noise
that disturbs other people, you know, this is the thing,
I don't mind quite frankly. Same with 3D and I separated
them into halves, one that would work and one that
wouldn't work, and I said to them one day, 'Look, you can
please yourselves whether you work or not, but I will not
have you disturbing the rest of the class. It doesn't matter
to me if you don't want to learn anything, this is up to you,
but you will not disturb others.' Now this is my sort of policy,
that you like to think you're teaching everybody and you'd
like to think that you give a perfect lesson where everybody
will learn something, but you don't. You can't hope for this,
not in this type of school. Not in the lower streams.
Really, as long as a child is not worrying other children,
not stopping him from working, then quite frankly I don't
care what he does.

I.   So you permit a fairly wide range of things that they
could do, provided you were sure they were working?

T.   Yes, as long as they stay where they are. I'm not having
them wandering around the room because they are disturbing
other people once they start to wander, because other kids
get up and wonder where they're going to for a start or what
they're doing. But if they stay where they are or lean over to
somebody's desk or even get up to the desk next door well
that is all right, but I don't want them wandering all the
way across the room.

(4) I.   When they're copying from the board, what would you
permit that you wouldn't permit when you were
demonstrating at the blackboard?

T.   When they're copying from the board, or even when
they're doing any written work, quite frankly I think that
anything that is outside the actual lesson shouldn't come into
discussion. For example, I don't think it's right and I don't

think it is contagious [*sic*] to good work for a couple of lads
to be discussing last Saturday's Cup Final when they ought
to be doing their work. These are my feelings.
I.   That's one thing you wouldn't permit?
T.   No, not if I came across it.
I.   What about talking?
T.   Well, here again, you see, talking. If I were satisfied
that—I'm speaking generally now, I'm not just talking about
blackboard copying, I'm talking about that they're on to some
written work—now if I were satisfied that two children
were sat together and they were discussing a question—
right?—I don't consider that talking, not talking to grumble
about. Obviously it is talking, but I wouldn't be averse to
two children discussing a question. But not to the point of
one leaning on the other and talking about—conversation
both ways—I'm not altogether in agreement with letting
that sort of thing go past—Johnny telling Jimmy *all* the time
how to do a question, I mean this can amount to somebody
copying. Really, I'm speaking about exchange of opinions
on a particular problem and I think this would be fair
provided it's done in a sensible way and not developing in a
rowdy state of affairs, which really speaking—the type of
thing I'm talking about where children are engaged in this
type of conversation, they are usually moderate, they usually
keep it down to a moderate level.
I.   What about movement?
T.   Well, here with movement, I'm not in favour of—I don't
like a lot of—. Well, for the type of work I'm doing it would
be a different matter. Obviously if you do some practical
work you've got to have movement then. But I think where
it's academic and book learning, then I think you should
have a reasonable amount of steadiness in the room, because
movement, when all's said and done, it doesn't help towards
keeping your room in an—keeping the volume of noise down,
anyway, and it doesn't take long for miscreants to start
making wrong use of the volume of noise in the room.
But if you're doing work of a practical nature, then of course
you've got to make a reappraisal of the situation.

(5) I.   When we were talking about the first stage, you
mentioned noise, something you didn't like them to be talking
to each other. What's the difference in stage two when they're
working by themselves?
T.   When they're working by themselves, well, obviously,

if people are working in groups they'll work and require
to discuss with each other what they are doing. To help each
other they have to use their voices to communicate one to
another. . . . Sometimes two groups will call over to each
other and they will be discussing together, which I wouldn't
mind for a short time. . . .
I.   What about movement?
T.   There will be movement in this stage. They will be going
about, they will want more material, they'll be wanting the
sinks to get more water, they'll probably be moving to get
more light—lots and lots of reasons why they should move
about, so there'll quite legitimately be movement. What
there won't be, of course, if they are to get on purposefully,
would be running around. Movement will be at a reasonable
speed and obviously with the aim of helping them to get on
with what I want them to do. If this movement consists of
chasing somebody, then no.

The third type of subphase in the lesson proper is a mixture of the
other two types. Both teacher and pupils are actively involved in the
task. Examples are question-and-answer sessions, discussions and
tests (where the teacher poses the questions orally). Question-and-
answer sessions are more common than discussions, but the two have
similar rules. The main rules of question-and-answer sessions are:

1. On the whole it is the teacher who asks the questions and the
pupils who contribute the answers.
2. Pupils should be willing to volunteer answers.
3. That a pupil is willing to volunteer an answer should normally
be signalled to the teacher by hand-raising.
4. Pupils must answer when called upon to do so, and normally
should not 'shout out' an answer on their own initiative.
OR
5. If the teacher does allow the pupils to take the initiative, several
pupils must not call out their answer simultaneously.
6. Pupils must not offer an answer whilst another pupil is stating
his answer.
7. Pupils must not talk to one another whilst (1) the teacher is
talking, or (2) a pupil is answering the question.

(1) I.   Then when you move on to the next stage, the discussion?
T.   This is different, I find this different. Very rarely do you
get just one child who has a comment to make by himself.
You generally get three or four wanting to have a comment
after what I've said, because sometimes I can be provocative

to the children generally and say, 'No wonder!' and I would
say to them that, 'You're in 4D and you're so thick you don't
know what day it is!' and this stimulates some of them when
I've given my talk on the revision on the book itself, and,
'None of you are articulate enough to get up!' Well, then you
get, 'We are! we are!' you see, and sometimes you get a
response and you get four or five talking at once. Now I
would try then to calm them down. Now I allow some laxity
in this kind of thing, because I say, 'OK, well, will you be
quiet while he says this?' and if they're eager to get up I
accept a more tolerant attitude. I take a more tolerant view
of the kid when he's trying to say something and someone
else is speaking, than I would do if I was reading or talking
myself, because I want all of them to say something and I
don't want to shout and frighten him off from what he's
saying. I'll say, 'Hold on to what you've got until he's
finished', and that kind of thing. I allow them to talk to
themselves if I feel that it's relevant to what we are discussing.
I.   How strongly do you feel about somebody who just
didn't answer, didn't attempt anything?
T.   Well, again I'm very tolerant. Very rarely do I get a good
discussion going. . . . I don't get angry with them all for not
making a contribution, but I do tend to get annoyed with
kids 1 know have a contribution to make but yet don't even
bother putting it forward . . . and maybe when we're writing
the essay, they may pop up and say, 'Well, what about such
a thing?' and I'll say, 'You ought to have said that in the
discussion stage!'

(2) T.   I come down like a ton of bricks if they call out when
I'm asking for answers, because it doesn't give the child a
chance who I wish to answer. So they have got the habit
now that they must not call out in my class; they must put
their hands up.
I.   Is this always true?
T.   I think most teachers ask for hands rather than calling
out for that reason, if I ask a child and am not sure that the
child knows the answer, I want to know, and if they call out
it spoils it. So it is a general principle that they must put up
their hands and not call out.

(3) T.   I like to bring in as much participation in the class as
possible, because I think this does help. I think it keeps them
lively. They're thinking and to my mind you've got a better
chance of getting interest and retaining interest if you get

them talking—in an orderly fashion of course. As you may
have observed, at times they get a little anxious to give you
an answer and they blurt out an answer instead of putting
up their hand, for which I check them, as on occasions this
morning.

In tests the principal rule is that each pupil must work independently.
This means that pupils are not allowed to talk at all; they must not
look at or copy from the work of a neighbouring pupil.

'We'll have a test to see how much hasn't sunk in,' says the
teacher, as the kids settle into their places.
'What does it mean when I say we're going to have a test?
Does it mean turning to your neighbour?'
'No, Miss,' answer the class.
'Does it mean copying from your partner?'
'No, Miss.'

(Observation notes)

T.   I don't object to boys looking over the work of their
colleagues. I don't want them to wander from one corner to the
other corner. I don't mind them looking over the work of
another boy in the vicinity. Of course, if it were a test it would
be different. Everybody would be rooted to their chair. . . .

The lesson proper, then, typically consists of a sequence of subphases
of these three types. Only on rare occasions is only one type of subphase involved; more typically several of them occur. Some com-
binations are particularly common, for example, teacher exposition
(type 1) + question-and-answer session (type 3) + group work or
working from books (type 2). Every transition from one subphase
to another is effected by means of a switch-signal. There is an infinite
variety of these, even though most individual teachers betray
particular preferences.

I.   One more question, how do you get the pupils to switch from
either listening to you to doing work by themselves, or from
doing work by themselves to listening to you?
T.   Fairly difficult. I've had many ways of doing this. One way is
if I want them to stop work I say, 'Stop work please', and
perhaps, even though I've raised my voice only three-quarters
they will stop and then I'll pick out those who have not stopped
and shout further to them and even after that there might be
one boy who is determined to carry on and finish what he was
doing. I've put this down to no fear of the consequences and
perhaps in the old days a boy could be punished physically or

in any other way. I, of course, don't punish physically these days and I don't give them any punishment in any other way. Sometimes I bang on the blackboard with a ruler. I find that a sharp noise will stop them better than even my voice. I think that perhaps it is familiarity. . . . At one time in my career I even tried a whistle. I said to myself that they immediately respond on a football field, so I got my whistle out and gave a quiet whistle and lo and behold everybody stopped. I tried this for a week or two and then I thought, well, it's not done so I'd better discontinue the practice, but it certainly works, just like any sudden shock will stop people and, of course, as I said my voice is too familiar to them and some of them don't stop for it. Very often I've gone right up to a boy who has deliberately kept on, and just banged a ruler in front of his face to give him a shock and that's stopped him of course.

If the pay attention rule is in play, as is the case if a type 1 subphase is ending, the teacher can proceed to give the task indicator directly.

'Now what I want you to do is to answer the question on the board.'
'Right, now form a circle round the desk.'

Sometimes the teacher is able to assume that the pupils know the subphase that is to follow, in which case the switch-signal can be reduced to:

'Right, carry on.'
'OK, get on with it.'

If the pay attention rule is not in play, then such statements will be preceded by an instruction to stop the activity of the preceding phase and to put the attention rule into play.

'Right, leave what you're doing, put your pens down and face me.
'Stop work now and look this way.'
'Right, look this way now.'

The last of the subphases of the lesson proper is followed by the fourth phase, the clearing up phase. In those lessons where the pupils are not using equipment of any kind, this phase may be very brief, but in most cases the pupils do have some kind of equipment. Usually, the transition to the clearing up phase is marked by a clear switch-signal, which directs them to stop work and to clear up whatever equipment has been in use during the last subphase according to the rules operated by the teacher in charge. Examples are:

'Right, it's time to stop work for break.'
'Close your books now.'
'Put the rulers and pencils away please.'
'Now can I have all the papers in?'
'It's time to stop now. Pass your books forward.'
'Right, everybody pack up and put the equipment straight.'

Most teachers permit talking during this phase, and frequently the clearing up requires considerable movement.

(1) I.   How do you end a lesson?
    T.   Well, about five minutes before the end I'll say, 'Right, 2C, that's it', and it's finished like that, the lesson comes to an end abruptly, you know. 'Let me have your books in. Jeffrey, can you collect the rulers? Peter, will you collect the pencils? Anyone else had a pen of mine can you bring it back now? Let me have the books on the side table.' And they just go and sit.

(2) T.   If the room is needed for another class I don't have the equipment collected. I ask them to spread out the equipment on the drawing board in a set pattern and I have this set pattern so I can quickly check. I don't just say all your equipment on the board, I have the equipment in a set pattern. . . . I then ask the boy nearest to the remainder of the equipment in the racks to check the remainders, so he knows how many are out in the room. . . .

(3) T.   As soon as I have said that it's time to stop, be finishing off your work, I don't mind if they do talk. I think they know that. Once they are collecting books, and pencils they do talk. I think they need it. I think when they have had their heads down quietly as they had, I think they need to have a little break.

(4) T.   Yes, well when I stop the lesson—if there is to be no further class in the room that particular session—I have a routine for putting the materials, all the equipment they use into little racks, self-counting racks to save time. If there are any losses, everybody has put what they think everything away, I then make them search for the missing things. . . . Then when everything is away they return to their seats.

The switch-signal that is used to usher in the clearing up phase does not need to be very explicit, since the pupils know that the lesson is near its end from their own watches. As one teacher said:

Well, some pupils will have been watching the clock. They'll be aware of the time. They know when the bell goes, so towards the end of the lesson they'll be looking towards me like spectators at a football match blowing their imaginary whistles.

Pupils are thus able to fill in that a statement, such as 'Right, stop now' is in fact the clearing up phase switch-signal.

> **T.** Before the end of the lesson, perhaps five minutes before the bell is due to go, 'It's time to collect up.' Having said it's time to collect up I'd probably detail one or two boys to collect specific items from the groups so I'll say, 'You collect all the. . . . You go and get all the watch glasses. You go and get all the forceps and count them.' At this stage if I find any lads doing nothing at all, I usually try to remind them that they too should be putting things away, tidying up, picking up odd things that may be lying about. The aim of that is to have everything away so that I can have them back in their places before the bell goes. This is an ideal of course, usually they are moving about, but I would hope to get them together. Often it will be necessary for me to say something. I might even have to point out why we have done the thing if I thought it needed emphasizing and why we had done the lesson at all. I might emphasize that this case of an organism what looks like nasty slime in a pond, when in fact it's delightful, you know, and they can apply this sort of thing to other things. . . .

The exit phase is complementary to the entry phase and is concerned with the accomplishment of leaving the classroom. The main rule is that pupils may not leave the room until the teacher indicates that they have his permission to do so. And the teacher will not grant this permission until the bell has rung, for this is one of the rules that the teachers must follow.

> (1) I. Do you always wait for the bell before you say that?
> T. Oh yes. I would be in trouble if I let them out.
> [The headteacher] does not want to see any child outside the classroom before the bell goes.

> (2) I. Are they allowed to just leave the room?
> T. I don't let anybody leave before the bell. I don't let anybody go before my say, even though the bell has gone.

But the sound of the bell does not in itself permit the children to leave, even though it signals the official end of the lesson.

> I. At the end . . . you turned round and said, because they

started moving, 'Somebody say leave?' and they said, 'But, sir, the bell's gone', and you said, 'That's for me not for you.'

T. Yes. I honestly feel that this is slackness if teachers let them get up and wander off without either looking for some sort of expression from the teacher that it is the correct thing to get up and go. I think it is impolite, really, for behaviour in school. Nothing to do with teaching a subject, but I think they should say, 'May we go?' I don't mean that they should stand on their hands or anything silly, but at least look towards the teacher and get some sort of acceptance from the teacher that it is time to go. . . .

Permission to leave is signalled by phrases such as:

'Right, away you go.'
'Off you go then.'
'Right' ('you can go' being filled in by the pupils).

With older children, teachers generally do not impose any further rules for the exit phase, except that the pupils are not expected to push or run during the exit. Typically in these cases the teacher will say, if the bell has gone, 'You can go when you're ready', or, if the bell has not yet rung, 'You can go when the bell goes.' But with the younger pupils, there are many more rules governing the exit.

(1) 'Right, get in line,' says the teacher. Pupils get up from the seats and line up by the door waiting to go out. Bell goes. 'Right, you can go.' Teacher follows them out into corridor and dismisses them.

(Observation notes)

(2) 'I'm waiting for everyone to be quiet.'
'I've some pencils and rubbers missing, so we'll just wait for those to be found before we think about going out.' This is done.
'Stuart, will you shut up.'
'Now we'll have everybody sat straight, arms folded and we'll have a period of silence.' There is still some talking.
'We still have some person in the room who doesn't understand the word silence.'
When this occurs, the teacher lets them go. They later line up in the corridor, and then off.

(Observation notes)

(3) I. Do you have any procedures for leaving the room?
T. I vary, I personally vary. If I think a class is being unduly noisy then I might be rigid and enforce some sort of organized

exit from the room. If the class is not particularly noisy I'd rather not, I'd rather see them going out when they say, 'May we go?' I let them go as they are ready provided the bell's gone—which will be in twos, threes and fours. If I suddenly find a mob charging for the door, I'd stop them all probably and line them up and tell them that they're not acting as I would expect of their age and so on. Until they can do it sensibly then we'll have to do it this other way.

(4) T. And they just go and sit . . . they don't always go back to their desk and sit, it just depends how near the end of the lesson we are because I don't like holding other people up for lessons for this performance where they all must be sitting in their desks with arms folded before they go. I don't approve of this quite frankly. I'd rather if—they drift back and they just sort of sit around with a little bit of chat for a couple of—well not even a couple of minutes, it might be about thirty seconds and then the bell goes and then I have them going down the stairs and, of course, having to go down stairs here you've got to go down with them to make sure that they are not larking about on the corridor, so you've got to more or less follow them down, and this is the end of the lesson.

This material illustrates the variations in, and the complexity of, the exit phase rules. For some teachers, especially those with younger pupils in large classes, the exit phase may extend well beyond the physical exit through the door and sometimes almost runs into the entry phase of the pupils' next lesson.

I. So you say you have to see them down the stairs, you get them all together. . . .
T. Yes, at the door, they line up at the door going down and then they go down, supposed to go down the stairs in single file because by the time they've got to the first landing there's half a dozen of them collected and then you've got to try and get them going down the corridor in single file so that they're not interfering with people coming the other way. I always ask where they're going next so that I know where they're going when they get to the bottom of the stairs, either up or down. It's confusing if you don't, and then that's the end of the lesson.

Individual teachers may vary their exit rules not only by the age of the pupils, but also in relation to special contingencies.

I. At the end of the lesson everybody just seemed to drift out of the class. Is that what typically happens?

T.   No, not with every class. You see 3E live next door anyway
so at dinner-times they go and collect bags or go and put them
in for dinner-time so it isn't always necessary to make them
line up and they are such a small form anyhow. So what I
usually do is say, 'Come on 3E', and I go down to the end of the
line, just sort of token really as you have to do with a full form
so you don't get cross currents in the corridor. It's not usually
necessary, most of them turn off into Mr ——'s room which is
right next door and only a few go straight out.
I.   Well, I was wondering, do you expect them to know what to
do?
T.   Oh yes, well by now, I have had them for two terms for
maths so they know.
I.   You don't find that it is necessary unless you think they are
going to get up to something on the way out and can't be
trusted?
T.   I think 3E can, they can be trusted to go out in an orderly
fashion.

The analysis of lessons in terms of these five phases is essentially
a structural analysis. As such it is perhaps of interest in its own right,
and makes an interesting comparison with the way in which a cur-
riculum developer or a classroom interaction analyst might seek to
examine a lesson. Our analysis stems directly from our need to
understand classroom rules and proposes that every phase or subphase brings into play a distinctive combination of rules. Pupils
know which rules are in play because they know which phase they
are in—though they would describe a phase in terms of the activity
of that phase. Phases—and their rules—are changed by switch-
signals, which are usually verbal statements made by the teacher.
All this constitutes part of teachers' and pupils' common-sense
knowledge of classrooms, and it is on this basis that members can
make sense of deviance-imputations which invoke unstated rules
which are known to be in play at particular points of time in the
lesson. Yet the five phases do not account for all the rules that are
in play in a lesson, and many events occur which cannot be made
sense of by members with reference to the five phases and their rules.
The five phases account for much of what happens, but by no means
all. The rest of the chapter will be concerned with making some
important qualifications and additions to the phase analysis which
has been presented.
    Switch-signals act as a 'bridge' between phases, terminating the
one in existence and ushering in the subsequent phase. But switch-
signals can be used in another way, namely as a 'suspension'. In this

case instead of effecting a transition between phases, the switch-signal is used to create a temporary hiatus in the middle of an on-going phase. The teacher sometimes finds that a problem has emerged during a phase, which requires that he should reinforce, clarify, refine, or add to, the instructions of rules governing the pupils' activity. He may discover, for instance, that the pupils have mis-understood or forgotten his directions or that he has failed to give adequate instructions. Clearly he has to intervene. Typically, this suspension has three elements.

1. The attention-drawer, e.g. 'Right, now look this way.' This switches off all the rules in play, directs the pupils to stop any current activity, and requires that the pupils should conform to the pay attention rule which is now in play.
2. The refining instruction, e.g. 'Now remember to start each new problem on a new page.' It is here that the rules are refined in some way.
3. The restorative instruction, e.g. 'OK, now carry on.' This indi-cates to the pupils that the suspension is terminated and that the original phase and its rules are restored completely, except for the refining instruction.

I.   Then you said, 'Could you just give me your attention?'
T.   Sounds as if I was having a difficult time! But sometimes when children are doing an activity which is perfectly legitimate—they may be doing various things—if I want to say something, because something's occurred to me, or somebody's asked a question not in the hearing of the whole of the class, I may think it's important that others become aware of what's been said. It may influence what they've been asked to do, and I may then have tried to get the attention of the class in this way. . . . On the other hand, it may just have been a sign of impatience on my part because somebody has been persistently not listening. I can't tell you the particular incident.

This passage neatly illustrates a suspension, but the most significant part of this passage is in the last two sentences. This teacher cannot recall the context of utterance of the remark that is being fed back to him by the interviewer. It is only through the context of utterance that the teacher can recognize it either as a deviance-imputation (which is the teacher's second interpretation) or as a suspension (the teacher's first interpretation). But to demonstrate that de-contextualization makes interpretation difficult is not to reveal what it is in the context that makes correct interpretation possible. How do pupils know how to distinguish the two? In practice, a verbal clue is provided in a suspension which would not occur in a phase switch-signal or a deviance-imputation. In the example given above, the verbal clue is the word 'just'. More commonly it is provided in the words 'for a moment' as in 'Look this way for a moment' or 'Put your pens down for a minute', for such phrases give an indication that a temporary interruption is about to take place—and it is this which is characteristic of a suspension. If such a clue is not given, then the pupils will not know whether a phase change or a suspension is taking place until the teacher clarifies the position with further talk.

Many phrases used by teachers can be either a switch-signal or a deviance-imputation. Again, it is the context of utterance which allows the pupils to make the correct interpretation. If the teacher says, 'Look this way' in any phase where the pay attention rule is not in play, then it cannot be a deviance-imputation, which by definition must implicitly invoke a rule in play at the time. In this case the 'Look this way' must be a switch-signal as part of a phase change or a suspension. But if the pay attention rule is in play as part of the current phase, then it must be a deviance-imputation invoking that rule, and will be interpreted by the pupils according to the procedures set out in the last chapter. In short, the phase structure allows us to make considerable clarification of the rules that are invoked in deviance-imputations; it also demonstrates that the interpretive work done by the pupil is more complex than was indicated in chapter 3.

There is a second kind of interruption to a phase in addition to the suspension. It is similar in that its source lies in an emergent problem for the teacher; it is different in that it changes one of the basic phase rules. In a type 2 phase, where pupils are working on problems alone or in groups, the pupils are commonly allowed to indulge in a certain amount of talk. One of these talk rules is that the pupils must talk quietly. It quite often happens that the noise level grows slowly but steadily as the phase proceeds. The teacher will probably intervene with a warning, such as, 'There's too much noise, 3B.' When the noise continues to rise after several such interventions, the teacher may feel the need to take more radical action. It is this which we call the 'ad hoc'. Whereas the suspension involves a relatively minor refinement to the detailed rules in play, the 'ad hoc' changes one of the basic rules in play. In the present example, the teacher may say, 'From now on there will be no more talking at all. You must work in silence for the rest of the lesson.' The normal rule of this phase has been changed or put out of play. However, it is important to note that unless the teacher states other-wise, it is assumed that the ad hoc-ed rule is only temporary, i.e.

applies only to this phase on this occasion. When the same phase occurs in another lesson, the previous phase rules will be in play once again. In another form of ad hoc-ing, an utterly new rule may be introduced to cope with an emergent problem. For instance, the teacher may have instructed pupils to come out to the teacher's desk with their work as soon as they have finished. After a while, there may be several pupils waiting by the side of the desk, chatting in groups. The teacher may then instruct that the pupils should 'stand in a line and stop talking'. If that were a normal rule of 'having work marked at the teacher's desk', then the statement would be a deviance-imputation. If it is not a normal rule, then the teacher is putting a new ad hoc rule into play. In most cases, its status will be temporary. If the teacher continues to ad hoc this rule on future occasions, then it may be transformed from an ad hoc rule into a normal rule, which is automatically seen by teacher and pupils as in play during such an activity.

Anyone familiar with classrooms will recognize that our conception of the five phases and their rules fails to give an adequate account of all the rules that are in play in classrooms. The value of the concept of phases is that it allows us to deal with certain rules which come into play at particular times but then go out of play later. But are there not rules which are in play all the time; rules which in the terminology used so far might be described as multiphasic? In chapter 3, it was suggested that schools contain some general rules, which we called institutional rules, which are in force for most of the time in most situations (assembly, corridors, playground, dining-hall, etc.), obvious examples being rules about clothing and appearance. It will be recalled that some of these rules have a general applicability. For instance, the punctuality rule, which states that pupils must conform to the time-schedules laid down by the school and not arrive late, or the property rule, which states that pupils must treat school property with respect and care. Other rules apply only in certain situations, such as the rule against eating sweets which applies in assembly and the classroom, but not in the playground. These institutional rules are not operative all the time, nor are they brought into play by teacher-initiated switch-signals. For example, the property rule is in play at those times and on those occasions where the pupil's activities directly involve the use of, or have a specifiable relation to, school property. If the pupil is using a piece of school equipment, he knows that he must treat it with due care. If he is playing with a ball in the playground, he must handle it in such a way that it does not damage school property, for example by breaking a window. For the pupil to be able to conform to the property rule, he must acquire the capacity to recognize what constitutes school property and what activities involve or relate to school property, for only on the basis of this knowledge can he know when the property rule is relevant and in play. Equally, of course, he must know what constitutes the proper use of property and what constitutes a misuse of it. In the case of the punctuality rule, the pupil must understand the nature of the school's time-schedules and the occasions when the rule is in play—the beginning of the school day, the beginning of lessons and so on. A pupil cannot understand what it is to be 'late' unless he knows that at certain times there is a rule in play which requires him to be at a particular place at a particular time. Certain scheduled movements (in and out of school, between classrooms) bring into play the rule which requires that the pupil accomplish this movement within a given time.

But this addition of some institutional rules to the phase rules does not exhaust all the rules in classrooms. We discovered this by examining all the deviance-imputations we witnessed and finding ourselves unable to account for the rule being invoked in terms of what we had classified as institutional or phase rules. These rules appeared to operate outside classrooms, but they were also in play during lessons, where they interpenetrated with phase rules in complex ways. On the other hand they were not linked to the performance of tasks-in-lessons, as was the case with phase rules, nor were they brought into play by switch-signals. The dominant feature of these rules seemed to be that they were concerned with the relationship between teacher and pupil and between pupil and pupil. For this reason we shall call them 'relational rules', following Denzin (1970, 1971) who has built upon the pioneering work of Goffman (1963, 1971). We shall distinguish two kinds of teachers' relational rules: teacher-pupil relational rules, which specify how pupils are to relate to teachers, and pupil-pupil relational rules, which specify how teachers expect pupils to relate to one another. Naturally we shall have to ignore many of the relational rules discussed by Denzin and Goffman, which undoubtedly do operate in classrooms as they do elsewhere, and shall concentrate on the main relational rules that are of special significance in the setting of the classroom as a distinctive arena of social relationships between particular persons, namely teachers and pupils.

Before we state these relational rules, it is important that we specify the data we collected and then used as a source for formulating the rules. How did we make the transition from the teacher's statements —the deviance-imputations—to our formulation of the set of relational rules which we are about to present? From what we observed we made a list of the prescriptions and proscriptions which were explicit or implicit in the teachers' statements. Our natural temptation was to infer from these the rule that was being invoked in the deviance-imputation. This appears to be a reasonable enterprise, since it was our assumption that a deviance-imputation by definition invokes a rule. Our task was therefore to discover which rule was being invoked. The outcome would then be a list of relational rules which could be invoked in a variety of ways and the deviance-imputations would constitute illustrations of such rule invocation as experienced by us in our role as observers. The argument would then be that these rules must implicitly be known by the members, otherwise they would not be able to recognize a deviance-imputation as a deviance-imputation.

The weakness here lies in the assumption that the teachers do have a clear set of relational rules which they invoke in their deviance-imputations. But we argued in the last chapter that the teachers' common-sense knowledge of rules need not be clear and consistent and logical at all. All a practising teacher needs is knowledge which permits him to 'get by' in the classroom, that is, a knowledge which works for all practical purposes in everyday life. Thus it is potentially a mistake on our part to infer that a deviance-imputation invokes one, and only one, rule. Deviant acts observed by the teacher might be codable or subsumable under several rules. In this case a deviant act would be definable as deviant not because it breaks *a* rule, but because it can be interpreted as a breach of *some* rule. A deviant act would be describable in several possible ways, because several rules—and possibly several very different kinds of rules—can be invoked to make sense of that act.[2] So we accepted that it would be an error to search for the particular rule that was being invoked in a deviance-imputation. The only legitimate course would be to ask a teacher which rule was being invoked in a particular deviance-imputation, since there might be several rules that could be invoked, but the verbal statement of the teacher would often give no clue as to the particular rule being invoked on that occasion. Even here we are in difficulties because such an account, given to us by a teacher some time after the deviance-imputation had taken place, bears a problematic relationship to his thinking at the time of the deviance-imputation. Indeed, his account to us is inevitably a social construction *sui generis*. In itself the account is not the same as the original action of making the deviance-imputation and so it is not possible for us to know the precise relationship between the deviance-imputation and the teacher's later account of it. This is a central problem at the heart of all phenomenological research which makes extensive use of members' accounts.

The implication of this is that the relational rules being presented by us must be seen as our constructions, derived from observed deviance-imputations and teachers' commentaries upon them. We do not want to suggest that these are the rules that teachers invoke. The relational rules created by us have a problematic relationship to the rules of the teachers. Our purpose in presenting these relational rules is social scientific; that is to say, we wish to convey to an outside group (the readers) some insight into the range of acts which are defined as deviant in classroom and the kind of rules which are being invoked in such definitions; and we must do this in a way that is relatively parsimonious and logical. We shall return to these problems after presenting the relational rules.

Teacher-pupil relational rules

1. The rule of obedience. Pupils are expected to do as the teacher orders them, and they are expected to do so without arguing, without 'answering back', and without undue delay. The rule of obedience refers to those situations in which teachers give orders to, or make requests of, pupils in the expectation that they will be carried out.

2. The rule of good manners. Pupils are expected to display good manners towards the teachers. This is a comprehensive set of rules, with inevitable variations between teachers. At the simplest level it is concerned with saying 'please' and 'thank you' at appropriate times. It covers modes of address—especially the use of the terms 'sir' and 'Miss'. Of particular interest to us is the concept of 'cheek' or 'insolence', which we are placing here since it is a school form of the more general social rule against being 'rude'.

3. The rule of permission-seeking. Pupils are not expected to initiate certain acts without seeking prior permission from the teacher. This is one of the most complex of the relational rules, since a pupil has to learn whether or not an action is or is not within his discretion at a particular time. Leaving the room (e.g. to go to the lavatory) almost always requires explicit permission, whereas leaving one's seat (e.g. to sharpen a pencil) varies not only by teacher, but also by phase (e.g. no permission-seeking would be expected during a 'group work' phase, but it normally would be during a 'teacher demonstration' phase). Teachers show irritation against a pupil who seeks permission 'unnecessarily', just as they show it against the pupil who fails to seek permission when it is expected.

4. The rule of telling the truth. When a teacher asks the pupil a question (of a non-academic kind), the pupil is expected to respond truthfully and not tell lies.

5. The rule proscribing violence to the teacher. It is always forbidden for a pupil to strike a teacher in any way.

6. The rule requiring co-operation. A pupil must always 'co-operate'

with the teacher. This is a complex rule which we can merely illustrate. For example, if a teacher asks a pupil a question, then the pupil must always answer, unless silence on his part can be interpreted as ignorance ('I don't know') or guilt ('Yes, I did it'). If the pupil does give an answer to a teacher's question, it must be relevant and 'sensible', i.e. not a wild guess, or not patently absurd. Similarly, questions put to the teacher or suggestions offered must not be 'foolish' ones. To take another example, if the teacher is helping a pupil with some work-related problem, then the pupil must co-operate by allowing himself to be helped. Clearly, this is a wide-ranging and diffuse rule which has links with the obedience rule and the good manners rule.

None of these teacher-pupil relational rules appeared in a written form, nor were they reported to us as such by any of the teachers. They are based on statements made by teachers and events observed by us, but it is we who suggest that these are discrete rules which are always invoked in a distinctive way in specific deviance-imputations. For example, pupils are often described by teachers as being 'awkward'. This term can be used to describe pupils' conduct which breaks one or several of the rules as elucidated by us.

I.   What's his behaviour like in class?
T.   Awkward to say the least. Last Friday is a case in point.
He sat in a certain place behind another boy—I'll call him boy A.
Now boy A asked if he could go to the toilet so I said, 'Yes', this
was near the beginning of the lesson, 'just for one minute'.
And during this minute he came in and went straight to boy A's
place and I said, 'Will you go to where you were earlier this
morning', and he said, 'I was here this morning', and I said,
'You weren't', and he was adamant that he was, and of course
I knew that he was wrong. I made a kind of something out of
this and sent him out. In came pupil A and sat in that very place,
proving that I was right.

Now it could be argued that this pupil is breaking the rule of obedience, or of telling the truth, or of co-operation, or that he is breaking two or all of these rules. Our interest is not so much in assigning this event to one or more of the rules—though the teacher's own account would be most interesting—but rather in showing that both the researcher and the teacher were able to make sense of this event as one of pupil deviance by invoking some rule(s) which is neither a phase rule nor an institutional rule.

Infringements of the rule of obedience, which are typically described by teachers as 'disobedience' or 'defiance', involve a refusal

to carry out the teacher's orders or an attempt by the pupil to negotiate ('argue') whether or not he should comply with the order, and
are often accompanied by what the teachers describe as a surly or
resentful attitude in the pupil. These events are often interpreted by
teachers as a threat to their authority.

(1) The pupils are working at their tables. 'Have a look and if
   you think you have finished one, come to me,' says the
   teacher. Some pupils form a queue at the teacher's desk.
   The teacher says to one pupil, on looking at his work, 'You
   can't multiply 17 by 23 without setting the sum out', she says.
   'Now go and do it.' The pupil replies, 'I did do it in a sum.'
   The teacher says, 'Don't argue, go and sit down and do it.'
                                              (Observation notes)

(2) T.   There are times when he won't accept a bit of correction
   and it's not just the business of answering back, you know,
   like when he said, 'I am listening', when I told him that he
   wasn't. Sometimes he accompanies this by a terrible scowl
   or sour look. . . . I once made him come back—he'd left
   books and rulers and pens littered all over his desk and I told
   him to move them just before the end of the lesson. Then
   they went out and lined up and they were still all there, so I
   told him to go back and clear up his desk and I got one of
   his filthy sullen looks from him and I almost had to drag
   him with force and stand over him, so he cleared them away
   as slowly as he dared. . . .

(3) T.   I might go down the corridor and find him chasing a girl
   down the corridor and grabbing her handbag or schoolbag,
   taking it from her and refusing to give it back, and if I say
   to him, 'Barry!' he'll turn away and won't do it immediately,
   he won't respond like this. He has his own way of dealing
   with authority. He might eventually give it back, but he'll
   expect you to stand there and wait until he does it in his own
   time, to show that he himself has authority. Of course, some
   of us are hoping that he'll toe the line army-style, but this
   can't be achieved.

With regard to the rule of good manners, one of the most common
forms of deviance is that which is called by teachers 'cheek' (or
insolence, rudeness or impertinence). As in the case of disobedience,
cheek as an act hinges upon the status differential between teacher
and pupil: it is an act, either verbal or non-verbal, which by its
content or manner threatens, jeopardizes or denies the superior
status of the teacher. Cheek occurs in three main forms. The first

might be called 'familiarity', in which the pupil denies the teacher's superior status by an action which is appropriate only to status equals. The classic case is an intrusion into what the teacher regards as his personal life, but swearing is often seen in this light.

I.   Well, what about cheek? What sort of things would a kid have to do for you to decide that he was being cheeky?
T.   Well, I personally, especially with the older boys, I believe in being quite friendly, you know, I don't believe in second names or anything like that. I like to be called sir. I think really the main thing is if they speak to me as if I were one of their friends, you know—it's a complicated situation really. You try and it's difficult to do to try and win their confidence so that you don't have to wield the big slipper all the time and you can get work without wielding the big slipper you know, and still maintain, what?—respect. I think that is the main thing, when they speak to me as if they were talking to the person next to them, then I fly off the handle and I say, 'Now that's enough.' Occasionally people, if I have just told somebody off, I hear them mimic me under their breath when I have turned my back, you know, they repeat what I've said and that makes me very angry as well, I won't stand for that. I don't mind kids making jokes at my expense, that's not cheek, it depends on the whatsit. They can have a bit of a laugh at you if you make a mistake. I wouldn't say 'How dare you!' or anything like that. I don't think that is cheek. Of course, things like boys swearing under their breath in a lesson I regard that as cheek and insolence on their part. I don't believe in boys being saints or anything like that because they all swear and you are bound to hear it as you go round the school, but I won't tolerate them, you know. You can hear odd whispers at the back, I always find out who that was and haul them over the coals for that. I could say that was cheek in a way because they are not meant to use a swear word in a lesson however quietly.
I.   So it wouldn't be cheek outside the classroom?
T.   It wouldn't be cheek to me, no. I'd pull them over the coals for it, but I would not regard it as cheek because you know boys playing football and these days they can't avoid it. . . . They can't win, I think they are almost taught that it is natural, that it's normal to swear, especially when someone gets kicked when playing football and you're on duty and you're walking round the playground and someone comes out with a mouthful. It depends, sometimes you turn a blind ear and another time you call him over, it depends. If I think he has seen me, you

know, and knows I am there and he still swears I'd have him for it, but you know everybody swears really.

A second form of cheek is the more overt insult, which betrays a contempt for the teacher or affronts his dignity.

T. There is one particular boy who was just very rude and had been rude previously, but he got away with it because I could not sort of prove it. . . . Well, he told me to 'Get stuffed' once . . . and he's got this thing that I just pick on him, and I suppose it's obvious that I don't like him. You can't help these dislikes, although at one time I couldn't understand how teachers could dislike children, it's awful really, but they do. I told them to sit down and he said, 'Get knotted' sort of under his breath but loud enough for me to hear. So I just walked over to him and said very quietly, 'That's the second time you've insulted me and the last time. Get down to [the headteacher].' So he immediately jumped back at me and took on the aggressive sort of attacking thing as though I was in the wrong, and said, 'It wasn't me, it wasn't me.' I said, 'You can lie. I heard you and everybody else heard you.' So he said to me, 'It's you, it's you, it's your fault.' So I said, 'What do you mean, my fault? I told you to sit down. You're the one that's being rude to me.' Maybe I should not have started arguing with him, but then he just got very aggressive and said that it was my fault, I was always picking on him and that he was fed up with me. So I said, 'Are you going down to [the headteacher]?' And he said, 'No.' So I couldn't let him get away with it.

This pupil added the insult of breaking two further relational rules, of obedience and of telling the truth, to the injury of the insult.

A third form of cheek arises when the pupil assumes the rights or prerogatives of the superior. In this illustration we see the importance of the status differential despite the teacher's attempt to minimize its significance.

I. Can you remember that particular incident when you said that this morning about going down to [the headteacher], because afterwards you said, 'Keep your cheek to yourself.'
T. That was because he told me, 'Can we get on with the lesson', and I had been standing there waiting for him and it was a cheek to turn round to me and say that, moaning at me, which annoyed me. I don't think it was anything to do with discipline. It was just a personal thing that annoyed me. I don't like having to talk to them like that. I don't feel that they should necessarily be cheeky to me because I can be rude to them. I

think that is partly why I don't like being rude to them and shouting at them, and why I ask them politely, is that I don't want to have to be nasty to them and therefore I don't expect it back and therefore I have a good reason for telling them off if they are rude to me. If I was rude to them I wouldn't have a conscience that I could say it was wrong of them to be rude. I often say to them, 'I don't put up with this from anybody, let it be another teacher or anybody, let alone a little punk like you.' I'm trying to say it's nothing to do with me being a teacher and them pupils, just a thing between two people.

It is relatively rare for a pupil to break the rule which proscribes violence towards the teacher. In this research we recorded only one instance.

Relational rules are not brought into play by switch-signals made by the teacher. The rules of obedience and telling the truth are brought into play whenever a teacher issues an order or asks a question. To know that these rules are in play, a pupil must have the capacity to recognize an order as an order and a question as a question. The rules of good manners, non-violence and co-operation are brought into operation whenever the pupil is in interaction with a teacher. The rule of good manners is of particular interest, since politeness is not so much a task in itself, but a manner in which certain tasks should be accomplished. It is for this reason that this rule interpenetrates with other rules, including phase rules. Thus in a question-and-answer subphase of the lesson proper, the pupil must not only answer the question, but he must also do so in a polite manner and truthfully.

The permission-seeking rule is a complex one in that conformity to it rests upon the pupil's capacity to recognize that the activity which he seeks to initiate is one which requires permission. The pupil must learn when it is appropriate to ask permission as well as how to ask permission in conformity to the rule of good manners. For example, pupils in the secondary school soon learn that they must seek permission to go to the lavatory, whereas such permission is often not required in primary schools. They also learn that such a request is unlikely to be granted immediately after the beginning of the lesson, since the pupil is expected to go before arriving for the lesson, or immediately prior to the end of the lesson, since the pupil is then expected to wait. Permission is usually denied in certain subphases of the lesson proper, such as a teacher exposition or a test. A refusal is also likely if the request is made immediately after the teacher has permitted another pupil to go, since the teacher believes that if two pupils go together they will delay one another en route.

Whilst leaving the classroom always requires permission-seeking, pupil-initiated actions within the classroom sometimes do and sometimes do not require permission. Often pupils intentionally initiate such action without seeking permission in the hope that they will 'get away with it', i.e. the teacher will not notice.

Pupil-pupil relational rules

In addition to the teacher-pupil relational rules, teachers also enjoined on the pupils a variety of pupil-pupil relational rules. Our data on these rules are less extensive than with the teacher-pupil relational rules. One reason for this is that lessons in both our schools were organized along fairly 'traditional' lines. This meant that in the lesson proper, type 1 and type 3 subphases (that is, those subphases in which any pupil-pupil interaction is prohibited) were highly prevalent. It is only in the type 2 subphases, which were less common, that informal pupil-pupil interaction is officially permitted, and even here it is meant to be task-related. It follows that many pupil-pupil relational rules are distinctly phasic in character rather than having the generally pervasive quality of the teacher-pupil relational rules. In 'progressive' secondary schools and some primary schools, type 2 subphases would be much more common and we would expect teachers in these schools to have more elaborate conceptualizations of pupil-pupil relational rules, and to talk about them with greater frequency than was true in the case of the teachers in our schools.

The pupil-pupil relational rules may be conceptualized as follows:

1. The rule proscribing aggression. This rule proscribes a variety of acts. At an obvious level this proscribes acts of physical violence, including fighting with other pupils, hitting other pupils with physical objects such as rulers and books, or with parts of the body such as the fists or the feet.

(1) T.   He hit a kid in this class, so I got up and walked over to him and I said, 'Look, pack that in or else you'll have me to deal with, OK?'

(2) T.   If somebody gets up and belts somebody else across the head, it's not a school rule that they mustn't do it but nobody would stand for it.

(3) T.   Well, I did notice at first he would walk past people and punch them as he was passing and tap girls on the head with anything he was carrying, paper or newspaper, so I thought I'll have to watch this boy.

Another class of proscribed aggressive acts includes the use of threatening behaviour for manipulative purposes.

(1) T. He came in last time and he kicked a kid out of his chair and said, 'I'm sitting there', and he sat there!

(2) I. He makes the pupils get gear for him and put them away?
T. Not every time.
I. Could you possibly suggest why he might be doing this? What is your opinion?
T. Well I think he is able to do this so he just does it and he knows they'll respond to his power.
I. You think power lies behind it?
T. I do, yes.
I. What do you think of a pupil doing this sort of thing, kids doing his work, totting for him?
T. I don't think much of it. When I spot it or hear of it I just say, 'Get your own, Grimes', or 'Put your own stuff away, Grimes', which he does.
I. What are you trying to do in this when you treat him in this way? What is your objective?
T. Well, I think, of course, that it's not right that one should have small boys working for one in such a way especially in school. Of course, I know he knows that he shouldn't do this but everybody knows that. But he just does it.

This rule also proscribes acts of psychological aggression such as making jibes, calling pupils cruel names, making fun or mocking other pupils, ostracizing and victimizing them.

(1) I. You had to speak to him yesterday?
T. Yes, I did, but that was about something different. The deputy head asked me to do that. That was about his behaviour towards another boy who was a bit ill, you know, and he was making jibes at him and had to be told to stop.

(2) T. I told him once, that's all, the very first time I met him I told him once and I've never had to speak to him again, only this week when he called Martin 'Specky', and he came out with a remark, I can't remember who else it was once, and I told him then, he mustn't do this, it isn't very nice and 'You wouldn't like it, would you?' and he said, 'No, I wouldn't', and that was it.

(3) T. I will not tolerate kids taking the mickey out of one another. I will not stand laughing when someone gets something wrong. That's the first thing, I stamp on that

straightaway at the start, I say, 'I don't care whether you
get an answer right or wrong, put your hand up and have a
go; if you are wrong, you are wrong', and if one person
laughs I always tell them. I don't care if they are the cleverest
in the class you know. I say words to the effect that they
are not cleverer than him; you have absolutely no grounds
for laughing, even though it's often a downright lie and they
are cleverer and they know it, you know, but I regard that
as bullying. That's mental bullying more than anything.
That's trying to make somebody feel small and it might even
be worse than actually pushing somebody about in some
cases.

2. The rule of good manners. This rule prescribes behaving in a
'civilized manner' and 'showing respect for others' and proscribes
the use of 'rude' words, swearing and not acting in a ladylike
manner (for girls).

3. The rule proscribing theft. In terms of this rule the pupils are
not permitted to take possession of items belonging to other pupils
without the consent of those pupils. This, of course, applies to the
most 'trivial' items such as pencils, pens and rulers as well as items
such as pupils' bags, coats and bicycles.

4. The rule proscribing 'telling tales'. This rule proscribes tale-
telling or 'sneaking'. Pupils should not attempt to get other pupils
into trouble with the teacher by reporting their minor misdemeanours. From teachers' point of view to break this rule is to
show disloyalty to fellow pupils.

I. A girl called Joanne shouted out to you, 'Sir, Boyle did . . .'
. . . actually got a pencil. Now when a pupil says this to you—
presumably you hadn't seen this incident?
T. I hadn't seen it.
I. When a pupil says this to you, what is your immediate
reaction?
T. Again I feel if you look at the classroom situation and the
kind of class you are teaching, it's half a dozen of one and
six of the other. To avoid any friction both ways between the
kids because I hadn't seen the situation, and knowing the type
of people who had said this. They are always trying to get each
other into trouble. I don't recall what I did at the time—could
you tell me? No, I don't know what I did, but I probably said
something to Boyle. I don't recall quite frankly.
I. I'm interested in your reaction to what is commonly to be
seen as sneaking or tale-telling on the part of Joanne. How
do you react to this situation?

T.   I have always been appalled, being a comparatively new
teacher, at the way children do tell tales on each other. Trying
to recall my childhood, I don't think we told tales on each other
the way the kids do today. I don't know, maybe I'm wrong.
But I don't care for tale-telling, in fact I do say, 'Well if you
weren't watching him or her then you wouldn't have seen
anything would you? You would be getting on with your work.'
I don't like tale-telling generally.

There are, however, exceptions to this general disapproval of tale-
telling. In particular, in the case of offences in terms of the property
rules, it would appear that it is perfectly legitimate to tell tales.

Clearly these relational rules, in the form in which we have conceptualized them, do not represent the rules as might be stated by
the teachers, or even as they are stated by teachers in their commentaries. Our rules are highly condensed versions of many first-
order rules. It is possible to subsume under our rules large numbers
of prescriptions and proscriptions as stated by teachers. We have
introduced some sociological order by classifying many first-order
rules as having certain common features. It can be argued that we
should specify the criteria by which we have made this classification.
We shall not take space to do so because any sociological classification would be very arbitrary and would exhibit a feature which it
shares with the first-order constructs, namely the interpenetration
and overlap that is present in such rule formulations. Demonstrating
that common feature is, in our view, much more important than
trying to justify our own classification, whose purpose is to convey
to others the complexity and nature of deviance-imputations-in-
relation-to-some-rule in the work of both members and sociologists.
At the level of our sociological analysis, it is readily apparent that
there is an overlap between what we have called phase rules and
also an overlap between the relational rules that we have specified.
For example, when a teacher orders a pupil to pay attention when
that rule is already in play, it is possible to code this as a deviance-
imputation invoking the phase rule of paying attention, but it is also
possible to code it as a deviance-imputation invoking the relational
rule of obedience in that the pupil is not being obedient to the order
previously issued by the teacher. Similarly, should a pupil poke
another pupil during a lesson, the teacher might say to the pupil,
'Don't do that, it's not nice', apparently invoking the pupil-pupil
relational rule. On the other hand the pupil might be ordered by
the teacher to 'Get on', apparently invoking a phase rule. This 'Get
on' can only be used in a phase; it would not be a meaningful
deviance-imputation in, say, the playground, whereas the first

deviance-imputation would, since this is an arena where pupil-pupil relational rules are notably in play. Such inconsistencies and contradictions at the level of the sociological classifications reflect—and inevitably reflect—the inconsistencies at the members' level. Classificatory order by a social scientist could be achieved only by tacit agreements between different coders (the so-called 'reliability') to exclude overlap by the creation of mutually exclusive categories. But in so doing—and there may be reasons for so doing—they inevitably misrepresent, distort or dispense with the common-sense thinking of the teachers themselves.

We, as phenomenological researchers, must not lose sight of the incoherence, inconsistency and overlap in the teachers' common-sense thinking. It is our concern to show that teachers, far from using mutually exclusive categories, can and do describe deviant acts in multiple ways. That is, one act is describable in a variety of ways in relation to a variety of rules. Our judgment is that a teacher can invoke one rule by describing the deviant acts which break it in various ways—and we shall analyse this in the next chapter. It is also the case—as has been already shown—that the verbal deviance-imputations may be formulated in the same way even though different rules are being invoked. It is for this reason that the attempt to find some order in the relationship between deviance-imputations and rules is so very confusing to the observer in the classroom. An outstanding example of this is the teacher's use of the term 'wasting time' in deviance-imputations. At first sight, the obvious solution is to infer that there is a rule which proscribed wasting time. But then one is led to examine why some pupil acts which are described as 'wasting time' in the deviance-imputation also can be described as breaches of other rules, since the act which is alleged to be wasting time can be interpreted as a breach of many other phase and relational rules. A pupil who is 'talking' when there is a rule against talk in play can be described as breaking that rule and/or as 'wasting time'. In short, many deviant acts can be described in varied ways and several rules can be invoked by a single imputation of deviance.

The problem is not how we as researchers are able to code a particular deviant act as an infraction of a particular (or even of several) sociologically formulated rule, but rather how it is that an act is codable as rule-breaking at all. Our purpose is to explicate the common-sense knowledge by which teachers are able to link acts to rules and thereby define the acts as deviant. In so doing, we shall perhaps, as we have done so far, also throw light on our own research practices.

5   *The imputation of deviance*

Teachers rarely state in any explicit way the rules which are broken by pupils. Rather pupils (and by implication, ourselves as researchers) are required to fill in the rule or rules which are being invoked by teachers' utterances on any particular occasion. Thus, in the case of the pay attention rule it was shown that such a rule may be invoked in a variety of forms; for example,

'Pay attention.'
'Look at me.'
'You're not looking at me.'
'Stop looking through the window.'
'Are you listening?'
'Stop talking.'
'Jones!'

These, and other such utterances, can be coded as deviance-imputations in terms of the pay attention rule, and in so doing we have made use of our common-sense knowledge of the context in which the utterance is made. We were able to make sense of, that is 'code', teachers' utterances as imputations of deviance from a particular rule on the basis of our knowledge that a particular rule was in play in a context or phase of the lesson. In doing this coding we were engaging in a form of interpretive work and thereby making use of our common-sense knowledge in terms of which such coding may be accomplished, and it is the organization of this knowledge which is involved in our earlier analysis.

In this chapter we wish to turn our attention away from the problem which we shared with pupils, namely, how did we recognize teachers' utterances as deviance-imputations, to a problem which we shared with teachers, namely, how did we recognize or know that a given act was deviant? In addressing this problem, our attention will be focused on the interpretive work which is carried out by teachers in making deviance-imputations, and in particular, on some of the interpretive rules and strategies whereby pupil conduct is linked with the classroom rules to provide for such imputations.[1]

Before proceeding with this analysis, however, it is necessary to explicate further the nature of tasks and rules in play in the classroom situation since, as we shall demonstrate, it is teachers' common-sense knowledge of these tasks, and the rules whereby they may be accomplished, which constitutes the basis of the interpretation of acts as deviant and which therefore underlies teachers' deviance-imputations.

Many of the rules in play in the classroom situation refer to tasks which are either pupil-initiated or are enjoined on pupils by the teachers. To understand the processes of recognizing that deviance from the rules embodied in the tasks is taking, or has taken, place involves us in clarifying how any normatively enjoined task is accomplished by a person and recognized as such, or is recognized as a failure to fulfil that task, by another person. Before proceeding, therefore, to analyse the imputation of deviance in relation to tasks and rules in the classroom situations, we wish to illustrate the generality of the problem with reference to a non-classroom task, namely, driving a car. We are using this illustration because we ourselves found it useful in clarifying our own thinking.

If we ask the question: how do people accomplish the task of driving a car in a way that would be recognized as competent driving, there are essentially two answers, both of which involve the concept of rule. The first answer is concerned with the driver's knowledge of the Highway Code. In the light of this knowledge, the driver keeps to the left, stops at traffic lights when they show red, does not park on double yellow lines, and so on. As every learner-driver knows, whilst it is impossible to pass the test without a thorough theoretical knowledge of the Highway Code and without an ability to follow these rules in practice, this type of knowledge alone is not sufficient for driving in a way which would be recognized as competent driving by a driving examiner. In addition, the driver must be able to follow a set of rules which are never mentioned in the Highway Code, but which are essential to following the Highway Code rules in the first place, namely the rules of controlling the car as a complex piece of engineering. These rules consist of the rules of steering, brake work, gear changing, and so on, and conformity to the rules of the Highway Code presupposes them. The first set of rules consists of what are essentially normative rules, conformity to which constitutes being able to drive properly, that is, in the socially approved and sanctioned manner. The second set of rules, which is presupposed by the first set, consists of technical rules, often in the form of physical skills, conformity to which constitutes being able to drive the car adequately or effectively or at all. Both of these sets of rules must be adhered to if the driver is to accomplish the task of driving a car in a manner that would be assessed as competent by a driving examiner.

A task, then, is accomplished by following rules and we shall call these 'implemental' rules, since it is only by following these rules that the task can be implemented or accomplished. We have distinguished two kinds of implemental rules: normative implemental rules and technical implemental rules. Failure to follow either set of rules prevents the competent accomplishment of the task—and therefore would constitute deviance from a rule which enjoined that task.

The relationship between these two sets of rules, where their object is competent driving, is highly complex. The learner-driver must master both sets during his period of instruction, though a basic grasp of the technical implemental rules is a prerequisite to a practical grasp of the normative implemental rules. It is of course possible for a driver to be driving adequately or effectively (that is, following the technical implemental rules) whilst he is driving improperly (that is, breaking the normative implemental rules embodied in the Highway Code). Similarly, of course, it is perfectly possible to avoid breaching the Highway Code, even though the technical dimension of driving may leave much to be desired.

Before proceeding with our analysis of the rules in relation to pupil conduct in the classroom, it is important to point out that whilst the distinction between these two types of rules does seem essentially clear, many driving rules are somewhat difficult to assign exclusively to one category or the other. For example, we experienced some difficulty in attempting to assign the rule which prescribes the regular use of the rear-view mirror exclusively to either the category of a technical implemental rule or to the category of a normative implemental rule. This difficulty arose because it was clear on the one hand that such a rule is enjoined by the Highway Code which suggests that it is a normative implemental rule, whilst at the same time it may also be viewed as an aspect of technical proficiency in relation to the avoidance of collisions with other objects, particularly other vehicles. In spite of this cautionary remark against the possibly premature acceptance of the conceptual categories we have devised, it is clear that to be a competent driver a person must follow a highly complex set of rules and that one possible useful way of looking at these rules and attempting to bring some general sociological order to them is provided by the above scheme. Thus, to reiterate: in driving competently the driver must follow a set of normative implemental rules which enjoin a variety of tasks in different situations (the Highway Code), and each situation brings into play particular normative implemental rules (for example, when approaching traffic lights slow down and stop on red) which

are themselves accomplished by following relevant technical implemental rules (for example, taking one's foot off the accelerator,
depressing the brake and clutch pedals).

As it is with a non-classroom task such as driving a car, so it is
with classroom tasks as well. In order to be a competent pupil, a
person must follow a set of rules, which we have hitherto referred to
as the classroom rules, which enjoin a variety of tasks in particular
situations, and which we have conceptualized as phase and relational
rules. Conformity to these rules (for example, pay attention, no
cheating, be polite) is accomplished by following the relevant set of
normative implemental rules which is itself accomplished by following the appropriate set of technical implemental rules. To clarify
these remarks we offer the following examples.

One of the most common classroom rules is the phase rule which
prescribes that the pupil pays attention to the teacher. How does the
pupil accomplish conformity to this phase rule? Our analysis of the
rules-in-context in chapter 4 revealed that it is possible to distinguish
three types of phases in which pupils are enjoined to conform to the
pay attention rule. First, pupils are expected to pay attention to the
teacher in those phases when the teacher talks directly to the pupils,
as when he is narrating a story, giving a dictation, or engaging in
verbal explanation or instruction. Second, the pay attention rule is
operative in those types of phases when the teacher is not engaging
in verbal communication only but rather is demonstrating, either on
the blackboard or on a piece of paper, as when drawing a diagram
or a picture, or working out a sum. Alternatively, in this type of
phase the demonstration may be an item of equipment or its use,
such as in the case of the specialized tools of woodwork, needlework
or metalwork, or when conducting an experiment in a science lesson.
Third, the pay attention rule is operative in those phases which
involve not only verbal communications on the part of the teacher
but demonstrations as well, so that in many situations in the classroom we would expect to find a combination of the first and second
types of phase in which the pay attention rule is in play. Having said
this we can now explore further the features of these phases and in
particular the methods of accomplishing paying attention which
are detectable within them. Our question is, given these different
types of phase in which the pay attention rule is in play, how does a
pupil accomplish paying attention?

It is clear that there is not merely one simple method of accomplishing conformity to the pay attention rule, but rather the nature
of, and the method of accomplishment of, paying attention differs
according to the type of phase in which paying attention is enjoined,
and more significantly, according to the object to which the attention

is to be paid. In the situation where the teacher is reading, dictating, or giving verbal instruction, paying attention is accomplished by following the normative implemental rule which prescribes that the pupils 'listen to the teacher'. By implication, of course, to engage in listening is to refrain from any other action which would preclude[2] listening and as a result there are sets of normative proscriptions associated with any normative prescriptions, such as the listening rule. Thus, in the case of the listening rule there are associated with it rules about talking to other pupils while the teacher is talking (that is, rules about the object being listened to—that it should be the teacher rather than another pupil) and also rules about refraining from 'doing nothing at all' (for example, pupils are not supposed to fall asleep while they are supposed to be listening). The essential point is that these proscriptive rules serve to proscribe activities which teachers regard as incompatible with listening; activities which, were the pupil to engage in them, would preclude him from accomplishing conformity to the listening rule and thereby to the pay attention rule as well.

Underpinning the normative implemental rules, whether they are prescriptive or proscriptive, lies the set of technical implemental rules. Conformity to these rules is essential to, and is a prerequisite of, conformity to the normative implemental rules, and thereby of conformity to the phase rules. In the case of the listening rule, these technical implemental rules deal with such matters as turning and maintaining auditory consciousness in particular directions, namely towards the teacher's spoken words and away from, say, the sounds of the birds in the trees outside, the workmen in the yard, or the whispering voice of the pupil seated at the desk behind.

In the second type of phase, where the teacher is engaging in some form of demonstration, paying attention is accomplished by following the normative implemental rule which requires that the pupils look at the teacher or the objects which are being demonstrated by the teacher. As in the case of the listening rule, prescriptions imply proscriptions, and as a result the pupils are expected not only to look at the teacher but also to refrain from looking elsewhere, that is, away from the teacher or at objects other than those which the teacher intends. And similarly, as in the case of the listening rule, there are further sets of technical implemental rules underpinning normative implemental rules. These technical implemental rules constitute the basic set of procedures which have to be performed in order to accomplish the act of looking in the first place. Here the pupil must follow the technical implemental rule of giving eye contact to, or turning and maintaining visual consciousness towards the teacher and/or the objects which he is demonstrating.

A few brief examples will serve to illustrate the applicability of the above analysis to other types of rules as well. Take the rule which prescribes that pupils be polite to the teachers; how does a pupil accomplish conformity to this rule? Depending once again on the particular context in which politeness is expected, the pupil may accomplish conformity to the politeness rule by performing a variety of acts which constitute being polite in that particular situation. Thus when the pupil wants something from the teacher, say an item of equipment or the answer to a question, he must remember to make a request of the teacher and not simply order the teacher to comply with his wishes, and furthermore, the pupil must usually supplement his request with the word 'please' or 'sir', or put his hand up and await the teacher's permission to speak. Similarly, in those situations where the teacher poses the pupil a direct question it is often the case that the pupil must incorporate the word 'sir' into his reply. Generally speaking, being polite is accomplished by displaying deference and respect towards the teacher on the part of the pupil. The occasions when such politeness is enjoined have implicit in them the imple-mental rules whereby politeness may be accomplished. Thus, in the case of asking the teacher questions, the pupil must make requests and must not give orders. Underpinning the normative implemental rules are the technical implemental rules whereby conformity to the normative implemental rules may be accomplished. With regard to the rule about making a request the pupil must follow the technical rules whereby talk is organized in the form of requests rather than in the form of commands which involves following rules of word organization, voice intonation, and the like.

In the case of the phase rule 'do not cheat' in a test, the normative implemental rules are, first, that the pupils should not copy one another's work; second, that the pupils should not crib; and third, that they should not ask other pupils for answers to test questions. In order to conform to these normative implemental rules, the pupil must follow the technical implemental rules of not cheating. In this case these rules are concerned with proscribing ways in which cheating could effectively be accomplished should the pupil wish to do such a thing. For example, the pupils, in order not to copy, must refrain from looking at another pupil's answers. In other words, in order to conform to the normative implemental rule of not copying, the pupil must conform to the technical implemental rule of not looking at another pupil's work, and in order to conform to this rule the pupil must conform to the technical implemental rule whereby his visual consciousness is focused in one direction rather than another, that is, on his own work rather than on another pupil's. Similarly, in the case of the rule, 'do not crib', the pupil must refrain from the accomplishment of those types of act which constitute cribbing. This involves following the implemental rules whereby the pupils do not have in their possession and do not look at anything that gives the answers to test questions, wherever these answers may be located. Lastly, in the case of the rule which proscribes asking other pupils for the answers to questions, the pupil must conform to the implemental rules whereby the activity known as 'keeping silent' is accomplished.

A legitimate question which could be posed at this point in our analysis is, 'What has happened to the discussion of deviance?' Certainly the scheme as presented so far is mainly about how to perform normatively enjoined tasks in a competent manner, and we have concentrated on the question of how to be a competent pupil in terms of the rules in play in the classroom situation. The analysis presented so far tells us how to deviate only negatively; that is, deviation from the phase rules is achieved by not conforming to the implemental rules whereby conformity to the phase rule is accomplished. However, such an answer hardly illuminates the accomplishment of deviance by pupils in the classroom. It is to this matter that we now wish to turn, namely, how do pupils accomplish deviance in terms of the phase and relational rules we have already discussed? It is only when we have clarified this that we shall be in a position to move on to the main part of our analysis of how the teacher recognizes an act of pupil conduct as deviant.

In proposing that conformity to a rule is accomplished by following a further set of implemental rules, both normative and technical, we are apparently suggesting that deviance from that rule is accomplished by failing to follow its implemental rules. Yet to say that a person is not doing something gives little information about what the person is doing. Whilst it is true that a person may not be doing something because he is totally inactive, it is normally the case that we know that a person is not doing one thing because we know that he is doing something else. The accomplishment of deviance involves more than the mere failure to accomplish conformity; there are rules and skills to be learnt in order to accomplish deviant acts just as there are rules and skills to be mastered in order to accomplish conformist acts. So if we ask how a pupil accomplishes the offence known as 'not paying attention', it is clearly inadequate simply to propose that the pupil is failing to follow the implemental rules inherent in that task of paying attention. We need to know what that pupil is doing and how the pupil accomplishes that act. We will then be in a position to explicate how the teacher knows or evidences that the pupil is not accomplishing the enjoined task (and therefore not following the task's implemental rules) and is thus in a position to impute deviance to the pupil.

There is a variety of ways in which a pupil may not pay attention, but essentially these ways consist of acts which preclude conformity to the implemental rules of paying attention to the teacher. The following quotations illustrate this point:

(1) I. Things that you would be inclined to say, 'Stop doing that', if it happened whilst you were demonstrating. . . .
T. Well, for example, talking to their next-door neighbour, that's an obvious one, or if I caught anybody drawing, perhaps drawing an image of a football or something like that when he's supposed to be watching. To my mind I can't say that they can be taking sufficient interest if they're fiddling about with other things that are outside the classroom, thoughts which take them outside the classroom. I think whilst a lesson is on, concentration is necessary. You only need to think on these lines, you only need to think of, for example, yourself in a lecture or listening to a sermon in church anything like that, if you don't concentrate you won't take in all the lecturer is trying to put over or all that the preacher is trying to put over. I do think that anything that is detrimental to concentrating should be stopped.
I. You pointed out . . . what are the less obvious signs that lead you to suspect that somebody is not paying attention?
T. Well, I suppose, this is a fairly obvious one really, you've only got to catch somebody gazing out of the window, you see . . . they're not making a noise even but they are not paying attention. I don't really know of anything else that will come to my mind at the moment.

(2) I. Next one, 'X, will you stop playing with your money?'
T. Well, again it's inattention if he is playing with money. He is not listening to me or doing what he should be doing.

(3) I. What for you would constitute not listening then?
T. Where a child is obviously doing something—making pellets, for example, or trying to lean and touch someone else or looking over his shoulder doing this kind of thing, obviously it's showing signs of disinterest.

From the teacher's point of view the offence known as 'not paying attention' may be accomplished by engaging in a variety of acts: talking, drawing, fiddling with irrelevant objects, thinking about irrelevant matters, not concentrating, gazing through the window, moving around the room, and so on. All these acts can be accomplished only by failing to follow the implemental rules of paying attention. But to say that throws no light on how the pupil actually accomplishes those deviant acts, for the implemental rules of talking, drawing, fiddling with irrelevant objects, etc., remain unspecified. In breaking the rule of paying attention, the pupil may break the normative implemental rule which demands that he look at the teacher simply by looking elsewhere—through the window, at another pupil, at an object hidden behind the desk. (In so doing, of course, he is continuing to follow the technical implemental rule of looking, namely turning and maintaining visual consciousness in particular directions at particular objects, for this rule is inherent in any act of looking.) Alternatively he may engage in actions which break both the technical as well as the normative implemental rules, for instance by closing his eyes and daydreaming or sleeping. In accomplishing any of these acts the pupil must follow their implemental rules. He must know how, i.e. by what rules, it is possible to look at something else or to daydream or to fall asleep.[3]

Similarly, in those contexts where the pay attention rule requires that the pupil listen to the teacher, the pupil can break this rule by listening to something or someone else, such as another pupil or a workman outside the classroom, in which case he is continuing to follow the technical implemental rule, namely the rule of how to listen, but breaks the normative implemental rule, which requires that he listens to the teacher's voice.

In the case of other types of act cited by teachers as constitutive of not paying attention—playing with money, fiddling with a crisp bag, moving around the room—all these acts can be accomplished by following known implemental rules, none of which is involved in listening to and/or looking at the teacher, which is what constitutes paying attention. In the case of the rule which proscribes cheating in tests, the pupil may break that rule by breaking its implemental rules, and in order to accomplish this he must follow the implemental rules whereby cheating may be accomplished. The pupil may cheat by breaking the rules against copying, cribbing and asking other pupils for answers, and to break these rules the pupil must follow the implemental rules of copying, cribbing and asking neighbours for answers. If a pupil wants to accomplish copying he must look at his neighbour's work, and write down what he has seen on to his own paper. Of course, both this looking and this writing presuppose following the technical implemental rules whereby both looking and writing are accomplished. Similarly, in the case of cribbing the pupil must first of all devise a crib, such as a small piece of paper hidden beneath his test paper; he must then look where the crib is located, and then write down the information so acquired on to his test paper. Such methods, of course, comprise only a small number of the many ways of accomplishing cheating, and it is not our intention to provide an exhaustive catalogue of such methods for the prospective cheat, for that would exhaust the reader as well.

This analysis applies also in the case of relational rules as well as phase rules. We shall consider the good manners rule of teacher-pupil relations which requires that the pupil be polite. Here the pupil can be impolite merely by failing to follow the implemental rules of being polite. He may, for instance, simply decline to use the word 'sir' in his remarks to the teacher. But more common than such sins of omission are the sins of commission, whereby the pupil acts in a 'familiar' manner, thus denying the teacher's status by treating him as 'one of the boys', or by ordering the teacher to do things rather than making requests, thus making an attack on his dignity and rights. In performing such acts which break the implemental rules of being polite, the pupil must follow different sets of implemental rules by which they can be accomplished: he has to learn how to be impolite.

Deviance, like conformity, must be recognized as a task much like any other, and any deviant act is accomplished by following complex and interrelated constellations of rules. In making this point, we wish to draw attention to what is a much neglected dimension of the phenomena of deviance as viewed from current perspectives in this field, and in particular, the labelling approach. This neglected dimension consists of the practical accomplishment of deviance from the members' point of view, that is, how deviance is done as an activity or task. We feel that this aspect of deviance has been obscured, or rather taken for granted, by those who would view deviance as merely the failure to conform to rules or as merely the process of imputation based on the observation of rule-breaking. We have emphasized this dimension not only because we feel that the accomplishment of deviance from members' points of view is interesting and investigable in its own right, but also because it is the members' taken-for-granted knowledge of the typical methods whereby deviance is accomplished which forms the essential basis of deviance-imputations. In our own work, it is the pupils' common-sense knowledge about how conformity to and deviance from phase and relational rules is accomplished that allows them to conform and deviate. More important to the theme of this chapter is the fact that the teachers share this common-sense knowledge of conformity and deviance, for they draw on it constantly in recognizing or knowing that acts are conformist or deviant. Without it, they would be quite unable to make deviance-imputations.

The shared nature of this common-sense knowledge of conformity and deviance is demonstrated by an examination of the deviance-imputations which we quoted at the beginning of this chapter. When the teacher says to the pupil, 'Pay attention' as a deviance-imputation, he is simply stating the 'phase rule' in play at the time of utterance. In so doing, he is drawing on his knowledge that the pupil's act—whatever it is—involves not following implemental rules of paying attention but does involve the following of implemental rules of some other incompatible act. The pupil understands the teacher's statement as a deviance-imputation because he too shares the common-sense knowledge of paying attention. Yet the teacher may say to the pupil, 'Look at me', where the teacher is citing the 'normative implemental rule' of paying attention, not the phase rule itself. Or the teacher may say, 'Turn your head this way', where the teacher is citing the 'technical implemental rule' which underlies both the normative implemental and the phase rules. To both teacher and pupil, all these statements have the same meaning, only because both teacher and pupil share the same knowledge of the relationship between what we have called the phase rule and its underpinning implemental rules. Our development of the concept of implemental rules to explicate the members' common-sense knowledge of conformity and deviance not only allows us to understand how teachers know that a pupil is being deviant—about which much remains to be said in the rest of this chapter—but it also allows us to understand how members (and we researchers) are able to interpret a large number of different verbal deviance-imputations as having the same meaning.

From our analysis so far it is clear that teachers possess a stock of common-sense knowledge about the accomplishment of deviance and conformity. We must now examine in more detail how, on the basis of this knowledge, the teacher is able to recognize that deviance is occurring or has occurred. The interpretive work involved here is highly complex: it consists of a variety of capacities and practices. We shall concern ourselves with a limited aspect of this interpretive work, namely the application of 'interpretive rules'. These rules consist of collections of assumptions by means of which members are able to classify, typify, identify and name, objects, persons, acts and events as being of a certain kind. In this present analysis we are concerned with two kinds of interpretive rule. The first refers to those rules by which a member is able to interpret and define acts as certain kinds of act. It is by means of these rules that members are able to recognize talking as talking, looking as looking, writing as writing, running as running and so on. The second kind of interpretive rule—in which we are much more interested—refers to those rules by which members are able to link those acts which they have recognized as certain kinds of act to the rules which they know to be in play, and thereby interpret those acts as being in conformity to, or deviating from, the rules in play. In short, for our purposes, the interpretive work consists of two analytically distinct processes which involve the application of two kinds of interpretive rule: (1) the interpretation of an act as a certain kind of act, and (2) the interpretation of that act as a rule-breaking act. Since our particular interest is in the second kind of interpretive rules, rather than in the first kind of interpretive rules which underpin them, we shall for obvious reasons call them 'evidential rules'.

Teachers, like detectives in the police force and like all of us in our more mundane everyday detective practices, use evidential rules to identify rule-breaking. In classrooms, as we shall see, because the deviant status of pupil acts is often shrouded in ambiguity from the point of view of teachers (and of ourselves as observers), the application of some of these evidential rules eventuates in a suspicion rather than a conviction that the pupil's act is deviant. We shall show that teachers attempt to clarify their knowledge about the act and its relationship to the rule in play by means of what we shall call 'evidential strategies', which consist of investigative actions taken by the teacher as a method of resolving such ambiguity.

From our interviews and observations of teachers' imputations of deviance, it would appear that teachers possess an extensive collection of evidential rules whereby pupil acts are recognizable as deviant. In order to describe these we shall first take the case of the pay attention rule and ask the question: how do teachers recognize that deviance from this rule is occurring or has occurred? In order to answer this question we shall present examples of teachers' accounts about their interpretive work whereby they are able to recognize deviance in terms of this rule, and we shall show how this interpretive work involves the use of evidential rules and evidential strategies. It will then be shown how these various first-order evidential rules may in turn be reduced to a much smaller number of second-order, abstract, sociologically formulated evidential rules, and how these latter rules can then be used to make sense of teachers' accomplishment of deviance-imputations not only in terms of the pay attention rule, but also in terms of a variety of other phase and relational rules as well. To this end we shall examine the rules about cheating, aggression, politeness, obedience and punctuality. In our exposition, as will become apparent, the recognition of deviance in terms of these other rules reveals the use of other types of evidential rule as well as those employed to recognize not paying attention.

How then do teachers know that a pupil is not paying attention? How are they able to recognize and code the observed pupil action as an instance of deviance from the pay attention rule? Let us examine some further accounts by teachers.

(1) I. How would you recognize that somebody was not paying attention?
T. Glassy eyes, a vague look, and probably looking out of the window. Other than that, fiddling with his bag, probably either anticipating or not realizing, anticipating something I was going to say, therefore he is not paying attention. Taking out their books when they are supposed to be listening. This is not paying attention.

(2) I. What would be signs of not paying attention?
T. Well, not looking at you for a start, looking away from you. Either looking down at their feet or looking at the person next to them, or just—er—that is the main one— not looking directly at you.

These accounts clearly confirm our earlier analysis. The pupil is held not to be paying attention if he is not following the implemental rules of paying attention and/or is following the implemental rules of some action which is incompatible with the task of paying attention. 'Looking away', 'looking through the window' and 'looking at another person' preclude looking at the teacher. The teacher draws on his ability to recognize and code these acts as such and on his common-sense knowledge that one cannot look at two things or in two directions simultaneously. In those contexts where the pay attention rule in play requires that the pupil look at the teacher, such acts will constitute an infraction of that rule. In other words, the teacher has at his disposal a large collection of evidential rules, all of which take the form: if the pupil is doing action X, then he cannot be doing action Y. Examples would be:

'If the pupil is looking through the window, then he cannot be looking at me.'
'If the pupil is looking at the person next to him, then he cannot be looking at me.'
'If the pupil is looking at his feet, then he cannot be looking at me.'

The teacher is able to recognize a large number of acts that necessarily preclude the pupil from committing the action that is normatively enjoined by the rule in play. From our point of view we can reduce all these evidential rules into a single, abstract, sociologically formulated second-order rule, from which all the teacher's first-order evidential rules can be derived. We propose the following evidential rule.

If an act is perceived to be following the implemental rules of an action which necessarily involves infraction of the implemental rules of the (classroom) rule in play, then that act is deviant.

At a later stage we shall test out the general applicability of this second-order evidential rule by trying to fit it to other classroom rules. Before doing this, we want to show that an examination of teacher's accounts brings to light other evidential rules in addition to the 'conviction evidential rule' which we have just formulated. We can begin by considering another form of the pay attention rule, namely where the pupil is required to listen to, rather than merely look at, the teacher.

(1) I.   The first one, 'Are you listening?'
    T.   You want to know why I said it? I probably said it
because he looked as though he wasn't listening. It's
something on their face that you could tell and it calls their
attention to what you are saying.
    I.   When you say something on their face, could you be more
explicit about that?
    T.   Yes, well they are staring round the room or out of the
window or they have got their head turned away from you.
I find it annoying to try to talk to children when they are
not looking at me, probably because I'm used to performing
on the stage. I like an audience to be attentive.

(2) I.   What for you would constitute not listening then?
    T.   Where a child is obviously doing something—making
pellets for example, or trying to lean and touch someone
else or looking over his shoulder doing this kind of thing,
obviously it's showing signs of disinterest.

These accounts show that teachers cite the same evidence for not listening as for not looking; indeed, not looking is thought to constitute grounds for the judgment that the pupil is not listening. In this they are drawing on the common-sense knowledge that we normally look at persons to whom we are listening. Yet they are fully aware that not looking does not necessarily preclude listening. The teachers say that the pupil 'looked as though he was not listening' and that he 'showed signs of disinterest'. The conviction rule clearly does not apply in this case. The teacher is not convinced that the pupil is being deviant; rather, he suspects that the pupil is being deviant.

    I.   How would you recognize that a pupil was not paying
attention?
    T.   Well, it's hard sometimes because it may look as though,
I mean it's really hard to tell even if they are behaving perfectly
quietly whether they are listening. The only way is if you get
feedback from them, which you can. As I say, in class discussions

we always discuss a piece of writing before we do it and there
are some boys that you can't drag—I say, 'Well, what do you
think about that?' and they shrug their shoulders, and mostly
when you get the written work you can tell whether they have
been listening, most of the class, but a slipshod piece of work
might not prove that they haven't listened, it's just that they are
too lazy to do a better piece.

I.   Actually in a situation where you are telling them something
say, what would be a sign that they weren't paying attention?

T.   Well, the obvious sign is if they start looking at somebody
else for any reason. Mind you though it's not always proof that,
because sometimes I have said to somebody, I have directed a
question at them, and they have been listening even though they
had been—so they had got one ear on me and one ear to see
what's happening there, so I have tried that out and it doesn't
always work. They say, 'Ah I was listening, you see', even though
they were looking away, and you know you can sometimes
subconsciously be listening so it doesn't always prove that they
are not listening. It's very hard to tell whether a boy is actually
taking in what you are saying.

I.   What do you usually do when you suspect that a boy is not
listening?

T.   I'll direct a question to him if it's a class discussion and see
whether they can answer it, but as I say sometimes they can!—
hah hah hah—in that case I sometimes make a joke of it and say,
'Just let me know that you are listening next time.'

I.   So they are meant to be looking as well really?

T.   Well, I mean it is disconcerting if you have got a class in
front of you and somebody is not looking in your direction. It's
very hard to tell whether they're listening then, and the only way
is to direct a question to them. And sometimes they can tell
you word for word what you have said even though they have
not been looking at you, or they seem to be looking at what,
not talking, but seem to be looking at what some boy is doing,
you know, so you have jumped on them, but they know what
you have been saying. . . . It's surprising when you meet boys
that are supposed to be not particularly bright. They are bright
in doing things that *they* think matter, you know—not getting
caught out . . . they use their brains in the wrong ways sometimes.

These accounts betray several significant features. The most
obvious of these is the appearance of a number of first-order
evidential rules by which teachers become suspicious that—as
opposed to being convinced that—a deviant act is taking place.

Examples of these are:

'If a pupil is not looking at me, then this is grounds for suspecting that he is not listening to me.'
'If a pupil is making pellets, then this is grounds for suspecting that he is not listening to me.'
'If a pupil has his head on his hands and his eyes downcast then this is grounds for suspecting that he is not listening to me.'

These, and many other similar first-order evidential rules, can be given an abstract formulation as the evidential rule of suspicion.

If a pupil is perceived to be following the implemental rules of an action which *could* constitute infraction of the implemental rules of the (classroom) rule in play, but which does not necessarily involve an infraction of these implemental rules, then that act is to be suspected as deviant.

Where the evidential rule of suspicion is applicable to an act, but the conviction rule is not, the teacher has insufficient grounds for making an overt imputation of deviance. Were the teacher to make such an imputation, he would open himself to denial, contradiction, or even accusations from pupils. Before the teacher can make such an imputation, he must transform his suspicion that the pupil is possibly or even probably being deviant into a firm conviction. Like a detective, he must seek further evidence to resolve the ambiguity. In other words, he must discover sufficiently more about the act to make the conviction rule the appropriate and relevant evidential rule. In order to collect and collate this evidence, the teacher must employ an 'evidential strategy'.[4] These strategies can take various forms; in the extracts above the particular strategy used is the interrogative strategy—directing questions at the suspected deviant with the intention of culling the required clarificatory information/ evidence.

That teachers commonly employ interrogative evidential strategies in evidencing deviance from the pay attention rule, is attested to by one of the pupils in the study:

I. What do teachers do in that situation?
P. Say you're talking, you're not taking no notice, they'll ask you a question on what you're supposed to be doing, what they're teaching you like. Say in Maths, like, he's doing a sum on the board and you're talking behind a book, well he'll just say, 'Right, Shaw, how do you do such and such a thing?' If you're listening you know how to do it but say you're talking to somebody else they'll say, 'You're too busy talking to know how to do these.' If you can't answer they say that you've been talking.

These interrogative strategies—whose strategic nature is fully recognized by the pupils—are often successful in that they elicit the relevant evidence which permits the transition from suspicion to conviction. But of course these interrogative strategies presuppose other interpretive work. For instance, when a teacher asks a pupil a question to ascertain whether or not he has been listening, he must be able to recognize an 'incorrect' answer when he hears one. Every evidential strategy is built upon such interpretive capacities.

The evidential strategies do not always resolve suspicion into conviction. As the accounts presented show, the teacher's suspicions may prove to be groundless: the pupil, as it were, 'passes' the test implicit in the evidential strategy and demonstrates that he was indeed conforming to the rule in play. In such cases the teacher abandons—or at least partially abandons—his suspicions. The act is now retrospectively redefined as conformist, though teachers often advise the pupil to make his conformity more evident in future.

Because evidencing not listening is accomplished by the use of the interrogative evidential strategy we may say that it is only evidenceable indirectly and retrospectively. Hence we may subsume the use of this evidential rule under a more general category of interpretive work, namely, retrospective interpretation.[5] Retrospective interpretation deals with matters which have occurred in the past and by engaging in it the teacher is able to infer that deviance has occurred, as opposed to inferring that deviance is actually in the process of its occurrence. The example just mentioned in the case of listening illustrates the use of one set of interpretive rules whereby retrospective interpretation is accomplished; the following quotation illustrates the use of another.

> T.   The classic, of course, is you know immediately when they are not paying attention when you say, 'Right I want you to take your book out, I want you to write the date and the heading, and I want you to draw me a picture, and it's to be a full side picture', and so the kid immediately comes out and says, 'Look, sir, I've got a half side here, should I draw my picture on here?' I mean he wasn't paying attention and this happens about 90 per cent of the time, and you can be certain in any classroom that at least two or three people will not be paying attention. I don't know, maybe it depends on how good a teacher you are but I've yet to find anybody that has found a solution to this, so that everybody is paying attention all the time, because you know as a student your mind wanders, it's bound to.

Here the teacher argues that because the pupil in question asks him for instructions it is possible to infer that pupil could not have been listening when he originally gave instructions, because the pupil's question had in effect already been answered by him. Consequently, if the pupil then provides evidence that he could not have been listening, by asking the teacher a question about matters already dealt with, then the teacher finds it reasonable to infer that the pupil could not have been paying attention.

In cases like this the deviant nature of the act emerges some time after its commission. At the time of the act the teacher was not suspicious, however, and therefore no investigative strategy was initiated. In the above account the commission of a later pupil act becomes comprehensible only if the teacher makes a retrospective application of an evidential rule by which the earlier act is defined as an instance of deviant conduct. The present act is seen as the natural consequence of an earlier undetected, unsuspected and uninvestigated act which is now defined as deviant. These retrospective applications of evidential rules occur in the case of both conviction and suspicion rules. When the pupil act which is observed in the present can be accounted for only if an earlier and undetected deviant act is imputed to the pupil then it is the conviction rule that is applied. But in many cases other interpretations are possible. For instance, if a pupil asks the teacher a question about previously stated instructions or explanations, the question may spring from the pupil's failure to pay attention or from the teacher's failure to make his explanation or instructions clear. In these cases, it is the suspicion rule but not the conviction rule which can be applied retrospectively.

We made the point earlier that teachers and pupils share the common-sense knowledge of how conformity and deviance are accomplished. One important consequence of this fact is that pupils also share an understanding of the evidential rules and strategies which teachers employ to detect or suspect that deviant conduct is taking place. So in order to escape being suspected or detected, they must engage in conduct which is designed to conceal or mask behaviour which can be used by teachers as grounds for applying the evidential rules and thus for making deviance-imputations. Consequently, many deviant acts carry with them a range of appropriate concealment strategies. For instance, deviant talk can be masked by whispering, covering the mouth, the passing of notes, etc. Not surprisingly, the teachers are again one step ahead of their pupils, for they too share this knowledge about concealment strategies. So if a teacher observes a pupil committing an act of concealment, or following one of the implemental rules of that act of concealment, then he has grounds for suspecting that a deviant act is taking place. Moreover, since the teacher knows which concealment strategies are linked with which deviant acts, he is still in a good position to suspect the precise form of the deviant act that is taking place, even though he may observe only the concealment behaviour rather than the deviant act itself.

The capacity of teachers to recognize deviant conduct, then, is grounded in their common-sense knowledge which is organized in terms of a set of evidential rules. We offer as a summary of teachers' interpretive work the following sociologically formulated evidential rules.

The Conviction Rule
If an act is perceived to be following the implemental rules of an action which necessarily involves infraction of the implemental rules of the rule in play then that act is deviant.

For example, if the teacher perceives that a pupil is looking out of the window, or is talking, or is fast asleep, acts which necessarily preclude conformity to the implemental rules of paying attention, then that pupil must be deviant in terms of the pay attention rule.

Further, this evidential rule may be used retrospectively to infer that deviance must have taken place. In its retrospective form the conviction rule may be stated as follows:

If an act is perceived to be the consequence of an earlier act which entailed the following of implemental rules which necessarily involved infraction of the implemental rules of the rule in play at that time, then that earlier act must have been deviant.

For example, if the teacher perceives that a pupil cannot answer an easy question or cannot repeat what the teacher has just stated then that pupil could not have been paying attention at the time the teacher made the statement.[6]

The Suspicion Rule
If an act is perceived to be following the implemental rules of an action which could constitute infraction of the implemental rules of the rule in play, but which does not necessarily involve infraction of the implemental rules of the rule in play, then that act is to be suspected as deviant.

For example, if a pupil is perceived to be looking out of the window or at another pupil or fiddling with an object, acts which do not necessarily preclude conformity to the implemental rule of paying attention, which prescribes that the pupils listen to the teacher, then the pupil's act is to be interpreted as suspicious and to be suspected as deviant.

As in the case of the conviction rule, the suspicion rule may also be used retrospectively. In its retrospective form the suspicion rule is as follows:

If an act is perceived to be the consequence of an earlier act which could have involved infraction of the implemental rules of the rule in play, but which does not necessarily imply such previous infraction, then that act is to be suspected as deviant.

For example, if the pupil cannot answer a question, which may well be accounted for in terms of his deviance from the implemental rules of the pay attention rule, but which could also be accounted for by virtue of the fact that the pupil is 'stupid' or failed to understand what the teacher was talking about, then that pupil may be suspected but not convicted of having been deviant.

In addition the suspicion rule is used to infer that a pupil may be committing a deviant act when the teacher observes the pupil engaging in acts of concealment. In this case the evidential rule may be stated as follows:

If an act is perceived to be following the implemental rules of 'covering up' or concealment then the pupil is to be suspected of committing, or having committed, a deviant act.

For example, where the pupil is perceived to be hiding his mouth from the gaze of teacher by covering it with his hand then he is to be suspected of talking.

We shall now take these sociologically formulated evidential rules and show how they are used in recognizing deviance from a variety of rules in play in the classroom, and in conjunction with evidential strategies mentioned above. We shall take each of the evidential rules in turn.

First let us examine the use of the conviction rule, both in the way it is used to recognize the deviant act whilst it is occurring, and in the way it is used to infer retrospectively that deviance has in the past taken place. This rule is used to impute deviance in terms of the phase rule proscribing cheating in tests when the pupil provides immediately observable and unambiguous evidence that he is currently engaging in the act of cheating. Such evidence of cheating is provided when the pupil is perceived to be following the implemental rules whereby the various ways of cheating may be accomplished, for example, copying, cribbing and asking other pupils for answers to questions. Thus, if the teacher observes that the pupil is looking at another pupil's work and is then copying what he observes on to his own paper, then that pupil, from the teacher's point of view, is 'obviously' copying, since he is following the implemental rules of copying. The same applies to the teacher's perception that the pupil is currently engaging in cribbing, or is asking another pupil for answers. By directly observing that the pupil is accomplishing these acts the teacher is able to infer that the pupil is 'obviously' cheating because these acts necessarily break the implemental rules whereby conformity to the no cheating rule is accomplished. On the basis of such directly observable and unambiguous evidence, the teacher is able to use the conviction rule as a basis for imputing deviance in terms of the no cheating rule.

Similarly, in the case of the teacher-pupil relational rule which requires that pupils be polite to teachers, the teacher may use the conviction rule to impute deviance when the pupil provides directly observable evidence of his following the implemental rules of an action which necessarily involves infraction of the implemental rules of conformity to the be polite rule. Thus where the teacher directly observes unambiguous evidence that the pupil is following the implemental rules whereby 'disrespect', 'rudeness', 'cheekiness', 'insults and so on, are accomplished, then the teacher can employ the conviction rule to organize these perceptions and thereby impute deviance to the pupil. In chapter 4 we quoted an instance where a pupil told a teacher to 'get stuffed'. Most teachers in this study would almost certainly define this as an unambiguous infraction of the rule, since it is very difficult to give any alternative interpretation to the pupil's statement other than to make an overt, direct and intentional insult. However, it is often quite difficult to apply the conviction rule in the case of good manners and politeness rules. In part this is because there are considerable variations amongst teachers in regard to what constitutes politeness and 'cheek', since they vary in the degree of formality/informality they allow into their relationships with pupils. What is defined as 'cheek' by one teacher may be interpreted as 'friendliness' by another. In part this is because of the structure of accomplishing some forms of politeness. For instance, pupils are expected to add the word 'sir' to some of their statements which are addressed to teachers. The frequency with which this word is to be added is problematic. A child can be defined as being cheeky if he never uses the word; but equally he will be defined as cheeky if he uses the word excessively in a kind of super-conformity. So the teacher may well rely on other cues in his interpretive work, such as the intonation of the word 'sir'. In part also it is because the interpretation of an act as cheeky involves an imputation of intent by the teacher to the pupil. The imputation of intent is implicit in all deviance-imputations, of course, but teachers appear to find it more problematic in the case of certain rules, of which the good manners rule is a prominent example.

(1) I. He was shouting out for you to move the board for some
other girl. . . .

T. It's like that all the time and we have a very casual sort
of relationship—they are not cheeky because their attitude
isn't cheeky except on occasions when they go a little bit
too far. They do things like that—'Hey, move the board,
Miss.' They don't say, 'Please could you move the board?'
like other kids might. They don't do that, they are very much
at home and I think that is quite natural. It's the third year
of having me and I don't mind it and frequently they call me
'mum' and to me this is all part of 3E although they are
getting a bit older now, aren't they, to be doing that sort of
thing?

I. Is that cheek?

T. No. They don't intend to, they get carried away.

(2) I. What sort of cheek do they give you?

T. They give you kind of off-hand replies, you know, not
really the sort of thing you would expect. I mean it's not that
I am against cheek, but I just think, it grates on me because
it undermines you, . . . it just grates on me because I don't
mind them being cheeky but I think there again they should
not be, so I have got to make something of it, and he has
got a particular kind of devilish glint in his eye, Steve Roberts,
that really, I don't know whether you know the look I mean.
I don't know whether you have seen it, you know he can look
at you really cheekily as though, you know, he knows he is
being cheeky—I don't know, things only strike me as cheeky
only after it has happened usually. . . .

I. Do you think he is being cheeky on purpose?

T. No, I don't think he is being cheeky on purpose, but
there again he should know what is being cheeky. I don't
think he knows when he's being cheeky. . . .

As in the case of the other rules considered above the teacher is
able to use the conviction rule to impute deviance in terms of the
pupil-pupil relational rule which proscribes aggression.

(1) I. What would be a sign of bullying?

T. In a lesson . . . I will not tolerate kids taking the mickey
out of one another. I will not stand laughing when someone
gets something wrong. That's the first thing, I stamp on that
straightaway at the start. I say, 'I don't care whether you
get an answer right or wrong, put your hand up and have a
go; if you are wrong, you are wrong', and if one person

E*

laughs I always tell them. I don't care if they are the cleverest in the class you know.

(2) I.   Well, what about bullying, how would you recognize a case of bullying?

T.   You know a lot of these questions are downright intuition, you don't know it but you know it.

I.   Well, what sorts of things would the kids have to do to suggest to you that bullying was occurring?

T.   Thumping, or else you know, the raised fist, and the other kid obviously showing signs that he is going to get thumped if he doesn't do what the other kid tells him to do. A boy's look towards another one will usually tell you that this kid is either in fear of the other one or he knows that in the sort of scheme of things, in the line of peck if you like, and there is always one of these in a class, you know, there is always some poor beggar that gets thumped and everybody can thump him, and then, of course, there is the cock of the class and then from there there is the cock of the year and no matter how much we try to stamp that out it still exists. You can usually tell excessive bullying, you know, the odd, 'You do that or else I'll thump you,'—that you can see.

In these two extracts it is clear that deviance from the aggression rule may be conclusively imputed when the pupil follows the implemental rules of accomplishing acts of either mental or physical aggression which necessarily preclude conformity to the rule proscribing aggression. We might note here that teachers draw not only upon the evidence which is provided by the individual pupil, but also upon evidence which is provided by both parties to the interaction; that is, from the conduct of the 'victim' as well as from the conduct of the 'aggressor'.

Often offences cannot be directly witnessed in the process of their occurrence, but rather are retrospectively inferred from currently available evidence. If the pupil act which is observed in the present can be accounted for only if the teacher imputes to the pupil an undetected earlier deviant act then the teacher can use the conviction rule retrospectively. The following extract illustrates its use to impute deviance in terms of the obedience rule:

I.   No, the previous instance when he came in. Then you said to him, 'Go back and walk.'

T.   Because he and the girl ran all the way up [the corridor] and I made them go back and then he came back too quickly and I knew he hadn't done it.

In this case the teacher had observed two pupils running in the corridor, which was a breach of the school rules. So the pupils were told to go back and walk along the corridor. The teacher did not observe this, but concluded that the boy had reappeared at the classroom so quickly that he could not have conformed to (been obedient to) the instruction that he should go back and walk, i.e. either he went back and ran or he did not go back at all. In claiming that the pupil took 'too little time' to accomplish the act, the teacher is making use of the common-sense knowledge about how long it takes to accomplish given tasks in given situations. The teacher is convinced of the validity of the deviance-imputation because there is no possible method by which the pupil could have conformed to the instruction and yet returned to the classroom so quickly.

So far we have dealt with the question of the imputation of deviance on the basis of unambiguous evidence by the use of the conviction rule in either its present or retrospective forms. We now turn to the imputation of deviance on the basis of much more ambiguous evidence, that is, to the evidential rules whereby acts may be endowed with the quality of suspiciousness, and also to the evidential strategies that are used to clarify evidence or to acquire further evidence, so that the teacher is able to apply the conviction rule instead of merely remaining suspicious.

Acts may be endowed with the quality of suspiciousness when the teacher observes the pupil committing acts which could involve infraction of the implemental rules of a particular phase or relational rule, but which do not necessarily preclude conformity to such rules. Probably the best example of the use of the suspicion rule is the case of the rule which proscribes cheating during tests. A pupil is to be suspected of cheating if he provides evidence that he is following the implemental rules of an act which could constitute the offence of cheating, but where the teacher is as yet unsure as to whether or not such an act is constitutive of cheating. Where the pupil engages in talking to another pupil during a test, such an act may be indicative of cheating but this need not necessarily be so, because the pupil could quite easily be asking another pupil for a rubber rather than asking the pupil for the answer to a question of the test. Similarly, the pupil could be observed looking down at his lap deep in thought, but the teacher may be suspicious that this is a case of cheating, since looking down at the lap could be one of the signs that the pupil was using a crib placed on his lap. In the use of the suspicion rule the teacher is inferring from the pupil's conduct that he could be performing a deviant act but he could also be performing a conformist act. In some instances resolution of the ambiguity of these acts is achieved by the use of an evidential strategy, such as the interrogative strategy. Thus, the teacher can simply ask the pupil, 'What are you doing?' and infer from the pupil's reaction to his question whether or not the pupil had been cheating. Alternatively, the teacher can employ another type of evidential strategy, namely moving to check visually if the pupil has a crib hidden on his lap or not. Or the teacher can simply 'wait and see' if two pupils' answers are the same when the test is completed, though we should note here that such a similarity of answers can only, as it were, provide corroborative evidence of the suspected cheating, rather than establishing as a matter of fact that the pupils had been cheating.

Another excellent example of the retrospective use of the suspicion rule is in relation to the institutional rule that enjoins punctuality. Offences in terms of the punctuality rule are interesting because it is not possible for the teacher to infer that a child is deviant in terms of this rule merely by observational interpretation alone. To be sure, the teacher has only to look at the positions of the hands of the clock to ascertain whether or not the pupil is in fact a 'late arrival', but the simple fact of the late arrival is insufficient grounds for an imputation of deviance in terms of the punctuality rule. To ascertain whether or not the pupil is deviant in terms of this rule the teacher must acquire more information, and in particular, information about the grounds for the late arrival since if the pupil has 'good' grounds the act will not be defined as deviant. The late arrival in itself is a basic pre-condition of deviance in terms of the punctuality rule but for deviance to be imputed to the pupil who has arrived late, an account of the act must be provided by him; deviance may or may not be imputed depending on the nature of that account.[7] The first step from the teacher's point of view is to establish the grounds for the late arrival. Usually the teacher will ask the pupil to account for his late arrival. On occasion, however, the teacher's knowledge of the type of person the pupil is enables him to dispense with such evidential work because he is sure that the pupil concerned will have a legitimate reason for being late. On the other hand, some pupils are more likely to be called to account because of the teacher's knowledge that they typically do not have legitimate reasons for being late.

> A boy comes in after the lesson has started. As he comes in he goes towards the teacher's desk, presumably to explain why he is late. Before the pupil can say anything the teacher says, 'Sit down', and the boy goes to his seat.
> Immediately after the lesson I asked the teacher why he had not allowed the pupil to explain his late arrival. He said, 'In this case I assumed that he had been legitimately delayed. There are other lads who I would have asked where they had been.'
> (Observer's notes)

With regard to the imputation of deviance in terms of the punctuality rule, accounts for late arrival may be defined as legitimate or illegitimate. Legitimate accounts are those which are acceptable to the teacher and do not result in a definition of the late arrival as deviant. Illegitimate accounts are those which are unacceptable to teachers; they are 'excuses' rather than 'good reasons', and do result in a definition of the late arrival as deviant. Teachers possess a stock of knowledge of typical accounts provided by pupils such that any particular account may be legitimate or illegitimate. Some accounts are just not acceptable from the teacher's point of view, and any pupil who provides such an account is likely to have his late arrival defined as deviant.

(1) I.   This is an interesting thing about the people who come too late to lessons. Two lads came in and in fact they immediately volunteered an explanation. You did not have to ask them. They said they had been to [the headmaster] and you said to them, 'What for?' Why did you query that?
T.   I had to know whether they had been sent for over some legitimate thing that I would know something about, or whether this was an excuse. I didn't expect in the case of these two lads that it would be an insufficient reason. I expected it to be a reasonable explanation and I was satisfied when I got it, that it was something not directly in their control. They were not simply going off to see him simply to waste time.
I.   What would have constituted an unsatisfactory explanation?
T.   Well, not in this class, but in some classes lads would come in and say, 'I have been to ask if I could get off to go for my football tackle', or, 'Can I do something relative to games', towards which the answer would have obviously been 'no', and they had gone and should have known that it would have been negative, so the only point in going would have been to waste time. People saying, 'I went to see if I could go home for my PE things', and they know they are not allowed to do this in lesson time. So I expect them to be aware of this and not to go and ask.

(2) I.   The boys who came in late and you asked, 'Where have you been?' They accounted for themselves in some, what. . . ?
T.   Yes, but it was wrong, they had been to the toilet and this is what dinner-time is for, you see, and I told them I would report them to [the deputy head]. I knew he was busy and I knew he wouldn't thank me for sending him more

you see. Then one boy told me about his pen but he hadn't
explained that to me when he came in. He never apologized
and said where he'd been.

I.   Then two girls came in and they made an excuse. You
accepted that?

T.   Yes I did, it was something that was quite legitimate.
They'd been to a teacher about something.

I.   I was just wondering what the difference was.

T.   Oh yes, it was a legitimate excuse. You see this business
of going to the toilet. That should all have been done during
the dinner hour. There's no excuse for that. These two girls
had been to a teacher about something she wanted to see
them for.

Whenever a pupil comes late to a lesson, he becomes subject to an
investigative evidential strategy in terms of the punctuality rule; that
is, is the pupil justifiably late? As the above extracts illustrate,
teachers distinguish between legitimate ('good', 'adequate', 'reasonable') and illegitimate ('bad', 'inadequate', 'unreasonable') accounts.
Of course, the fact that some accounts of lateness become recognized
as legitimate and others as illegitimate does raise the possibility that
this common-sense knowledge may be drawn upon by pupils. They
come to know what types of accounts are appropriate in typical
settings and thereby may come to use them fraudulently. In addition,
then, to the type of account offered by the pupil, there is this issue
of whether or not the account is authentic. A late arrival by a pupil
is normally subject to the suspicion rule, which the teacher seeks to
resolve by an examination of the account proffered by the pupil.
But since it is possible for the pupil to proffer an inauthentic account,
the accounting itself may become subject to a further suspicion rule.

(1) I.   What would an excuse have to sound like for it to sound
inauthentic?

T.   Well, you get things like, suppose I was teaching in the
main building, you know, someone will say he kicked a ball
in the river or something like that, you know, in the brook
that runs past my room, you know. And when it comes down
to the truth they have just been strolling along and the ball
has never been in the river at all, and they say they couldn't
leave it there because someone would see it and take it so I
had to go and get it, you know. Things like that, most of
the time, are just fabrications and just don't happen at all.

I.   What are your grounds for suspecting that it hasn't
happened at all?

T.   Well, anything like that I just doubt. The only thing I am not doubtful about is if a teacher has kept them or possibly they have gone to the toilet. I'll accept that in between lessons because they are told that is the time they must go but they must still get permission from the teacher that they are just leaving, and perhaps if it is very muddy they might go and wash their hands if they have got mud all over them. I'll accept that. But apart from that, though you can't be absolutely definite on that, I would start to think that things were starting to get a little bit fancy, just as in the morning if someone is late for school and says, 'Oh my brakes stopped working', or something like that, you know.

(2) I.   What if they came late to lessons?
T.   Well, if they come late to lessons the only excuse I accept is that they have been seen by another teacher and I always check on that. If they say they have been to see so-and-so [deputy head], you know, or the headmaster then I check with the office or check with the teacher concerned to see whether they've been where they say they have been. This happens quite a lot.
I.   Do you always check?
T.   Not always, no. But if I have any doubts, if I think, well, why would he be seeing him? Well, you see, every break there are always meetings, sport meetings. I check if I have any doubts, if I think someone is trying to have me on. If I say, 'Well, why did he keep you?' and it doesn't sound authentic then I check up with the teacher concerned.

Should the pupil be discovered to have provided a false account, he will not only be defined as deviant in terms of the punctuality rule, but also in terms of the rules which proscribe telling lies. These investigative strategies allow the teacher to move from these two cases of the suspicion rule to two cases of the retrospective conviction rule. The pupil was deviantly late and he told lies: he is doubly deviant.

The use of the suspicion rule with respect to the observation of acts of concealment is most clear in the case of the phase rule which proscribes cheating in tests.

T.   ... Er, signs of cheating—well, I don't know, some sudden movement behind my back, you know sudden movements, just as you are about to turn round somebody suddenly takes a quick jerk away from you and you think well he is trying to cheat. We don't find boys whispering. They are more subtle than that, they will try and have a quick look while your back is turned, you know, for a fleeting instance some of them, and there is a penalty for it and I either dock the marks or if it is an important test just cancel it altogether and just give them none.

This extract illustrates the use of the concealment evidential rule by which the teacher suspects that cheating may well be taking place by observing that the pupil is following the implemental rules of an act of concealment. The teacher does not directly observe copying, cribbing, or asking neighbours for answers; rather, the teacher observes an act which can be rendered accountable as an act of concealment in the context of the rule against cheating. The act which the teacher perceives is interpreted as an act of covering up, an act which the teacher knows would be committed only by a pupil who did not want to be discovered in the commission of a deviant act, in this case, cheating. The teacher knows that one typical method of accomplishing cheating is to sneak a look at another pupil's paper when the teacher's back is turned, and thus when the teacher observes an act which could constitute covering up such a method of accomplishing cheating then the teacher may be reasonably sure that such an offence has just taken place. We may note here that in rendering the pupil's act as a suspicious act in terms of the rule against cheating, the teacher is imputing a motive to the pupil for his directly observed conduct, and it is only when that motive is imputed that the pupil's conduct becomes possibly deviant, since sudden movement in itself need not be constitutive of deviance at all. The imputed motive derives its applicability to the act that is directly observed by virtue of the fact that there is a rule in play regarding cheating.

The evidential rules that we have developed so far have drawn upon the teachers' knowledge of the structure of deviant action. But it appears that teachers' knowledge of the identity of the perpetrator of the action can also be a source of evidential rules. Part of a teacher's knowledge that a pupil is a certain kind of pupil, is that he commits certain kinds of acts in certain kinds of circumstances. If, then, the act is ambiguous but the teacher is able to specify the nature of the circumstances and the identity of the perpetrator of the act, the teacher may be able to 'fill in' the probable nature of the act from his knowledge of the perpetrator's identity. This evidential rule hinges on the teacher's assumption that a pupil will normally commit actions which are congruent with the type of person he is. Essentially there are two evidential rules embodied here. The first relates the pupil act to the teacher's knowledge of the pupil in that the act is held to be incompatible with this knowledge that the pupil is a certain type of person. The teacher becomes suspicious because the act is 'type-discrepant'.

(1) I.   What about cheating, what would be a sign of that?
 T.   Well, in my classroom apart from test time I encourage
 them to work together. In test time if somebody is cheating
 then you can be fairly certain that they are cheating and,
 there is one case I knew that somebody had cheated but I
 could not prove it. Well, there was these two boys and they
 were as thick as two short planks, and they managed to
 get seventeen out of twenty. They just sat next to each other
 and they managed to get seventeen out of twenty. Now that
 was impossible absolutely. I was expecting them to get about
 four out of twenty but they managed to get seventeen. Now I
 couldn't prove how they had done it, and so I had to take it
 that they had done it. Neither of them could have remembered
 enough right answers to have pooled what resources they
 had. I mean I would have been quite happy for them to have
 done that, but they couldn't have done that. What they must
 have done was to copy down the answers from the book,
 anticipated what I was going to ask which for the first three
 tests is very easy for the first years because all it is is lists.
 So all they had to do was copy down the first seven days of
 creation and the sections of the Bible, which gives you two
 more on Adam and Eve, and of course they got those two
 wrong because they could not anticipate that, but they could
 anticipate all the rest. I couldn't prove that but you can tell
 if a kid is cheating usually if you just look round the
 classroom and there he is looking at someone else's book or,
 because they are not very imaginative, in the way in which
 they cheat. In grammar schools they are very imaginative,
 but not here, not usually, and the classes that do want to
 cheat, cheat in such a way that you can see it a mile off. The
 upper don't, it's not the done thing—it's the unwritten law
 that you don't, anything else is fair game but don't cheat.

(2) I.   Cheating?
 T.   Well it is not easy for them to cheat not in a proper test.
 They can cheat on classwork, but I always know.
 I.   How do you know?
 T.   Because I do a great deal of oral work and if they don't
 answer orally—I know the boys who can't answer orally and
 would answer a certain question in a certain way and if they
 suddenly produced a brilliant written answer when they
 can't, haven't been able earlier on to answer the question
 orally, I know they have been cheating, because all the
 written work is based on oral work which we have done

before so I can tell. If I have asked them in class and they
have got the oral answer wrong they can't possibly. It's far
harder to write than speak, so that always gives me a hint.
In a test I make them put their bags on the desks in between
each of them and I make them cover their work up with
another book as soon as they have written it and as soon as
the test is finished I make them close their books up, and I
also walk round all the time, so it's difficult for them to cheat.
Occasionally one or two of them might.

Thus it is that teachers often do not directly observe acts constitutive of cheating, but rather infer retrospectively that cheating
must have taken place. This retrospective interpretation is accomplished by the teacher by linking together certain information which
he has already acquired about the pupil concerned in the act. In the
cases cited above, the teachers judged that the results of the test
were other than those which the teacher would have expected the
pupil to attain given the previous performance of the pupil. Where
the pupil's current conduct is not consistent with the teacher's typing
of the pupil the teacher asks himself: how is this unusual and unexpected event to be accounted for? Given that the pupil is of a
certain type, he can be expected to behave in typical ways in typical
circumstances. From the teacher's common-sense knowledge of the
identity of the pupil, he would expect him to obtain a typical set of
marks—marks congruent with the teacher's prediction based on his
prior typing of the pupil concerned. When the pupil does not conform
to the teacher's expectations, then this needs to be accounted for.
In the context of the test the range of alternative explanations is
two-fold: first, the pupil could have swotted up the answers, but
here the teacher concludes that this is unlikely given this type of
pupil's lack of propensity for hard work; or second, he could have
cheated. Since this seems to be the only tenable explanation, given
the type of pupil, then the teacher is able to infer that it is highly
likely that cheating has taken place. We should note here that the
teacher cannot reach a firm conclusion by using such an evidential
rule, which we may refer to as the 'type-discrepancy rule'; rather, this
type of evidential rule serves only to make acts possible or even
probable, and the teacher only suspicious, rather than certain, that
deviance has occurred.

The second evidential rule deriving from the teacher's typing of
the pupils allows the teacher to 'fill in' the nature of the act on the
grounds that such an act is typical—that is, a natural and normal
product of the pupil's being a certain type of person. The act, in
other words, is 'type-congruent'. The following extracts illustrate the

use of the 'type-congruency rule' in the case of imputing an offence in terms of the rule about telling lies, and in particular, providing false accounts:

(1) I. What would make you doubtful?

T. Prejudice more than anything, I should think. With most boys it would be prejudice, you know, I would think he is a likely lad to be doing something else and has not been where he said at all, either he has been dawdling or skiving. Then again you find a lad who is normally a very good lad suddenly goes and starts for a week or so coming late and things like that for no apparent reason.

(2) I. What sort of excuses do you accept if a child comes late to lessons?

T. Well, if all the class are there and an odd one comes afterwards, I mean they have all come from the same place, and I will ask why. Sometimes there is a good reason, perhaps they have had a word with the teacher after a lesson. If they—mm—very rarely get it actually without there being a good reason, you mostly get they have been somewhere, it is something the teacher has told them to do.

I. So you would accept that?

T. Only if I can prove it. Now last year I had a class that once I had to check up on because I had reasons for doubting that they were telling the truth. I know it is a terrible thing to say but you can't believe all the boys, and because I knew the particular boys I checked up afterwards on them, and it wasn't true sometimes, you see.

I. So you suspected that it wasn't true?

T. Yes, because of the boys, you see. Because you get to know the particular boys, I mean you know which boy can tell the truth and which, well you just know that they may not be telling the truth unfortunately, so you check up.

I. What leads you to suspect that they are not telling the truth?

T. Well, it's just the type of boy they are. There were one or two in the class I took last year that I knew would do this sort of thing if they got, I mean they did this, I mean there were one or two boys in this particular, boys in this class they just went home, and [deputy head] got on to them. It was rather strange. One boy, we were talking about in the staffroom and I said, 'Oh well, he is not in today so he can't get into trouble', and so-and-so said, 'He is in school', and so I said, 'Well he wasn't in my lesson, I haven't seen him.'

This is the trouble you see, you don't check every boy if he is just away. And you see they are very loyal of a fashion, I suppose you would call it, but they don't tell on each other. I mean they knew there was two of those boys who skived off, but it was just sheer accident that we found out that particular time. He said, 'Wasn't he in your lesson?' and I said, 'No', so he looked into it, and he had gone home.

I. You say you just know it's the kind of boy that makes you doubt?

T. Oh, from your experience, I mean you know that they don't always tell the truth, when you prove them, if you see them do something and they say they haven't and you know that they are the type that would, would—I mean I knew some of them not by person, I knew from repute you know.

(3) T. ... one tries to ensure that any late arrivals are brought to book about it and made fully aware that they are late, you see. In certain cases, of course, as you're aware, you can get quite legitimate answers for the late arrival. With others, of course, perhaps some dilly-dallying has taken place and you've got to take the necessary action to try to minimize this thing or cut it out as a matter of fact.

I. Sorry, could I ask you to explain one or two things, you said sometimes it would be a legitimate thing, how do you know when it's legitimate?

T. Well, I mean accepting—this has to be very fine, of course, I mean the reason given on the spot would appear to be legitimate which naturally one would follow up with, for example, if a reason given was that, 'Well, Mr so-and-so asked me to do this,' all right, you know the child. The class I've taken this morning, well, the majority of them I could trust because I know them and if, for example, Billy Lomax or any of these girls here, there are one or two doubtful characters but in the main, this class I've taken this morning I know them pretty well, well I feel I do, and in the main I could just sort out just by, I suppose intuition if you like, which ones I ought to follow up very intensely and others where I'm pretty certain that they're telling me the truth.

These extracts illustrate the use of the evidential rule whereby the deviance that is imputed is not based on the atypicality of the pupil's conduct but rather on the typicality or type-congruency of that conduct. The teachers would become suspicious that a particular pupil was committing a deviant act on the grounds that they have come to expect such deviant conduct on the part of the pupil concerned—the pupil, in other words, is renowned for the commission of this type of deviant act. Nevertheless, as in the case of the type-discrepancy rule, the use of the type-congruency rule only permits interpretation of the act in question as possibly or even probably deviant; as a case of suspicion, rather than conviction. For this suspicion to be transformed into conviction the teacher must once again employ an evidential strategy whereby the evidence necessary for conviction may be acquired. In this case, the most efficacious strategy consists of 'checking the pupil's story' with other teachers. Where the 'facts don't fit' and where, as a result, the teacher is able to 'prove' that the pupil lied, then the use of the conviction evidential rule is warranted.

As we indicated earlier in this chapter, teachers' use of evidential rules and strategies consists of the application of only two of the interpretive devices which the teacher has at his disposal for making sense of pupil conduct. A fuller analysis of the interpretive work undertaken by teachers in making deviance-imputations would require us to look more closely at the interpretive elements underpinning the use of evidential rules and strategies. Some attempts at this closer examination of the phenomenon of interpretive work have been, and are being, made. Because in this study our interest is the substantive area of deviance, we have limited ourselves merely to indicating some of the more generic problems of the phenomenon of interpretation which require further analysis. To continue at this point with the investigation of the fascinating complexities of these generic problems, however, would deflect us from a thorough analysis of the substantive interest which originally inspired this study, namely, the phenomenon of deviance in classrooms.

6   A theory of typing

In chapter 4 we examined the rule-governed contexts in which deviant acts and deviance-imputations take place. In chapter 5 we built on this analysis by showing how, within these rule-governed contexts, teachers come to know or evidence that some pupil acts are deviant. Acts become defined as deviant when, through the teacher's interpretative work, they become linked in particular ways with the rules in play. We saw that part of this interpretive work rested upon the teacher's common-sense knowledge that the offender was a certain kind of pupil. Yet so far we have not explicated how the teacher comes to typify pupils in this way. This topic, which springs naturally out of our work on the imputation of deviance, also connects with the more general question of the relationship between deviant acts and deviant persons. How does an actor come to be defined as a deviant person? i.e. how do teachers make the transition from X pupil is a person who commits Y deviant act(s), to X is Y type of deviant person? For there is an important difference between recognizing (knowing) that Jones is telling a lie and claiming (knowing) that Jones is a liar. What is the link between deviant acts (talking, cheating, fighting) and deviant persons (chatterbox, cheat, bully)?

Our thinking prior to the beginning of the research suggested that this topic of pupil identity in the eyes of the teacher was of crucial significance—and not merely for a 'labelling theory' approach to deviance in school. Other approaches to the study of classroom life also suggested that the identity the teacher imputes to the pupil has important consequences for the analysis of teacher-pupil interaction and the development of pupil careers. Perhaps the most striking parallel for us is the work of Rosenthal and Jacobson (1968) on 'self-fulfilling prophecies' in the classroom, which generated considerable interest as well as further research. The close relationship between labelling theory and self-fulfilling prophecy theory can be clarified by reducing them to a schematic summary.

Self-fulfilling prophecy theory

1. Teacher believes X about a pupil (e.g. that he is very intelligent).
2. Teacher makes predictions about the pupil (e.g. that he will make outstanding academic progress).
3. Change in teacher attitude and behaviour towards the pupil.
4. Change in pupil self-conception and behaviour in line with the teacher's attitude/behaviour.
5. Fulfilment of the prediction.

Labelling theory

1. Pupil commits X deviant act.
2. Teacher labels the act or person as deviant.
3. Problems experienced by the pupil as a result of the labelling.
4. Commission of further deviance by the pupil as a means of resolving such problems.

It is interesting to speculate why these two approaches, which have so much in common, have tended to remain as separate strands in the literature. We think that the main reason is because Rosenthal's work was concerned with positive self-fulfilling prophecies. It is true that there has been considerable interest in negative self-fulfilling prophecies (e.g. Rist, 1970), but if the research is experimental, as was true in Rosenthal's pioneering studies, then there are good ethical grounds for taking an interest in the positive rather than the negative self-fulfilling prophecies. For who would dare mislead teachers into believing that certain pupils were likely to deteriorate academically, and risk bringing about such an effect, merely to demonstrate that negative self-fulfilling prophecies can occur? Labelling theory, on the other hand, is part of deviance theory and therefore neglects the consequences of the labelling by teachers of pupils and their acts as 'conformist'. Yet these two approaches have a common theme: how do teachers come to formulate pupils as being certain kinds of persons, and what are the consequences of such formulations?

To bring the two together requires the development of a 'theory of typing'. In attempting this we shall be predominantly concerned with deviant typing, but we believe that our conceptual scheme has a more general applicability to the typing of pupils. In Rosenthal's original study, the teachers were given information about pupils' academic potential 'from the outside', that is, from the judgments made by psychologists on the basis of tests administered to the children. This gives us no indications of how teachers make their own judgments in the natural situation where psychologists do not intervene with the provision of expert opinion. Similarly, other studies, which will be referred to shortly, tell us how teachers type pupils at a particular point in time, but fail to explain how the teacher came to such judgments. In other words, these studies offer a static analysis, whereas we are concerned to develop a dynamic or process theory which examines what happens between the point when a teacher says 'I don't know Smith' or 'I know Smith by sight, but that's all I know about him' and the point when the teacher confidently states 'Smith is a troublemaker'.

In presenting this analysis we must broaden the scope of our enquiry and the range of our data. In earlier chapters the data were presented in a somewhat fragmented form, since we took teacher utterances and observed or reported incidents as focal points for analysis. Most of our material thus has an isolated, unhistorical character. The present process theory should help to redress this balance, for it restores the single instances of deviance-imputations to the historical framework of the teacher's developing conceptions of pupils. Particular deviance-imputations are regarded both as a contributor to, and as a product of, these teacher conceptions. To understand a deviance-imputation, for members and for researchers, requires us to see it not only in its immediate context of tasks, phases and rules, but also in the historical context of the kind of person the teacher believes the pupil to be and how the teacher came to such a typification over time.

Our first data on pupil typings, collected in school A, derived mainly from our interviews with teachers. These interviews were of two kinds. The first involved asking teachers for commentaries on events or verbal statements (usually deviance-imputations) that had occurred in lessons observed by the researchers. The second involved asking teachers directly about individual pupils. Sometimes the two kinds of data were collected in the same interview, when the discussion of an incident led to a fuller discussion of the pupil(s) involved in that incident. It was clear in this material that these teachers had over the years developed highly elaborate typifications of pupils and that these typifications formed part of the teachers' commonsense knowledge of pupils and their acts in classrooms. Whilst we asked teachers to reconstruct their acquisition of this knowledge from the first time they had met a particular pupil—and such reconstructions are very significant data—such material gives little insight into how the teachers actually developed their conceptions during a much earlier period. For this material we turned to school B, where we followed first year pupils and their teachers during the early days of these pupils in the secondary school. Our theory will present the data in an order which reverses the order of its collection, and which also reverses the order in which we developed the theory.

Before embarking on this, an important caveat is in order with reference to our use of the term typing. This concept in its popular, everyday usage has distinctly pejorative connotations. If one were to ask teachers directly, 'How do you type your pupils?' many would reply that they do not think of their children as types but as individuals or as persons. In saying this teachers are asserting that they do not think of pupils merely in terms of labels such as 'bright', 'lazy', 'highflyer', or 'troublemaker' which fail to do justice to the complexity and individuality of the children they know. We do not wish to make any assertions to the contrary. We recognize that teachers do develop highly complex conceptions of their pupils, and we hope that our theory does justice to that complexity. Teachers do, of course, use terms or labels to think or talk about pupils—but that, as the teachers rightly claim, is only part of the story. For us, then, the concept of 'typing' is synonymous with the concept of 'person formulation'.[1] Our theory of typing must analyse how teachers come to recognize each pupil as a complex individual who is utterly unique. Whilst our theory is concerned with how one group of persons, teachers, comes to type another group of persons, pupils, and especially deviant pupils, there is also in our work an implicit general theory about how any person comes to type any other person. What teachers are doing with respect to children is not a phenomenon confined to schools; it is a phenomenon common to all people in all places at all times. Our present concern is simply one limited aspect of a universal practice.

One of the most basic ideas within the symbolic interactionist perspective is that man understands things (objects, persons, events) by naming them. The names we use are categories. A person can understand or know what is the round green object I have in my hand, when he has learned the category 'apple', which is a single name that is applied to a whole range of objects with certain characteristics. 'Apple' as a category is also understood in relation to other categories, such as 'fruit' and 'edible' as well as 'round' and 'green'. The ability to name the object is to understand it. These names or categories are evaluative; since we are creatures who need to eat, for an object to be described as 'edible' or 'tasty' is to make a positive value-judgment upon it. These names also direct our action towards the object; when we are hungry, we look for tasty, edible things to eat. So it is with persons. We use names or categories—or constructs, or labels, or types—with which we make sense of others. The names are evaluative, since some of these characteristics are held to be desirable, and they direct our action. We avoid 'obnoxious' people just as we avoid 'poisonous' fruits. To type other people—to name them, categorize them, label them—is an inherent part of understanding them. In itself, it is not something one should or could dispense with.

Labelling theory considers this process of naming or typing others in a particular way. It asserts that the naming of certain kinds of persons—'deviants'—and the treatment that often accompanies such naming, can have particular consequences. Implicitly it also asserts that these consequences are either unintended or undesirable (which is a value-judgment), and, paradoxically, these consequences can reinforce, strengthen or increase the deviant conduct which the labelling is perhaps intended to punish, diminish or remove. In this sense it is clearly utterly absurd to argue that labelling theorists are saying that we should never label, or even that we should never label deviant acts: that would be an impossibility.

Placing labelling theory in this wider context of naming makes it clear that there are distinct dangers in analysing the labelling of deviant acts and persons when this is extracted from the more general processes of naming acts and persons. We are of the view that for us, as social scientists, to understand how it is that actor X labels actor Y with the deviant label Z, we must also consider the wider and more general way in which X names, types or formulates Y. For this reason, we have tried to put forward a theory of how teachers (one kind of X) type pupils (one kind of Y), though much of this work, quite properly, is specially concerned with a particular kind of typing, namely deviant typing.

It is part of the liberal ideology of teaching that teachers should look at the 'whole child'. Be that as it may, teachers are still teachers and the child is still a pupil. People always encounter and interact with other people within specific role-relationships, of which the teacher-pupil relationship is but one example. A role-relationship is a way of saying that the encounter is governed by particular interests and purposes, takes place in particular settings, and is structured in particular ways. This is not the place to give a detailed account of this relationship, which has been analysed by many sociologists and social psycholgists interested in education. We merely wish to re-assert the simple idea that teachers tend to perceive pupils in particular ways and act upon them in particular ways. It has been argued elsewhere (Hargreaves, 1972) that teachers have two prime interests in regard to pupils. The first is an academic interest, for teachers have the task of ensuring that pupils learn. The second is a disciplinary interest, for teachers have the task of ensuring that pupils conform to the rules and regulations which aim to maintain social order in the classroom. These two tasks or interests are, of course, closely interwoven. The outcome is that many of the names or labels applied to pupils reflect those interests. It is in terms of these labels that teachers can understand and make sense of pupils. Naturally, teachers do not see children in school exclusively in terms of their teacher interests; they also have a much more general reaction to their charges. For instance, they make a general evaluative reaction to children in terms of their 'likeability', which is an aspect of almost all human encounters, whatever the particular nature of the role-relationship. But even this more generalized reaction takes place within the role-relationship. There is, quite naturally, a tendency for teachers to like those pupils who cause them the least trouble in realizing their interests. This has been amply demonstrated in the literature, and shows itself in the present analysis. [2]

The theory proposes that pupils are typed or formulated by teachers in three stages. The first stage, that of 'speculation', begins when the teacher first comes to know about and/or to meet the pupil for the first time. The third stage, that of 'stabilization', marks the point at which the teacher has a relatively clear and stable conception of the identity of the pupils. He 'knows' the pupil; he understands him; he finds little difficulty in making sense of his acts and is not puzzled or surprised by what he does or says. The second stage, that of 'elaboration', stands between the other two stages.

As will be made clear later, these stages should not be regarded as highly discrete or distinct stages that can easily be distinguished. Although the stages do occur in a sequence, they do not refer to distinctive periods of time. A stage is characterized by certain problems and processes. The stages fuse into each other, both in the sense that they can overlap in time and in the sense that processes from different stages can and do occur at the same point in time.

When we talked to teachers in school A, it was evident that they 'knew their pupils well'. They spoke confidently, unhesitatingly and at length about them. But we had no access to the ways in which they had come to know them. This was the result of two things. First, our interviews with staff were mostly about third or fourth year pupils who had already acquired a stabilized deviant typing. Second, though eventually sensitized to the need for study of teachers' reactions to new pupils, we had arrived at the school half-way through the school year and thus had no opportunity to study the ways in which teachers had 'got to know' pupils new to them. We therefore decided that we would go to school B at the start of the school year to observe and talk to teachers in relation to the first year pupils who had just arrived in the school. Our theory is thus not derived from a longitudinal study of one set of children. Subsequent research may reveal the consequential weakness of our theorizing.

When pupils arrive at their secondary school, they do not normally know their teachers and the teachers do not know them. It is tempting to think that as far as their new teachers are concerned, these eleven-year-old pupils are simply 'blanks', bare canvases that can only be filled in by the passage of time, or perhaps hidden pictures whose detail will be revealed by the passage of time. Yet this is not, in fact, the case. Certainly it is true that the teacher does not know them as individuals; at the first meeting they are pupils without names. But each teacher does know quite a lot about them in general or as a collectivity. They all have a history for the teacher, but it is a typical history, not an individual one.

In the first place, he knows that they are first year pupils. They have a common age-range; they come from a local area; they have recently left a primary school. If he has some experience as a secondary school teacher, he will have encountered first year pupils before. He knows what first year pupils have been like in the past, so he knows something about what to expect from this particular intake. Indeed he will probably use his past experience as a standard against which to judge these newcomers, and will soon be saying:

'They're the worst first year form I've ever had.'
'They're not settling down very quickly this year.'
'They're much more docile than the lot I had last year.'

He knows something about the school's catchment area. He knows that some pupils come from the 'better' districts, residential areas for professional people, and that others come from areas noted for 'problem' families. He knows something about the primary schools that 'feed' his school; that one school gives its pupils a 'traditional' education, whilst another is perhaps experimenting with highly 'progressive' methods. All this he knows from his typifications of schools and neighbourhoods, even though as yet he cannot attach particular pieces of information to any individual pupil.

If the teacher has record cards from the primary schools at his disposal, he may read them and discover the proportions of pupils coming from particular schools or areas—though in fact he is unlikely to do this unless he is the 'form-teacher'. (He may even have met the pupils on a visit to the primary school.) He may see a surname that he knows, and so realize or guess that this may be a brother or a sister of a pupil he has taught in the past. He may have some accidental information about a pupil. For instance, he may live in the same street as the pupil, or he may be a personal friend of one of the primary school teachers who has passed on some information.

So on the first day of term, when the teacher meets his pupils for the first time, he knows little about the vast majority of them. Over the next few weeks, he will 'get to know' them. He will learn to put names to faces and each pupil will emerge as a unique individual with his own personality and characteristics. Yet this formulation of pupils as persons is not a creation ex nihilo. Rather, each pupil is matched against some other material. First, he is matched against any pre-information he has of the pupil, which includes, as we shall see, any information that is passed to him by other teachers. Second, he is matched against the teacher's conception of the typical first year pupil, which is an anonymous abstraction derived from all his previous experience of first year pupils. Third, he is matched against his peers—all the other first year pupils. The first two or three pupils to emerge as individuals serve as a kind of yardstick against which an emergent individual can be matched; a pupil is described as being 'similar to' or 'the opposite of' or 'not at all like' those pupils who have already acquired a degree of individuality. In the teachers' terms, within the first few days one or two pupils begin to 'stand out' from the rest, who remain temporarily 'unknown quantities' precisely because they do not stand out.

To discover what it is that leads a pupil to 'stand out' is to discover some of the important forms or terms in which a pupil is typed by teachers. Their early descriptions, or more accurately their 'first impressions' of pupils, reveal the constructs they use to formulate pupils. We approached this problem in two ways. We asked teachers after two weeks of term which pupils had made any impact on them; and we also provided teachers with a list of pupils and asked them to comment on each name. Teachers, of course, varied in the speed with which they 'got to know' the pupils. Doubtless some teachers made a more active effort to do this than others. But more important, some teachers had special responsibility for certain groups of pupils, as tutors or form-teachers, and so made special efforts in this direction. Further, some teachers taught the pupils more often than others, and so naturally made more rapid progress.

The main constructs (or terms or 'labels') to appear in the early descriptions provided by the teachers are of five kinds.

1. Appearance. Naturally teachers noted facial appearance, size, dress and demeanour in their first impressions. Indeed, teachers often recalled a boy not by his name but by some appearance characteristic. They would ask us, 'Isn't he the little boy who sits at the back?' Amongst the constructs used were: tall, short, fat, thin, nice-looking, attractive, untidy, elfish-looking, athletic build, a vague look in his eyes.

2. Conformity to discipline role aspects. Common constructs were: awkward, difficult, truculent, resentful, cocky, cheeky, rude, hostile, disruptive, chatterer, talkative, noisy, sulks, familiar, fusspot,

messes about, doesn't toe the line, quiet, polite, co-operative, no problem behaviour-wise.

3. Conformity to academic role aspects. Common constructs were: intelligent, bright, clever, brainy, hard worker, eager to learn, keen, diligent, slow, dim, lazy, sleepy, lethargic, inattentive, time-waster, poor reader.

4. Likeability. This concerned a general positive feeling of liking that many teachers expressed. It was commonly mentioned, though the terms are almost always the same—'a likeable lad', 'a pleasant lad', 'a nice lad'.

5. Peer group relations. Whilst these were fairly infrequent at this early stage, they did appear occasionally: leader, ringleader, bully.

Two other groups of constructs were in evidence. The first might be called 'personality' constructs, such as aggressive, easy-going, extrovert, friendly, helpful, perky, shy, self-confident, withdrawn. An examination of their original context of utterance suggests that these terms are used to make indications which relate to one or more of the five main categories. The second group consisted of a set of highly general 'deviant' labels, such as nuisance, pest, naughty, fool, nutcase, trouble-maker, disturbed. We shall consider these in more detail later. Two other terms were used—'normal' and 'average'. At this stage these terms were used in a particular sense, to indicate that the pupil concerned did not as yet 'stand out' in any striking way, either positively or negatively. They were not used in the more narrow psychological sense of 'normal' as compared with 'disturbed' or 'abnormal'; rather they implied that the teacher simply knew little about the pupil.

'He doesn't really stand out as far as work or anything—he's just an average boy in the form.'

Our findings are clearly in line with earlier investigations[3] using very different methods for collecting and analysing data. After two or three weeks these teachers were able to provide brief portraits of individual pupils. Sometimes these are based upon a single incident or a single occasion when the pupil came to the teacher's attention.

(1) T.   I know him because when I was teaching him he was in such an agony trying to learn the school prayer. He worked so hard and was the first boy to try and say it, and he didn't succeed. But he's a lovely boy.

(2) T.   He emerged yesterday in the lesson. He's very good. A very pleasant, well-mannered boy.

Sometimes the teacher's knowledge is focused on limited aspects of the pupil, i.e. on one of the five types of construct.

(1) T.   He's a very small, very cocky little lad, who would take on
the whole world, and he's inclined to provoke other boys by
annoying them in silly little ways. For instance, he'll catch hold
of a boy behind the back of the neck and throw him down the
bank of the stream, and then be surprised that the boy
retaliated.

(2) T.   Yes, in his case it's his size that will be his biggest problem.
I think to some extent, without making it obvious, he's going
to have to be protected a little bit because it's no good boys
treating him like that. All right, they're not hitting him, I don't
think they are intentionally harming, they're just picking him
up and playing with him . . . he's just a plaything more or less.

(3) T.   He has stood out because he's generally one of the first
ones to finish and again he's one of the first with his hand up.

(4) T.   Now he's very quiet, very quiet lad. He seems very shy to
me, and a bit frightened. Doesn't like to ask me anything and
seems almost to apologize before he asks permission to do
anything . . . I think he's a little bit shy, doesn't like to put up
his hand in class, doesn't like to answer.

(5) T.   It's because he's a poor reader that I remember him, and
he's a bit absent-minded. A bit of a dreamer most of the time.
If you tell everybody, then you have to tell him a second time.
He looks absent-minded, he looks as if his mind's not on what
he's doing at all, ever. He does—he looks as if he's never
paying attention, anyway. His eyes look vague, dreamy and
vacant all the time.

(6) T.   Whenever I look at him I think he's going to burst out
crying. I don't know why. He's just got that expression on his
face. Seems a bit frightened and a bit nervous.

More typically the characterization of the pupil draws on several
types of construct and is based, like some of the cameos given above,
not on a single isolated event but on multiple observed events which
cumulatively contribute to the impression made. It is because the
pupil repeatedly behaves in a particular way that he is assumed to be
a particular type of person.

(1) T.   He stands out from the rest in the fact that he's a nice
looking boy, he's an athletic build. He works hard in lessons
and I think he's about the best boy in the class.

(2) T.   I have a feeling from his work that he can't express himself
at all. I think he's a poor reader and this reflects in his work
output. His behaviour's all right.

(3) T.   Well, possibly, I'd say, I'd pick him out as the cleverest lad in the class. Behaviour-wise no problem at all. Keen lad, hand up straight away when the question's asked.

(4) T.   He seems a very good lad at first impression, at first sight. He's a good worker, discipline-wise he's no problem, he's helpful. He seems, like I say, reliable. I've asked him to do several jobs. I don't know why, but he struck me from the start as someone who would do a little task for me and do it properly.

Many of these characterizations have qualifications built into them: 'I have a feeling that', 'he seems', 'possibly', 'at first impressions'. The teachers are very aware that their characterizations are built upon fairly slender evidence. The single incident may be atypical; an appearance factor may be misleading; even repeated incidents may be nothing more than part of 'settling down' in the new school. This 'first impression' can be no more than a temporary working hypothesis, whose validity will be tested by subsequent events.[4]

(1) T.   To me they are the only two to stand out at this stage as being sort of extroverts, that's all . . . they both seem intelligent kids, but I don't know if they are well above average at this present time. These two seem to me to be quite bright, and that's about all I can tell you at the moment.

(2) T.   He's another. A bit of a mystery at the moment. He's been away and I just don't really know him. He's no problem, or he hasn't been yet discipline-wise. Behaviour is good. I wouldn't like to say about him really.

(3) T.   Strange little lad. This is the one with fair hair, isn't it? I feel sometimes that he has trouble with other lads, but I don't know yet. I've not seen enough evidence of his behaviour, but he's either having a dig at them or they're having a dig at him.

(4) T.   Well, he seems to be one of the better boys. He seems quite polite, he doesn't chatter a great deal, his behaviour seems quite good, but then again he doesn't seem to be ultra-polite if you see what I mean. He seems quite a reasonable boy. Of course you can form this opinion of him now and you could quite easily change it by Christmas. But that's how he would strike me at the moment.

Although the teachers are often aware that the evidence on which the pupil is assigned a provisional typing is somewhat tenuous, the resulting speculative hypothesis points both to the past and to the future. The initial typing is used to make sense of what the pupil has done so far, but it also points forward in time by suggesting the kind of person the pupil will perhaps turn out to be. It is for this reason that we call this the speculative stage.

(1) T.   Very bright and seems a very nice lad. Now I think more than any of them he will go into the upper band in a couple of years quite easily. . . . He is very confident . . . without saying, you know, 'I'm the greatest.' He seems to be self-confident. . . . Mm, you find many in a class that you get to like by the end of the year. By like, I mean as you pick out someone you really like yourself. I reckon at the moment he could be one of the nicest lads I've taught, but then again that's the impression because he does his work, he doesn't fuss about you, you know, he doesn't make a big show of things, he gets on and does it well, yet you don't have to force him to answer and things like that. And that for me is just about—plus the fact that he is a good footballer, and stuff like that—that is just about the ideal, you know, and I think he'll be a good lad.

(2) T.   I get the impression he hasn't really settled into the class, that he's still a bit apart. Ability-wise he does not seem to be that good, but there again . . . I wouldn't like to say. I don't know, I don't think he'll be any trouble, but he has to be jumped on over books and work and forgetting homework and things like that.

(3) T.   Now he is bright. Of course, he lives in a good area of—— and he lives next to one of the teachers, next door, so he is in rather a difficult situation, I think. The family knows the teacher and I think [this pupil] is quite used to the idea of this school, knows a lot about it. And he looks the brainy type, just to look at him. Quite often, of course, looks can be misleading, but with him it works, he looks as if he would be good. He really looks the part, you know . . . and is probably the cleverest in the class. He is no problem at all behaviour-wise. He seems a very nice lad. Perhaps he doesn't contribute as much as he might, a little loath to answer when he knows, but he looks a bit quiet. I should say he will be a very good lad, especially when he gets further up the school.

(4) T.   I remember him, mainly because he caused a bit of bother in the past through inattention in class more than anything. He's a bright lad all the same, much brighter than the average in that class. Could be a nuisance in class.

F

(5) T.   I think he might be a problem later on. Yesterday he moaned a bit and was reluctant to do something outside school. We may get this later on. . . .

(6) T.   Nothing's come to light with him, but there again I think to myself sometimes that maybe if I've got my back turned to him he might try something. It's just an impression. Maybe I'm wrong in looking at that.

(7) T.   He's the most likely to be a discipline problem unless he's treated very kindly and firmly by the staff, because I feel that he's anti-social. Among the others one boy—and I don't know why I'm saying this—Tony someone or other, he gives me the impression that he's going to be a troublemaker and a lazy student. Why I don't know, but that's the impression. He's been no trouble in class and he's doing as much work as anyone else.

Once the teacher has made a working hypothesis about a pupil, then the typing process moves into the elaborative stage. This consists of several processes, the most basic of which is that of 'verification'. There is an attempt made by the teacher to find out if the pupil 'really is that sort of person'. It is concerned with the confirmation of the 'impression' or 'feeling' held by the teacher in the speculative phase. Like a good scientist, the teacher puts his working hypothesis to the test and attempts to verify it. It represents a movement from 'He may be, then again he might not' to 'He is'. But the teacher does not have to set up a special experiment for this; the hypothesis of the speculative typing can be tested against the successive revelations of subsequent events as they naturally occur in classroom life. The teacher adopts the wait-and-see evidential strategy as used in relation to ambiguous pupil acts, which we described in chapter 5. As in the case of acts, so also in the case of persons. It is assumed that 'time will tell' whether or not the teacher is right. So verification is concerned with the compatibility between what is hypothesized and predicted, against what is observed or revealed. It is not so much that very specific events or acts are anticipated. Rather, the teacher anticipates certain kinds of events or acts that are compatible with the provisional typing, i.e. events or acts that can be made sense of by the typing. If this occurs, then the typing is verified.

In effect this means that the teacher is specially sensitive to the repetition of the acts on which the original typing was based. If the initial basis for the typing was a single incident, then if that same (or more strictly, a similar) incident recurs, then this will be used as evidence for verification. If the original typing was based on repeated incidents ('he tends to . . .' or 'he's always . . .') then that conduct must persist if the original typing is to be substantiated. Additionally, the teacher can look for variations rather than repetitions of acts. If the teacher's original typing is that the pupil is 'lazy', based upon careless and untidy written work, then many subsequent acts can be seen as variations upon, and verification of, that typing—his tendency to come late to classes, the brevity of his homework, the inconsistent standards of his work, his unwilling attitude, and so on.

Should repetition and variation not occur, then the working hypothesis is likely to be falsified. The absence of typical acts, i.e. acts which can be made sense of by means of the imputed typing, challenges the validity of the provisional typing. In other words, the pupils must be 'de-typed'. This can be accounted for in a variety of ways. The teacher may believe that he simply made the wrong judgment in the first place—'I was wrong about him.' This is particularly so when the original typing was based on appearance and looks rather than on acts, or when it was based on a rather vague impression. In the light of subsequent evidence, the speculative hypothesis is rejected or modified.

> T.   Now his written work is very good and his exam and tests were very poor, so although he's been doing good written work, it's not been going in. . . . I liked him immensely at first, but now I'm a bit doubtful. He can write nicely so he enjoys writing, but if they don't learn the work and you have to tell them off, then he seems very miserable and unhappy. I was surprised because I suggested that he should be pushed up a class, incidentally, until these tests and then I found out that it was all written, it wasn't knowledge.

Alternatively, the teacher may believe that the original typing was in some sense correct at the time, but that it must now be rejected or modified, not because the teacher's understanding has changed in the light of evidence, but because the pupil has in fact changed.

> September interview
> T.   Ronald. I've never seen a lad whose work was so neat and level. His presentation is marvellous.

> January interview[5]
> T.   Did I mention any good ones last time? The ones that I would say are fitting in well with the system? Did I mention Ronald last time?
> I.   Yes, briefly.

> T. Well, he was working dead hard when he first came into the
> school and you thought that here's a lad who's really setting out to
> do well here in this school. You know, a fresh start and so on.
> And yet since then—I don't know if he's sensed that he's in a low
> stream or not, but somehow he's lost the zest for work that he had
> when he first came here, and it's a real shame. It might alter again
> next year . . . but you feel that if he carries on the same way he is
> doing now, then he'll really be working below his potential. . . .
> You can see somehow this loss of zeal from the initial few
> weeks. . . . The light has gone from his eye and that being the case
> I would detect that as a danger signal for that child.

There exists a hidden dimension to this pupil change. Part of the
teacher's common-sense knowledge consists of knowledge of what
we might call the 'newcomer status'. It is generally assumed by
teachers that coming to a secondary school is for many pupils, and to
varying degrees, a traumatic experience. They realize that pupils are
entering a new world, with new teachers, new subjects, new rules and
routines. Their 'senior' status at the junior school has given way to
the lowly status of 'new boys' or 'first year kids'. It is therefore
expected that many pupils will experience 'problems' in this process
of 'settling down' in their new school. Most pupils, it is assumed by
the teachers, experience nervousness and fear when they are
newcomers.

> T. First of all they are in sheer terror of this place. Most kids
> come into secondary school in sheer terror of what they come into.
> They would have been hearing fearsome stories of what happens
> in secondary schools from their older brothers and so forth. They
> will have to find their feet and after half-term they will probably be
> finding out how far they can go with the staff.

Thus a teacher can argue that a pupil has now 'settled down' or
'found his feet' and that the provisional typing was based on pupil
conduct which was unrepresentative of him because he was in this
abnormal and transient state of adjusting to his new environment. A
teacher may claim, 'I thought he was quiet, but he's really quite a
chatterbox' thus reading the provisional typing as 'quiet' as misleading and temporary, but justified at the time, because the pupil
was too nervous and apprehensive to be his 'real' self. Similarly a
pupil may prove to be 'troublesome' as part of this 'settling down'
but later turn out to be 'a very nice boy really'. It is assumed that
different pupils react to their newcomer status in different ways,
which need not be representative of the type in whose terms they will
ultimately be formulated. When they lose their newcomer status,

with time, then they come out 'in their true colours', which other boys, whose original typings are verified, have shown all the time.

September interview

T.   Gavin is more inclined to stand back once he's got a fracas going on and watch it. He's an inciter to action. . . . The three of them together could be a formidable gang if they were allowed to.

I.   Although you've lumped the three together, are there any differences between them?

T.   [The other two] are ready to help in class. They'll ask me if there is anything I want doing and they'll do it, but Gavin is inclined to sulk if you tell him off about anything. He withdraws into himself and then his whole approach to anything is that of a sulky nature. He's not prepared to co-operate. If you tell him he's done something wrong, he won't apologize. The other two will say they're sorry and be sorry, but Gavin doesn't. He rather harbours a grudge against you. . . . Several times I've had pupils complaining of being bullied and these three had their names given to me. Gavin is the one who resents being told. The other two will accept the fact that they have been accused of bullying and that's the end of it, but with Gavin he always seems to be saying, 'You're picking on me again.'

I.   Does he actually say this?

T.   It's the impression you get. You know, he shrugs his shoulders at you and he says, 'Well, I wasn't the only one' kind of thing.

I.   You say he shows resentment? What are the signs of this?

T.   Withdrawing into himself. He won't take an active part in an oral lesson. If he's speaking and you tell him to be quiet and get on, he'll withdraw into himself completely and take no further part in the lesson. . . . He's anti-discipline at the moment.

January interview

T.   Gavin's a nicer character now than when I first had him. He's not really stirring up like he was before. He used to be the main stirrer up then he'd sit back and watch the trouble that he'd caused, but now he seems to have settled down much more than he had before. . . . I think he's been channelled into lines where he's not looking for trouble. He's more sort of—well, he's fitting into the community of the school better than he did, or than I thought he would. He really was very definitely antagonistic to everything when he first came here, but now he seems to be working much better and has settled in. I wouldn't say that he was 100 per cent for school. He'll still on occasions stand up and say, 'Well, why do we have to do such and such a thing?' He's not anti-social now, except on the odd occasion when he feels he's been put on for

some reason or another. . . . Now he's joining in things more. . . .
Since then he seems to have become more like a normal school
boy. . . . He's even volunteered to do things, which came as a
great surprise to me to begin with. . . . I've changed my opinion
completely. . . .

A pupil may be de-typed because he has changed directly as a
result of the teacher's treatment of him during the early weeks.

T.   Now these two boys were inclined to be a bit silly, so I
punished them.
I.   When you say 'silly' do you mean chattering?
T.   Well, giggling as well, you know a bit of sniggers. I know this
boy will do this occasionally and you'll overlook it, but if it gets
too much then I will say something about it and I thought they
were going to develop so I gave them a punishment last week.
Well, since then . . . they've been quite well-behaved and worked
well.

On the other hand, some teachers expect pupils to change quite
unaccountably.

T.   I find that a naughty boy is a good boy next day for no
apparent reason and that they've developed into another stage and
it's possible that they could come along and be absolute saints
through no effort on my part or anybody else's. It just happens in
their development.

Clearly, if a pupil is 'de-typed', then he must be 're-typed'. The two
processes occur simultaneously, for as the provisional typing fails to
find verification, the teacher is creating new hypotheses to account
for the pupil. As the pupil is de-typed, no elaboration can take place
and instead the teacher must re-type by returning to the speculative
stage. But it must be remembered that the provisional typing often
consisted of several elements, and that some of these may be verified
whilst others are falsified. This is one of the reasons why the idea of
stages should not be taken to refer to discrete periods of time. With
one element of the typing the teacher may be in the elaborative
stage, whilst with another element the teacher may be in the speculative stage.

Sometimes the speculative typing itself contains contradictory
elements which will, the teacher trusts, be resolved by subsequent
events. In such cases the teachers seem to recognize the conflict
inherent in their initial typing.

(1) T.   If I just look at him, if I had to look round the class and
from faces alone say who was going to be the poorest one, I

would think of him. Yet his work is quite reasonable. It's a puzzle with him.

(2) T.   He is very quiet, yet he gives you the impression that he is not quiet really, you know, that he's just biding his time, sort of thing, or as soon as I am out of the way, you know—I don't know—he just does not look the way he behaves. It's a very prejudiced thing to say, I suppose, it's only my opinion. I just don't know, I wouldn't like to put him in any category at the moment. We'll just have to wait and see about him.

(3) T.   Now probably the most diligent boy, the hardest working boy. Whether or not he's quite as clever as some of the others, I don't know. But you always find his type, you know, who will sit down and get on and work hard, and just for the sake of trying to get everything right, not for showing off I think, or 'Just look, I've got ten out of ten!' He seems to be that sort of boy. He's very quiet but then he doesn't seem to hesitate to put up his hand and answer.

(4) T.   What can I say about him? Difficult really. At first I thought he was going to be very shy but when I ask him a question he doesn't seem to have any real problem answering. He doesn't seem self-conscious about trying to answer in French, yet he won't put his hand up even when he knows the answer.

These extracts indicate that teachers are prepared to speculate about some factor which might resolve the conflict. Normally, one part of the typing is verified and the other part is rejected to give way to a re-typing.

An important process in the elaborative stage is that of 'type-extension'. The provisional typing based on a single characteristic or cluster of characteristics now leads into a more extensive and wide-ranging constellation of 'multiple typings'. As the teacher sees more of the pupil, doing many different acts in many different situations, it becomes more difficult to understand the pupil—retrospectively, currently or predictively—in terms of merely one or two typings. The more the teacher learns about the pupil, the more he must resort to further types. Only a selection of the pupil's conduct can be used as part of the verification process. Some of the additional knowledge cannot be coded under the provisional typings, and is, in Schutz's (1932) phrase, 'type-transcendent', i.e. cannot be made sense of in terms of the imputed typing. New types must therefore be hypo-thesized to make sense of the conduct that falls outside, or is residual to, the provisional typing. These new types begin the process again at the speculative stage. We shall see ample evidence of this in the case-studies to be presented shortly.

As the typings are becoming more extensive, they are also becoming 'idiosyncratized', that is, related to a particular unique individual. This is much more than simply developing a typing which consists of a unique cluster of typings—for that was often evident in the speculative stage. Idiosyncratization refers to the process by which the teacher is able to specify the manner in which, and the conditions under which, a pupil exhibits typical (i.e. type-related) conduct. The teacher learns how a pupil commits his typical acts, for each pupil has his own way of 'being cheeky', or 'acting aggressively' or 'playing the fool'.

(1) T. If he comes in in a nice quiet mood, he will remain that way all the lesson and I won't have to say a word to him, but if he's acting the clown with [another pupil] at the beginning of the lesson, he never seems to settle down for the rest of the lesson.

(2) T. If you leave him alone to get on with the writing at his own speed, he's quite a friendly little chap. If you try to hurry him or push him at all, then of course he'll do absolutely nothing.

(3) T. He's a bit of a nuisance when he's not interested in the subject.

(4) T. She's terribly noisy. She's bubbling all the time, and you just can't quell her for any long period, and yet to a large degree she's an industrious member of the class and when you've got them moving on some written work, or even in oral work at times, she takes an interest in what I'm doing. . . . But I think she's easily disturbed by other interests very quickly and she's easily disturbed by others, nobody in particular.

Whereas idiosyncratization specifies how the pupil commits typical acts, motive elaboration is concerned with the question of why he commits them. Schutz (1932) has distinguished two kinds of motive. The 'in-order-to motive' which refers to the purpose, end or object which is to be accomplished by the act. From the point of view of the actor, the reference is to the future. Thus when a teacher says that a pupil lied to avoid getting into trouble, the teacher is imputing an in-order-to motive to the pupil. The 'because-motive' refers to the past experiences of the actor which have determined or predisposed him to act in a particular way. Thus when the teacher says the pupil lied because he comes from a bad home where he is not brought up to tell the truth, the teacher is imputing a because-motive to the pupil. As we shall see later, both kinds of motives are imputed to pupils as part of the typing, since both contribute to the elaboration of the typing. Because-motives help make sense of a pupil's typical act by explaining how the pupil comes to be that type of person who commits typical acts for typical in-order-to motives. Teachers, with their knowledge provided by sociologists of education, commonly see the home background of the child as a source of because-motives and what we might call the 'causal structure' which explains how a pupil has come to be a certain type.

In the speculative stage there is evidence that on occasions the teachers speculate about the motivational aspect of the provisional typings. For reasons we shall see shortly, these normally refer to because-motives, not to in-order-to motives.

(1) T.　I think that he must have been very spoilt, at home and in primary school, because he thinks he's so much better than anyone else.

(2) T.　I think he feels insecure and I also believe that he has an inferiority complex because of his home.

(3) T.　Another bright lad, very keen. He's the one who sits next to [another pupil]. He again seems very polite. Neat, neat worker. Gives me the impression that he is, that his parents have brought him up well. I've been wrong on this before. I've been so way out, but I get the impression that he's, erm, well done to, you know. He's a thoroughly nice lad.

(4) T.　He seems a bit nervy. Perhaps it's just me, but he does seem a bit of a ditherer. A bit shy, a bit loath to contribute. Might just be a phase, but he just gives me the impression that he's mothered a bit, I don't know why. I might be completely wrong. A little incapable of doing anything on his own two feet, but then again he's a reasonable lad, a reasonable worker.

Since our particular interest is in the typing of deviant pupils, we must now analyse this aspect in greater depth. What we as social scientists call 'deviant' pupils are, in the speculative and elaborative stages, described by the teachers as pupils who are, and/or who are likely to become, 'a problem' or 'difficult'. What is it that leads some pupils to 'stand out' from the rest—the 'normal' pupils—in this way and to be given such a typing? It is not simply that these pupils break rules, although that is true. It appears that there are several other factors which lead pupils to 'stand out' at an early point, which in themselves have no necessary relation to deviance, but which nevertheless play a very important role in the 'standing out' of deviant pupils.

The first of these factors we call the 'sibling phenomenon'. [6] When a teacher meets his new pupils for the first time, he is aware that some of his pupils may be the younger brothers or sisters of pupils he is currently teaching or has taught in the past. That a pupil is this other pupil's brother or sister makes him 'stand out' automatically. If a teacher recognizes a new pupil's name, or if he notices a facial resemblance, then he checks immediately if there is a family relationship. If so, he tends to remember that pupil. When we provided the teachers with a list of the new pupils in a class for commentary, teachers would remark:

'Well, of course, immediately the ones that strike me are the ones whose brothers I already know.'

Or as teachers were going through the list, they would say:

'Yes, I know him. He's got a brother here.'

So a newcomer pupil with a known sibling is likely to find his name learned by the teacher very quickly. But the sibling phenomenon extends far beyond this. If a pupil has an older sibling, then the older brother (or sister) acts as a yardstick or model against which the new pupil can be matched, which is quite unlike the case of the newcomer without a sibling, who can be matched only against the teacher's conception of a typical first year pupil or against other first year pupils. In the case of pupils with siblings, it is assumed by teachers that the newcomer will be like the older brother as much in 'personality' and conduct as in physical resemblance. Whereas the sibling-less newcomer has to provide positive evidence of his typing, the newcomer with a sibling is expected to be like the elder brother unless he gives negative evidence to the contrary. So not only does the teacher get to know the newcomer with a sibling very quickly, but he also tends to speculate and elaborate more quickly, because the older brother provides a constant source of comparison and contrast—and teachers are naturally rather curious to discover the extent to which they are alike.

(1) T. You know, you could almost do a study of how much does your attitude affect how you look at boys who have got brothers further up the school.
I. Do you think it does?
T. I think it does yes, especially in the case of —— who looks so much like his brother.

(2) T. Again, his brother is in my class, so that's why he comes to
my notice. But he is extremely—I noticed a sort of difference
in their attitudes, you know. [The elder brother] who is in my
class is very loud. He's always seeking attention, shouting out,
you know, 'I did this', or 'I did that', and this chap, he's only a
little lad—he must be about three foot odd—apparently some
people had been bullying. He seems very reserved, very loath to
say anything at all. . . . He just sits there, he's content to go
along, whereas his brother is always chattering, and is always
moving about—and this is in third year—moving about, you
know, and trying to take the mickey out of other people who
are stronger than him.

(3) T. Again, I know him because I taught his brothers. Very
good lad, you know, I wouldn't be surprised if he moves up,
although his actual work is not as good as I thought it would
be. This is the thing about the Harrison brothers, all of them.
None of them are very bright, they're all trustworthy lads, you
know, I've heard other teachers say this. They've looked at
people like Harrison and without knowing the brothers they've
said, 'Well, that lad looks OK.' I mean he just looks as if he
is going to be a reliable type, to me.

(4) T. He fits into the norms of the school better than most
people, probably because—or possibly because—his brothers
have been setting him an example, or it's probably because he
is well brought up anyway. I mean I'm probably prejudiced in
my view of him because I know the other two [brothers] who
are well brought up in my opinion.

(5) T. He forgets his homework, similar to his brother, but I
think we can arrest that before it goes too far. But he's different
to his brother in many ways. He isn't as cheeky as [his brother]
was, but he is more self-confident, he is more confident of
himself than his brother is, if that isn't a contradiction. His
brother was downright cheeky sometimes, but [this one] isn't,
he knows how far to go, he knows where the line is, which his
brother never did really.

(6) T. She's a bully. She'll use whatever means at her disposal to
get what she wants. She's been well trained by her sister. A lot
of trouble she was, as powerfully built as most of the boys and
she'd give one or two what for now and again.

One important effect of the sibling phenomenon is that if a newcomer with a 'good' sibling shows signs of being 'difficult', then this

can be interpreted as 'settling down' problems, on the assumption that he will ultimately turn out to be like the elder brother. On the other hand if the newcomer has a 'deviant' sibling, then early conformity may be interpreted as a temporary part of 'settling down' and any later deviance will demonstrate what he was 'really like' all along —his brother.

(1) T. I should think he'll probably turn out the same way as [his brother]. Yes, probably once this trouble is behind him, he will go the same way as his brother, because his brother was exceptionally keen on drama and that sort of thing.

(2) T. This is the first year one. He's got a brother in the second year who's been in a little bit of trouble now and again and I just wonder whether in fact that this is rubbing off on the younger one now, because he seems to be getting a little bit cocky. That's my opinion anyway. Apart from that I think that we'll have to keep our eyes on him. That may develop, I don't know.

We shall see the impact of the sibling phenomenon later in the case-studies, from which none of this material presented has been taken.

A second factor is staff discussion. Occasionally a teacher may know about a newcomer from a primary school teacher.

T. I had a letter from his primary school teacher about him. The father has a family of children and the widow he married has a family, so there are two families in one house. This boy in the primary school put years on his teacher and she felt terribly sorry for him. She wrote to me that when he came here I might take a particular interest in him.

Much more common is the discussion of teachers in the staffroom where teachers often 'compare notes' about pupils they teach. Teachers may seek confirmation or validation of their provisional typings in the opinions of their colleagues—and in the case of 'deviant' pupils some added consolation.

(1) T. I don't know why they're like this, but they're not just like this with me. This is a general thing with all the teachers that they have. I know, because we talk in the staffroom.

(2) T. I noticed him only because his work was better than others. I asked [a colleague] about him and he said he seemed quite bright so I think that he'd be one that we'd watch and see about getting him put in the other stream, because he does seem to be quite a good worker.

Naturally teachers gossip about 'good' pupils as well as 'deviant' pupils, but it is our impression, as former teachers as well as researchers, that there is more talk about the 'deviant' pupils, probably because such talk is simply more interesting. Inevitably, teachers hear these discussions and remember them even when they do not teach or know a pupil and an important source of pre-information is provided.

(1) I. Did you know anything about her at that time?
T. No, but amongst the staff we discuss particularly the new arrivals. You can see after they've been here only a few weeks they start showing their teeth and it's something you watch coming, yet you can't do anything about it. It's like a slow-moving lava bed, if you like, of trouble.

(2) T. I am suspicious of them anyway from mostly more of what I have heard than seen myself. . . .

(3) I. Was she the same in the first form?
T. I didn't teach her in the first form. Since I had her in the second year I should have said. Well, I was warned about her. All the teachers knew that she was a shocker then.

(4) T. She is a rebel in every sense of the word.
I. What do you mean—a rebel?
T. Well, from what I hear from the other teachers. She is a shocker.

(5) T. I got hold of him this morning in the corridor. I'd hear his name mentioned by somebody, some other teacher. He hadn't done the homework. I got hold of him and I said, 'I hear you haven't been doing your homework, lad.'

(6) T. I realized at first that he could fly off the handle, mostly from what I'd heard about him from outside the class, not in my own experience.

Such pre-information may well serve as a pre-typing, a second-hand provisional typing which the teacher can take over, actively searching for validation as if the speculation were his own.

(1) T. I'd heard his name mentioned, but he hadn't in fact stood out in my class. Then this morning we were going over some sentences and he said that 'his' should have a capital letter. So I looked at the sentence and I said, 'No, I'm afraid you're mistaken there.' And he said, '*You're* making the mistake, it should have a capital.' It was his manner—telling me, not asking me, 'Shouldn't it have a capital letter?' You know, I

thought, 'Oh. . . .' So I said, 'What's your name?' and he told
me and I thought, 'That's right, I've heard about you.' . . .
So that's how he stood out, because he definitely resents being
told.

(2) T.   He can be a nuisance. He never has been, but I can see. . . .
I'd heard his name and I didn't even know who he was. Now I
noticed this boy who'd start being giddy if Gavin did
something. . . . I'd heard his name mentioned in the staffroom,
so whether he—Mrs —— said he was one of those who'd start
trouble when they were on the corridor. . . . I think he will
always need watching and yet you see at first I hadn't noticed
him. It was a long time before I noticed that he was like
this. . . . I know he got off to a bad start with other teachers,
and because I heard his name I thought, 'Who is this lad?' And
I had a list with their names and where they sat and so I sort
of looked and thought, 'Oh, that's him, is it?' but he hadn't
done anything in my class.

This is not to say that teachers always accept the typings provided by
colleagues. They may have developed their own typing before hearing
the judgments of their colleagues or they may find that a pre-typing
that is taken over from others fails to be verified.

(1) T.   I knew some of them, not by person, I knew them from
repute, you know. I mean I've got a form this year, I've heard
some of their names bandied about amongst the teachers
before I ever met the boys. But mind you, I don't pre-judge.
I wait and see what they do with me. But all the same, you
can't help but bear it in mind. You know, you wait and see
how they behave for you. I don't believe in branding them—
they may react differently to another teacher—but all the same
it is at the back of your mind. You know you're only human.

(2) T.   He's not a noisy individual. He's crafty to a large degree,
but he's been quite an industrious boy as far as I'm concerned
and hasn't caused me any undue worry. He's done all that I've
asked him and worked well, producing good results and his
behaviour is quite satisfactory. From time to time I've heard
different members of staff mentioning his name, and yet I can't
line up my own experience of him on the same lines as theirs.
I don't know whether to put it down to the fact that he likes
maths. He does like maths, you see.

(3) T.   He's lazy, utterly lazy and he's anti-social. . . . I don't
know him all that well, you know, I've only had him in this

group. And apparently he doesn't behave characteristically with me at all, from what I hear of him from other members of staff, because he's never any trouble and he never causes any trouble in my group, which is odd really. . . .

Later we shall observe the significance of staff discussion in the case-studies of deviant pupils. At this point, however, we might indicate that pupils are aware of this staff discussion, either through over-hearing it or being directly informed by the teachers. Inevitably, perhaps, they see things in a somewhat different light from the teachers.

(1) I.   Let me put it to you that teachers are always picking on you because you are always doing things wrong?
P.   It's mostly what they've heard all the time. They go off other people, other teachers. Like they'll say, 'I've heard this in the staffroom about you today. Do anything in my lesson and you've had it.'

(2) P.   He [teacher] always picks on me because I'm always taking the piss out of him. Spicer's always taking the piss out of him but Spicer's his pet because he's in the soccer team. Spicer's his pet. He'd get away with murder with [teacher]. I heard [teacher] talking to some other teachers in the gym when they were playing volleyball, and he said to them that Spicer's not as bad. I mean [teacher] is at it, 'He's not as bad as he's made out to be', but he's worse than us lot put together. He's a back-stabber. He'll get you to do something then he'll say, 'Sir, look what he's just done.' He's a dick. He's a poof.

A third factor which may lead a pupil to 'stand out' at an early stage is that the child may have some particular problem about which the school is informed and which becomes widely disseminated among the teachers. A good example is when the pupil suffers from some disabling medical condition. One pupil had a kidney com-plaint, and teachers were told about this so that they would know that his frequent requests to go to the toilet were legitimate and necessary. Another instance was the pupil who suffered from epilepsy.

In summary, a pupil may 'stand out' at a very early stage if he has an older sibling, and/or is discussed among the staff, and/or if he has a medical condition. But that in itself does not, of course, make him a 'deviant pupil'. What does a pupil do to make himself 'stand out' in this way? Is it perhaps because he breaks the rules in a highly dramatic way in a single incident? In this research we came across only one such case.

The teacher was adopting his jocular manner with the pupils, and there had been no problems in the previous three-quarters of the lesson, no disciplinary events. The teacher was pressing the pupil to tell him the word that they had to remember—'conscientious'—and the pupil was obviously reluctant to do so, not because he didn't know it, but because he just didn't want to—in my opinion. Just prior to this the teacher had made a pun on his (the pupil's) surname, an innocuous one, pointing out his witticism to the rest of the class. The teacher did get him to say it, but only in a very quiet voice and he had to pull the pupil's hand away from his mouth as he was saying it. He then pushed the pupil further, firstly in trying to get him to say it out loud, which he wouldn't, and then by trying to make him spell it. The teacher indicated that the pupil was being a bit dull, because all he had to do was spell it from the board. At this point the pupil's control snapped and he lifted his fist to the teacher and said: 'Leave me alone or I'll bat you in the mouth!' The teacher was taken aback and just stood there. After four or five seconds the pupil said: 'You're always making fun of me and saying I'm stupid. You'd better stop it!' Throughout all this the pupil kept his fist raised. The teacher had to make a rapid decision. This he did by telling the whole class to say the school prayer out loud again. He made no comment and took no action at this time.

(Observation notes)

In a later interview the teacher commented:

T.   When I spoke to him the other day, when he came, I thought devil-possessed, I was just trying to be friendly and I made a pun on his name . . . and instead of accepting it as a joke, he came as if he resented being spoken to and I think he must be—well, I know he is unhappy at home, but it seems to me that after that he resents any type of discipline or being co-opted in and he's lost his sense of humour and I shan't forget him. I tell you, I prayed for that lad last night and this morning because it's really such a pathetic state. I've seen [headmaster] but personally I think he should see a psychiatrist. . . .
I.   Had there been anything in the previous three weeks to indicate that this sort of thing might happen?
T.   Nothing in the room at all, except that he was a Biggs, Terry's brother. I just knew that he was a Biggs and that you'd have to be reasonably careful, but I thought he was coming on reasonably well. He didn't show resentment. Something may have happened at home that we don't know anything about. I find that when a child is like this he's not well. It's quite likely that he'll be ill. But

I've taught two murderers and I hope that I'm not teaching a third. It's a bit depressing for an RE Department, isn't it?

This incident is of interest, because it shows how a pupil, on the basis of a 'dramatic' incident, can be re-typed as 'mentally ill' and as a potential murderer, incorporating the sibling phenomenon, a speculative motivation, and new predictions into the re-typing. Yet this is not the way most deviant pupils become typed.

Very large numbers of pupils break a variety of rules when they are newcomers and such rule-breaking is perceived by the teachers as 'normal' and 'natural'. In part this is because the teachers cannot be sure that the pupils know, or have formed the habit of conforming to, the rules of this particular school. The 'settling in' period is regarded as one of rule-teaching and rule-learning. Pupil conduct which technically breaks the rules is interpreted as possibly 'accidental' or 'unintentional'.

> T. In the first week I made a big point of stressing to all of them that this is not a primary school any more and they are to be taught in a different way, and won't be allowed to run about as freely and behave as freely as they were at primary school. And particularly that talking in class and moving about in class, which is a big problem. You know, I would never have dreamt of getting up in the middle of a lesson but at junior school these boys have been allowed to walk about and they just do it now and you can tell them off about it, and they do it unintentionally. They are just used to doing it, and without permission they will suddenly just get up and go and borrow a pencil off somebody.

So when pupils break such rules when they are newcomers, they are reminded of the rule, reproved in a mild way, but not punished. Such 'deviance' is accepted and tolerated as part of the newcomer status. The teachers do not need to find motives for such conduct, for there are typical motives (ignorance, poor memory, accident) which derive directly from their typing (newcomers). Further, it is expected that a certain amount of 'deviance' will spring from fear, nervousness and anxiety, which are additional newcomer typical motives. But once the pupils are no longer accorded newcomer status, it is assumed that they have now learned the rules and that they are no longer nervous and apprehensive: they have 'settled in'. Rule-breaking acts which are treated as normal during the newcomer period now become defined as deviant.

> T. They have had—what?—a month to settle in, it's not so new to them now. This is normally when you start to find out any potential troublemakers, or which boys are going to be good, the

sort of boys you put in plays and that sort of thing, you know. About this time, yes I think so. Just after they settle in, they get a bit of confidence and they think, 'I know where everything is now, I can start to be myself', sort of thing. If they are going to . . . I think between now and Christmas is the time you find out.

'Normal' pupils 'get over' their 'normal' deviance in the newcomer period; 'deviant' pupils do not.

I.   Are there any others you see as problems?
T.   Well, there's only giggling Roger. He's silly. He's a really silly little boy. He gets himself into trouble for laughing all the time. He can work really well when he sets his mind to it, one of the best in the class, but he always has to laugh and hee-haw like a donkey all over the place. If he settles down I think he'll be all right but the fact that he is so silly influences quite a few people in the class. . . . I wonder if really when he first came to the school he felt very insecure, you know, being in a school of this size, and his reaction to that was to giggle and to laugh to cover up the fact that he was feeling very insecure. But it's gone on, you see. It's not been eradicated even though he's been in the class for nearly a term. He's still giggling now and at times he can be really offensive with his giggling.

Many children who are regarded by the teachers as deviant are not typed with a label that refers to a specific deviant act such as 'giggler', 'chatterbox', 'bully' or 'insolent', nor do they come to the teacher's attention because they break particular rules. In the average lesson in schools there are many pupil acts which strictly speaking can be defined as deviant, but a large proportion of these are not overtly defined by the teacher as deviant by a verbal deviance-imputation. There are many reasons for this and we shall be considering them in depth in chapter 8. At this point suffice it to say that teachers often do not take action against pupil acts they privately define as deviant, because the deviant acts are often very minor, breaking relatively minor rules; the acts sometimes 'peter out' naturally within a short period; the status of the act as deviant is somewhat ambiguous. We can, then, distinguish two kinds of deviant act; those which result in an overt deviance-imputation of some sort and those which are simply ignored by the teacher, even though the act is defined as deviant or probably deviant. We shall call these 'reactional deviance' and 'subreactional deviance' respectively.[7] Whilst one particular pupil may commit just one or two subreactional deviant acts in a lesson, another pupil may commit many subreactional acts which break a variety of rules. In this case, we can say that the pupil commits multiple and variegated subreactional deviance. Our argument is that some of the pupils who become typed as deviant do not commit isolated 'dramatic' deviant acts, or even repeated deviant acts of a specific kind (as with Roger and his giggling). Rather, they commit multiple and variegated subreactional deviance. In addition, they commit some reactional deviant acts, but these acts in isolation are never regarded as serious because they tend to break minor rules. This subreactional and reactional deviance is not 'compensated' by any outstanding or noticeable acts of conformity, which might counterbalance the deviance. The cumulative result is that the teacher is left with a 'vague impression' that the pupil is deviant, even though he cannot 'pin it down to any one incident'. Often, he cannot in fact remember what the pupil has done, precisely because subreactional deviant acts and minor reactional acts are simply forgotten. A second result is that because the deviant conduct is variegated, no specific label is entirely appropriate to the pupil. In consequence he tends to be given a general or diffuse deviant typing, such as 'difficult', 'a problem', 'a pest', 'nuisance' or 'troublemaker'. None of these labels gives any clear indication of the acts that the pupil commits, whereas 'chatterbox' and 'bully' do. Specific labels may be used to talk about the pupil in detail, but it is the diffuse label which most adequately summarizes the teacher's conception of him. In practice, the teacher may not assign him one of these diffuse labels at an early stage, but expresses a feeling that he is likely to become such a pupil.

Although many of our teachers made statements from which we derived these ideas, one teacher in particular gave a highly explicit and articulate account, with reference to one of the pupils (Ted Lewis) who will appear in a case-study later. The interviewer was asking the teacher to expand on a comment that he had made in an earlier interview to the effect that he thought the pupil 'could be bothersome later on' but this was 'purely a feeling'.

> T.   Well, it's rather like driving a car with the seat of your pants, really. In your perception of children I'm sure there's a lot you don't note consciously, and yet all the time you're absorbing details of their behaviour at all times without this really registering. You're forming opinions even though you may say, 'Look, I can't say that I've had a big emotional upset with the boy', or anything like that. In fact, it's easier if you can say that, because at least you've got some really concrete evidence and this can always be used against the child later on. You start basing impressions of them on the basis of a lot of stimuli from them, and you make a note of it, subconsciously perhaps, and then you'll give an opinion

on that child that is based on what? On an accumulation of little bits and pieces here and there.

I.   Can you think of any particular incidents?

T.   None, except that we know his name. Of all the children in the class there aren't many that you know the name of at this stage. Yet his name has come to the fore, and not for anything academic or otherwise really. It's just that you do know him. Yet there has been no incident where you could say, 'Look. Dreadful boy', and there's been no incident where you could say, 'Lovely lad', and yet you do know him all the same. I reckon it's an accumulation of incidents that have brought his name to notice. . . . It's the little incidents that you don't sort of note but which you sum up in the end to making this kind of judgment about him.

I.   It's these sort of incidents I'm interested in.

T.   But there's nothing really. It's the things that are just not big enough to step into. Nothing there that you could say, 'Here's something that needs intervening over.'

We have now covered the main processes of typing in the speculative and elaborative stages, the factors which can lead a pupil to 'stand out', and the concept of subreactional deviance. These can now be illustrated not as separate strands of a theory, but as elaborately interwoven features of teachers' descriptions and accounts of selected pupils who emerged as deviant.

7 *The typing of deviant pupils*

We have so far outlined a theory of typing in its speculative and its elaborative stages. We now wish, in the first part of this chapter, to focus our attention on a more detailed exemplification of these processes. We shall present the data in the form of case-studies of pupils from the two schools, and in so doing we shall be able to demonstrate how the main processes of the elaborative stage—verification, extension, idiosyncratization and motive elaboration—fuse into a relatively coherent whole. In the second part of the chapter, we shall examine stabilization of deviant typings in greater depth and present case-studies to illustrate teachers' constructions of stabilized deviant pupils.

1 Ted Lewis—first year pupil in school B

In the September interviews, only four teachers talked about Ted. There had been no 'dramatic' incidents in which he was involved and he did not have a brother in the school. The comments are rather brief and are reproduced fully.

> T. I know him because we were waiting outside the class and I wanted something and he said, 'I'll go, Miss.' A perky little boy and he's a nice helpful little boy and that's how I noticed him. His was the first name I learned. The others were because they were too slow, but his was the other way.
>
> (Mrs O)

> T. I think that the three ringleaders who cause more trouble than anyone are Ted Lewis [and two others]. . . . Ted is the one with the large punch, rather like Muhammed Ali really. He's always ready with his fists and will punch first before he asks. The three of them could be a formidable gang if they were allowed to. I have broken them up several times. They pick on smaller and weaker boys in the class. Those are the most pugnacious boys in the class. . . . Ted and Peter are ready to help in class. They'll ask me if there is anything I want doing

171

and they'll do it. . . . They are more open-natured [than the third] . . . boxers, but they'll be tamed by the time they're in the third year. I mean they're open characters and you can do more with a boy who openly admits that he's wrong, than with one who mutters under his breath about discipline.

(Mrs N)

T.   He's another one that comes forward. He's keen to help out any time that you ask for volunteers. He's a rusher of work. I think that he's a boy that if you've got your back turned he'll be up to no good. Yesterday I asked him if he'd done his work and he said 'Yes', but when I asked him to bring it to me then he said that he hadn't. An instance of—well, a little lie. Whether anything can be gleaned from this for the future I don't know. . . . He clamours for attention—back turned could be poking somebody or provoking somebody to have a go at him, maybe. Maybe as he goes through the school he'll be one that you're always telling to turn round, shut up and get on.

(Mr Y)

T.   Lewis. A little blond lad. I suspect that Ted could be bothersome later on. I detect an air of sort of anti-establishment about him. That's just purely a feeling because at the moment he's very co-operative. He does as he's told; does more than he's told; does all that he can to help you, really. I just detect that in the end he might turn out anti-establishment. It's just one of those things.
I.   What I'd really like to know is what you are basing that on.
T.   It's experience of seeing other lads of a similar nature. It might be his relations—you see you can't always pin it down to any particular incident because you've never had a row with him. He's never been sort of bolshie with you. It could be in his relations with other children if he's more aggressive possibly. He won't be aggressive with the teacher at this stage because he's only a first year, but if he's showing some aggression to other children, then this might transfer to teachers later on in the school. That might well be it. And often you feel this rather than seeing anything. It might well be that. You've seen lads like this growing up. It might sometimes be the look of the child. I think that Ted has this look of slightly drawn cheeks; rather a hardened look and a slightly hardish look in the eye. These things give me the impression that he might be bothersome this type of lad.

(Mr Q)

These early characterizations display the tentative mixture of typifications that is a mark of the speculative stage. The four teachers agree on only one matter, namely that he is 'helpful'. The impression he leaves is not an entirely unfavourable one, for he is described as 'nice', 'open' and 'co-operative'. But two teachers note that Ted is 'aggressive' or 'pugnacious' towards other pupils, and a third describes him as 'provoking' others. This leads to the prediction that there will be 'trouble' at a later stage ('. . . who could cause more trouble . . .', '. . . if you've got your back turned he'll be up to no good . . .', 'I suspect that Ted could be bothersome later on'), but these predictions are tentative ('. . . just purely a feeling at the moment . . .') no doubt because the teachers are aware of the limitations of their first impressions based on a few incidents, and because some of the deviance is subreactional ('. . . you can't always pin it down to any particular incident . . .'). Mrs N believes that he will 'be tamed' by the third year, but neither Mr Y nor Mr Q appear to be so optimistic, perhaps because they are taking a more short-term view in their predictions. Mr Q links his typing with Ted's appearance ('. . . this look of slightly drawn cheeks . . . and a slightly hardish look in the eye'). This teacher also draws on his knowledge of typical first year pupils when he asserts that Ted will not be aggressive with teachers because he is in the first year when aggression is typically directed to peers; but when he has 'settled down' this aggression may well be directed to the teachers.

By January, the typings have become more elaborated. Mr Q does not find him to be a 'problem' in his own classes, though he has heard that this is not the case with other teachers. His own view is that the boy is 'lively' and 'high-spirited' rather than 'naughty', though he continues to sense problems in peer relations and now believes that he could under certain conditions be a leader of an anti-group, which confirms and elaborates his original prediction. He remains a pupil who is 'to be watched'.

> T. I think I mentioned Ted before. Now he's a character whose name always springs to mind, and yet I'd say that he's a lad that I can leave to work alone in my class. I know him very well, yet I still feel that here's a lad that has to be watched more closely than most. I think that he does cause trouble in classes, but I think that he reacts well to me. He's quite bright. Because of this we don't have—well, we don't have much to argue about really. I suspect that if something rubs him the wrong way then there will be trouble with Ted, and I think that this might have been proved so with other teachers. I've heard his name mentioned before.

I.   Would you still say that these were just suspicions about him?

T.   Well, in my class I know that he's not been much bother at all. He's a lively lad, fairly high-spirited, and I can see that— well, I know that in other classes it's been more than high spirits. He's been naughty and getting into trouble.

I.   You said that he might turn out anti-establishment.

T.   Yes. I still feel that eventually, if he gets stuck in a group of kids who are themselves turning out anti-establishment as a group, he'll be amongst them as a leader. His aggressiveness is still there and he also has this aggression towards other kids. From what they say they still figure that he is the best fighter in the class.

(Mr Q)

Mr Y links him with Peter, as Mrs N did in September, and whilst these two boys have tended to disturb other pupils, an improvement is noted since Peter left the class.

T.   He's been quieter this term because Peter's gone. Seems to have settled down more, but is another one who leaves his place and goes to interfere with other people. Peter used to work with him and they were very similar in this sort of thing where they were talking to each other. They used to go around the room and talk to other people and create a bit of friction with other groups. Now Ted hasn't done this this term so whether one has influenced the other I don't know, but I haven't had to speak to him as much.

(Mr Y)

Mrs N also believes that he has begun to 'settle down' and become less aggressive which is again attributed to Peter's removal to another class. He is described now as being 'sure of himself'. He is also differentiated from Peter in that Ted's aggression is seen as 'premeditated' whereas Peter is imputedly more 'spontaneous' in his aggression.

T.   He's not as belligerent as he was. He's still very, very sure of himself and he has a great opinion of himself but he doesn't fight everybody now and I think that's because Peter has gone into a different class. . . . He asks now before he punches anybody. Before he used to hit first and ask afterwards, but now he's not nearly as belligerent as he was. And his work's improved a great deal since then. He seems to have found his feet.

I.   You saw Peter and Ted as very similar characters.

T. They are, but of the two I would say that Peter has by far the more open nature. Ted is inclined to be surly about things whereas Peter will laugh them off. They developed along very different lines. I think I lumped them together because they were both quick off the mark with their fists, but I would think now that with Ted it would be premeditated in his fighting, whereas with Peter it wouldn't be. Peter would just sort of go off at anything and hit anybody—spontaneous I would think in his case.

(Mrs N)

Mrs O has extended and elaborated her original brief typing. Ted is no longer the 'nice helpful little boy'.

T. I think that Ted can be a bit—er—likes to be a bit of a know-all. I think that if he could he would influence the others if you let him. But if you say 'I'm doing this, Ted, not you', he does accept it. Whether he would when he got older, I don't know. He was very good last September. Now I think that it's mostly chipping in, you know, if you are talking to a boy. Or he will tell a boy. He thinks that he's in a position to tell another boy to do something. This if it went on, you can see it in some of the other boys, could become bossy, and I think that he could become that. Earlier on, as I think I said, he was a very helpful boy, and I thought that he was going to be very good. But you see it can work both ways that. Showing initiative to help can so easily become bossy, and I think that it could develop into that if it were allowed. . . . He thinks that he knows it all. He thinks he's the big 'I AM'. . . . I wouldn't let him go anywhere near Gavin or Peter because he could spark them off, whereas on their own they wouldn't do it. They would either be silly or resent each other.

(Mrs O)

Mrs O believes her early speculative hypothesis has been falsified ('I thought he was going to be very good'). She is now in a position to specify some of his deviant conduct and make tentative predictions ('. . . he would influence the others if you let him . . .', '. . . it could develop if it were allowed to . . .') and so alerts herself to the need to take preventive measures, without which his 'initiative' would easily become 'bossiness'.

We see Ted, then, in the middle of the elaborative stage. His typing is developing, but is far from being stabilized. He is possibly beginning to 'settle down' and the removal of Peter from the form is thought to have helped in this. Yet he still tends to create problems with other pupils. The teachers continue to have reservations about him and feel that under certain circumstances he might turn out to be more of a problem in the future. Since he is not a major problem at the present time, their outlook is one of a cautious 'wait and see'.

2 Fritz Benson—second year pupil in school A

The three teachers who talked to us about this pupil had all taught him for a full academic year; their typing of him is fully elaborated. Two of the teachers report that he is 'not really a problem' and the third points out that he is a 'special' kind of problem. Perhaps, then, we have no grounds for describing Fritz as a deviant pupil; he is more adequately described as near-deviant or potentially deviant. Like many pupils in the first two years of school, he is, in the teachers' eyes, someone who is likely to be a problem in the future.

I.   Did you know anything about him at that time?
T.   No. I'd heard the name bandied about occasionally, you know. You do hear the names in the staffroom from time to time.
I.   What sort of things?
T.   Well, I think that he's a bit of a bully and this was about all. He did create a rumpus occasionally in the form room, but then I haven't heard much of him, not from this point of view. I think I noticed him, of course, because he is a big boy for a start. He was all right, yes, all right. I think the first day he tends to be the sort of class comedian and I could see this come out in the first lesson I ever had with him. I said to him, 'Look you're not big enough to be awkward and don't start in my lesson', and that was that. I've never had any trouble with Fritz.

This teacher is able to elaborate extensively on these two features, 'bully' and 'comedian', by drawing on her common-sense knowledge acquired from her experience in industry.

T.   He's not witty, but he tends to make fun of other children, of their weaknesses in class and because he's a big boy and he obviously—well, I feel he's the sort of class bully, shop-steward, barrackroom lawyer all rolled into one. This is Fritz—he's sort of—if there was one in charge, he's cock of 2C and obviously a lot of the boys are smaller than him. This has happened before, but they eventually catch up in the fourth year and then he's no longer in awe as he was earlier down in the school. . . .
I.   You said shop-steward. That's interesting—could you expand on it a bit?

T.   Well, having been in industry, often you will find a
shop-steward will go round looking for bits of things that
people haven't thought about and they'll say, 'Well, you're not
getting paid enough for this are you?' and the person might not
have thought about it before. . . . Often you find shop-stewards
like this. They're not content . . . they often go round putting
ideas into people's heads that weren't there before and this is
sort of muck-stirring and this is the bit that I can see Fritz being
well fitted to do. . . . I'm always conscious that I couldn't walk
out and leave 2C happily if Fritz were there; (1) because he
might turn round and clout somebody or thump somebody and
(2) because he's a stirrer, you know. He's a big lad and makes
the most of it. I've noticed the boys in the class, if they're doing
anything, and they think it's clever or funny, they want Fritz to
see them do it. . . . But when I'm there teaching, he doesn't make
any difference at all . . . I've had no difficulty at all with Fritz.

Motivational aspects are elaborated by the teacher, who forges a
link between Fritz's activities as a 'bully' and his reaction to her
treatment of him ('He doesn't like to be told off . . .') with her belief
that he 'lacks affection' which she explains in the light of her knowledge about the home background. Note how the knowledge of the
home background is not used to explain that the younger brother
has 'a very sunny disposition' and is 'entirely different'.

T.   He doesn't like to be told off, especially in front of the class,
because he's being shown up. I find this often with the bully
and the class comedian. He'll have a go at somebody else but if
somebody has a go at him the only way he'll react is with his
fists and he's not witty enough often to come back with a remark
that'll flatten somebody like that. He hasn't got the wit about
him, he's no sense of humour about him. I think this comes
from his background of course.
I.   Have you been informed of his background?
T.   Yes, I know his junior school teacher—he's a friend of mine.
I.   What was he like then?
T.   He was the same. His younger brother is entirely different—
he's got a very sunny disposition. . . . I think his mother is
German and she admitted herself once that she had no affection
for her children whatsoever. . . . She will feed and clothe them and
give them all the necessary comforts that way, but she cannot
show any affection for them. And the father is very—if he knew
or was told the way Fritz behaved in school he would, you know,
really lace into him. . . . Yes, I think he does lack affection.

                                                                  (Mrs L)

The second teacher has relatively little to say about him, but does explain his deviant conduct as arising when he is not 'the centre of attraction'. The apparently imputed 'need for attention' can be compared with the previous teacher's imputed 'need for affection'.

> T.   As far as I can see this is not really a problem child. From the point of view of discipline, I have not had any trouble with him at all. He tends, if he is not being the centre of attraction with his own group, he tends to make a bit of a nuisance of himself then. . . . I don't have any discipline problems—violence or being naughty with other children. He seems to be all right.
>
> (Mr J)

The third teacher makes it clear that he shares this view that Fritz is 'a bit of a nuisance' and illustrates it.

> T.   Obviously Fritz is a problem. As I see it Fritz is a special problem that needs more of my time than the others do. He's different in many ways from the rest of his peers. His pattern of behaviour is different in that he'll move about and when spoken to will make some remark to the side, turn aside and make some remark, not aimed at a specific person but to the class in general, obviously to do something for him. . . . He will interfere with someone else's activities. He'll either pinch them, push them, have a kick at their legs as he walks past. Various things have taken place since the beginning of the year. At the back of the class he can be making various noises which may not be words, possibly having a little sign. All kinds of minor disruptive behaviours that you can think of, Fritz has done them. He pushes other boys and he takes other boys' pencils—all the little classroom annoyances. Then you'll find he's wandered off and is sitting in another place. You ask him why and he'll say that he's just decided to go. So you say, 'Sit there', and he'll say, 'I'm not sitting there. I don't want to sit there.' He feels that he has the special right to be peripatetic and wander about at will.

Various forms of minor or routine deviance are noted and these 'minor disruptive behaviours' make him 'different in many ways from the rest of his peers' who are not so 'disruptive' of their classmates. The result is that he 'needs more of my time than the others do'. In accounting for this in motivational terms, the teacher elaborates that he is 'insecure', which recalls the other teachers' imputations that he 'lacks affection' and 'needs attention'. Although this teacher discusses these issues uneasily ('I don't know what is going on in his mind . . .' and 'You're not expecting me to be a psychologist, are you?'), the imputed insecurity is explained and supported through his 'domestic problems' at home, and in its turn explains his classroom deviance which is interpreted as a means 'to establish his position' with his peers.

> T.   I don't know whether you're going to find a common factor
> in all this, but one is told by people who are responsible in the
> school that he's got domestic problems. I don't know if this is
> true, but this is a little boy who needs some sort of parental
> figure—I was going to say father figure—to look up to;
> somebody he respects and somebody to model himself on. I think
> he's lacking this and consequently he's lost and doesn't know
> where to go. . . . I don't know what is going on in his mind,
> but it's fairly obvious that he's always concerned with his own
> position relative to the group, the whole class. He always feels
> the need to do something about it. He's not satisfied that he's
> accepted as part of the group, and he's creating a special place
> for himself by performing all the time so that the rest of the
> class—and the teacher incidentally—notice him. . . . I should
> say that he's insecure. We read these things and say these words,
> but I think that the lad is insecure and seeking to establish his
> position. It's very difficult to remedy this, to make him like the
> others because you can't put back what's been lost over a number
> of years. . . . You're not expecting me to be a psychologist,
> are you? I've got to make some feeble attempt to try and
> understand what Fritz is doing if I'm going to do anything
> for him.

Yet this teacher does not experience any real problems in controlling Fritz in the classroom.

> T.   So he's just a silly little boy at the moment, and he'll
> probably become a very great nuisance when he gets older and
> bigger, because his little mischiefs may become physically
> dangerous if he starts being aggressive and so on. He's not big
> enough at the moment. You just say, 'Don't be a naughty boy
> and sit down.'
>
> (Mr K)

Fritz, then, is typical of the potential deviant. He is given a qualified deviant label ('a bit of a nuisance', 'a silly little boy') because in spite of committing variegated minor deviance with considerable frequency, the teachers feel fully able to handle and control him— at least for the moment. As in the case of Ted, some teachers hear the rumblings of distant thunder; in the future he may turn out to be much more of a problem.

3 Steve Roberts—first year pupil in school B

This third example of a potential deviant, about whom we were informed by six teachers, demonstrates the cumulative impact of the sibling phenomenon, staff discussion, the highly observable distinguishing characteristic of his red hair, and early subreactional or minor reactional deviance.

T.   Now there's a boy with sort of reddish hair whose name I don't know, who seems probably—he seems to—as though potentially he could cause trouble.

I.   I think you mean Roberts. He's the only one with red hair.

T.   Yes. He seems as though he could cause trouble, you know, in later years. I just don't know at this stage. It's all relative, and he's not that much worse than any of them. I've not had trouble with them [the form], but he—. If anything goes wrong, you know, if someone comes in late, or does something that aggravates me, you know, it's generally him. He doesn't toe the line and conform, like, I think, as much as the others. He comes in late occasionally and forgets things. I can't think of anything else. They're that trivial they barely register but just enough to notice that he's different from the rest.

(Mr P)

T.   Steve I know, partly because I had to speak to him once but partly also because he's got a brother that I taught last year in the third year. They've both got the same carrot-tops. I've only had to speak to him for slight incidents. You see, him and the boy who sat next to him yesterday, they weren't doing what they should have been doing—they were doing a bit of giggling instead of looking at the book, but I spoke to Steve afterwards and he was quite polite on his own and said he wouldn't do it again. He's quite a pleasant boy, I mean, I quite like him. I can't say I've had any trouble with him, no, I haven't. But I think he'll need watching. I think he'll be one, without making it obvious, you'd have to be a little bit, you know, keep your eye on him and see how he, which way he is going to jump. And knowing his background, which I did, I didn't know he was Steve until I asked him his name and then I thought, 'Oh yes, of course, I should have known.' I can tell from [his elder brother] but even that would not have made me wary because [the elder brother] is chirpy and not one of the worst in the form. He would always respond to a talking, you know, if I spoke to him, very obliging. So if Steve's the same way, he seems quite an obliging boy up to now, so . . . I've no grumbles about him up till now—

it's just the odd time I've had to say 'Steve' you know. So you
need to keep an eye on him to see if he's going to concentrate on
his work. But I think it's unfair to label them at this stage and
say he is going to be—I mean, there again, the very fact that he's
got ginger hair, I mean I sort of noticed it, you know, it might
be slight but it is, if a teacher is learning the names they are
likely to learn them for silly reasons and because he's got red
hair is a reason. I know I got blamed for things at school
because of my hair, so I know and you do notice those with
red hair.

(Mrs O)

T.   The other one that stands out, of course, is Steve Roberts,
Now with his brother I've had trouble in the past—he's a nice
lad, but he can be awkward sometimes, he'll try it on. Steve does
not seem to do this very much, not yet anyway. I think he is still
feeling his way. Nice lad. He does some of the same tricks as his
brother, things like everybody else will be listening and he
appears to be listening and then he will come out afterwards
and say, 'Now what do I do?' you know. And he also tends to
be very tired. . . . He falls asleep. I've had to wake him up
several times as you've noticed in lessons, because I've had a
word with [another teacher] and other people have mentioned
the same thing, and he's just not getting to bed on time. . . .
I think Steve's a stronger character than his brother. He tends
to be a leader within his own little group. You notice that the
other boys tend to look to Steve very often, whereas [the elder
brother] has always been a follower. He has been a loudmouth
and a class idiot, whereas I don't think Steve is. He does daft
things, but he's not the class idiot. I think in a way Steve has more
leadership than [the elder brother] has.

(Mr S)

T.   Now Steve. Unfortunately he's got a bit of a reputation
which isn't his own fault because he has several brothers who
have been here and they've been, you know, a bit of trouble.
Er, he strikes me as being much cleverer than his brothers—
the one I know, anyway—he's much cleverer for a start. You can
tell, you can pick out similarities with his brothers in behaviour.
Er, he's a—he likes to talk, and I think you were in one lesson
when I had to tell him. He likes to talk, he likes to chatter all the
time. He also has this characteristic, when you tell him off,
he's extremely sorry and repentant. He puts on this front, whereas
really deep down he really isn't bothered at all, I don't think,
you know. I don't think he's as bad as his brother, not as badly

181

behaved at all, but then again you get the impression that as soon as your back is turned he might be up to something, not anything really wicked I don't think, but I've got my eye on him.
I.   Was that the impression you had from the beginning?
T.   No, like I say, you're biased, you're prejudiced by the reports you get on some boys which you get before you even see them.
I.   Have you had to single him out for anything?
T.   Not actually single him out. He seems to have made a friend ... and they seem to sit next to each other in every lesson and they like to chatter and murmur, quietly, when they think the teacher's occupied with something else, you know. But nothing more than that. But he is the most untidy. Already his book is nowhere near in as good condition as the rest of the boys', it's bent up. . . . He just doesn't seem to have much respect for equipment and books. But he's quite interested.

(Mr R)

T.   He's obviously the biggest problem in the class because, you know, of his brother. I've come across him with his brother, and his brother saw me and started to give me a bit of cheek, because he knows that he can get away with it a bit, and I could see that Steve was laughing at the way that his brother was trying to score off me, you know. He likes to mouth and Steve is just the same I think. He's still pretty timid, but he's got all the answers. He's very cute. He knows you're having him on. The others you can put a stern face on, but he is very cute. He's quick, he knows, he'll start to smile. I think he can read the characters of teachers pretty well and he can see who to play up to and who not to. I'm not really experienced enough to say, but I wouldn't think he'd be as much trouble as [his brother]. I think possibly he's going to be affected by his brother's mystique, or whatever you want to call it. I've heard a teacher say this morning, 'Oh, Steve Roberts, he hasn't handed his homework in, that means he's going to be a nuisance the rest of his school life.' Well, I don't think that follows. It's probably in the back of his mind this prejudiced view.

(Mr T)

Whilst it is clear that Steve is seen to commit minor deviance—coming late, falling asleep, being forgetful, giggling, chatting—he is thought of as 'better' than his elder brother, as cleverer and as more of a leader. Although these are minor deviant acts, Mrs O nevertheless thinks 'he'll need watching' and Mr R says, 'I've got my eye on him'. Further, these extracts show that some of the teachers, like good labelling theorists, are aware of the dangers in taking 'a prejudiced view' of this pupil. Whilst they find it impossible to remove it from their early typing they sometimes try not to let it affect their treatment of the boy. Thus Mr R goes out of his way to account favourably for Steve's early misdemeanours.

> T. I should say Steve, if he's handled right, will be far better than his brothers, but he's got to be—at the moment I'm trying to be fair, fair to him, and only jump on him when he really annoys me and not jump on him for everything which some people do, and I think that only makes him worse. So, he's had a bit of trouble with [another teacher]. He's had to see him once about fighting already, yes, and he brought his radio to school which is against the school rules, but he didn't know much about that, or he said he didn't know about it. I think that's quite honest actually, because I don't think they'd been told. I didn't tell them. I think he's in a bit of an unfortunate position really, because several of the teachers know his brother and I don't think he'd really need much leeway to—it's a question of not jumping on him too much, I think.
>
> (Mr R)

By January, the teachers' typings of Steve have become more elaborated. He is now seen as 'a wise-cracking showman'; he has 'gone off the track of work altogether'; he 'regards himself as the top man in the class'. His deviant conduct is seen as persistent and more extensive. Some of the teachers believe that their early predictions have generally been confirmed, but their views of him are mixed.

> T. Steve's a nice lad, but he wants to show off, that's what it is mainly, I think. He's irrepressible, you know. If you've just settled them down he's—he's not a bad lad, he thinks he's a showman, you know, he likes to make what he thinks are clever remarks. . . . I've had to punish him once or twice lately, for speaking when he's not spoken to, you see, interrupting a lesson and speaking, or when they are doing a bit of quiet work. . . . I mean I don't punish them for talking but with Steve it goes beyond, the point of—it's too much. . . . He's a nice lad, but I've had to tell him off. He's irrepressible, as I say, but I've told him I'm just not having it. He's got to learn that when I'm speaking it's got nothing to do with him. You see I speak to another boy, 'Get on with your work', and Steve will say 'Yes, get on with your work', you see. He thinks, it's just this role that he thinks he is going to adopt.

I.   What role do you think that is?

T.   I think it's just a showman. He's just trying to get the approval of his fellows. He thinks he's creating, he's cutting a good figure in their eyes. I think that's what he's doing it for. . . . I think he'll be one you'll have to keep your eye on and make sure that he doesn't wobble over.

(Mrs O)

T.   Roberts, unlike what I said before, has developed into someone worse than he was before.

I.   How do you mean?

T.   Well, he's just refused to get down to any kind of work, and is continually chattering all the time. . . . I think it all stems from Roberts. He doesn't know where play ends and work begins, not in my lesson anyway. . . . If he's not careful I think he will go on to an entirely different track altogether. He seems to be going off the track of work altogether. This is the first time that I've seen his book this term. He just says he's forgotten it and looks blank. You know it's a lie really.

(Mrs U)

As the typing of Steve becomes more elaborated the significance of the sibling phenomenon appears to decline. Neither Mrs O nor Mrs U mentions Steve's brother whilst Mr R and Mr S stress the differences rather than the similarities between Steve and his brother.

T.   I think I said before that Steve might possibly be some trouble, but, well he has been in this trouble, but then again, it's been nothing serious. It's just, well, he regards himself as the top man in the class. It's more that than anything. And he's not as bad as I anticipated he might be by any means, because like I told you, his brother wasn't very good at all and there was always a chance of like father like son, but it doesn't seem to be like that at all.

(Mr R)

T.   Steve's behaving. Yes. Forgot his homework this morning, or rather said he'd been out so I told him to do his homework this dinner-time. Very little trouble. He enjoys lessons. He could be awkward if he wanted to be, but I think we can arrest that before it goes too far. He isn't as cheeky as his brother was, but he's more self-confident. His brother was downright cheeky, but Steve isn't. He knows where to draw the line, which his brother never did really. He's all right.

Another teacher (in the background).   Steve Roberts has gone worse this term.

Third teacher. I've clobbered him. I don't know what's
happened to him.
T. Has he gone awkward on you?
Third teacher. Yes, he was going quite good actually, towards
the end of last term and I thought, 'Oh, I've reached an
understanding.' But not this term. He's been really naughty.
I. (to first teacher) Your experience must be different then?
Second teacher. Great discipline you have!
T. Well no, it's not that as much, as I had little trouble with
his brother last year. Anyway, I don't have any trouble with
him. Whether he's a nuisance or not, I don't know.

(Mr S)

The teachers' typings of first and second year pupils are, as these
case-studies demonstrate, qualified typings. The characterizations
may be made with a degree of confidence and the teachers are willing
to make predictions about pupils, but normally there is also an
element of doubt that remains. The teachers accept that their
typing may be wrong or incomplete, and show themselves willing
to revise their typings in the light of subsequent developments. As
'time will tell' they can afford to 'wait and see'. Yet this is not a
passive period of waiting for teachers; they have a 'working
hypothesis', however provisional, which is constantly tested against
events. The very fact that the teachers are unsure about the potential
deviant puts him in a special category. No doubt there is the
equivalent category of the pupil who is potentially 'very good', but
provided that such a pupil is not presenting the teachers with any
current problems, they do not need to worry about him. They can
afford to 'wait and see' passively and optimistically. The special
status of the potential deviant resides in the fact that he typically
presents current problems, albeit minor ones, which if the teachers'
predictions are correct will grow into major ones. So the teachers
are actively concerned to avert such an eventuality. It is this determination to find preventive measures wherever possible that makes
the teachers suspicious of the potential deviant. In its turn this
suspicion results in an active surveillance, for unless the teachers
watch the pupil and events closely they may not notice the small
incremental steps which constitute 'getting worse', nor will they be
able to take preventive measures. They therefore 'keep an eye' on the
potential deviant. In the case of Steve Roberts, 'I think he'll need
watching . . . keep your eye on him and see how he is, which way
he is going to jump' (Mrs O), 'I've got my eye on him' (Mr T), and
this is to 'make sure that he doesn't wobble over' (Mrs O) which can
possibly be prevented provided that 'he's handled right' (Mr R).

As a result of this special surveillance, the potential deviant is elaborated more quickly than 'normal' pupils and the elaboration is in terms of the provisional deviant typing. Thus an appropriate biography and motivational backcloth is constructed for him and such information (having a certain kind of home background, having a deviant elder brother) can, should the speculation be confirmed, be used by the teachers as an explanation of him. They will be disappointed if he turns out to be a deviant, but they will not be surprised.

Over time these doubts and speculations diminish—though they rarely fade completely away—and the typing has entered the stage of stabilization. Essentially, it is a progression from 'he may be this kind of pupil, but then again he may not' to 'he *is* this kind of pupil'. This stage overlaps and fuses with the elaborative stage in that certain elements in the typing may stabilize fairly quickly whilst other elements are being elaborated or are being rejected and reformulated in the processes of de-typing and re-typing. Before analysing those features we have grouped together as the stabilization stage, we must emphasize that type stabilization is not the same as type permanence. In the speculation stage the teachers make hypotheses which may then become confirmed and treated as common-sense 'facts' in the stabilization stage. But such 'facts' too can change. In other words, the stabilization stage can give way to yet a fourth stage, namely the stage of type transformation in which one stabilized type is transformed into a different stabilized type. Our impression is that most pupils are stabilized by the second or third years. The teachers see such a stabilized pupil as changing as he gets older, and as they get to know him better, but these changes are perceived as 'natural developments', that is, as congruent with the way 'he always was'. Other pupils change more radically after stabilization. Pupils who were seen as 'difficult' in the first two years—such as the pupils in the case-studies presented—sometimes 'improve', for it is part of teachers' common-sense knowledge that there is a long-term version of 'settling down' apart from the adjustment that is typically made immediately following the newcomer status. Equally, other pupils originally stabilized as 'good' may 'deteriorate' or become 'unsettled', either temporarily (where stabilized typing can be retained) or more permanently (where type transformation takes place). There are many explanations teachers can use to explain type transformations in either direction—changes explicable by age (especially adolescence); changes due to the influence of friends and peer relations; changes in home circumstances; and changes in school, such as liking/disliking a subject or teacher, or the proximity of examinations, and so on. We witnessed no type transformations in school A, but that does not mean they were not taking place. All the deviant pupils we studied were in the stabilization stage. It is possible that type transformations are unusual in the case of deviant pupils, partly because, as we shall see, teachers see such type transformations as unlikely before the pupil leaves school, and partly because when the deviant pupil sees himself as being thus stabilized in the eyes of the teacher, he sees little point in attempting such a type transformation because he believes that the teachers will be unwilling to give up the stabilized deviant typings.

(1) P. I hate him. He's always picking on me. If anything goes wrong in the class he always picks on me or [another pupil]. [Another pupil] was going to give me something and he [the teacher] said, 'Don't give it to him you can't trust him.'
 I. Why did he say you can't be trusted?
 P. It's 'cos I've been in the nick that's why. There's more than him hates me because of that. Mr —— does. This girl were coming down the corridor and she stuck her shoulder out, this would be when I'd only been here about four or five weeks, so I twisted her arm up her back and he were on the corridor and he said, 'You'll be ending up on another long holiday if you keep doing that Grimes.' It got me mad that. I didn't like it. I didn't tell nobody but I'm waiting for him to say it again. I just want to forget about it, but people like teachers keep bringing it up. If there's any trouble in the school they think it's me.

(2) I. Do you think that you should start with a clean sheet each year?
 P. I'm not particularly bothered. It would be all right if we could in our last year start with a clean sheet, but some teachers don't give you that chance. Something happens and they'll say, 'Come here. Have you done such and such a thing? Do you know anything about it?' You've got a reputation. . . . I know that I'm a troublemaker, but it's the times that you get into trouble for the things that you haven't done that gets you down. I'm getting blamed for this and I'm getting blamed for that.

We shall analyse the stabilization stage by means of case-studies of stabilized deviant pupils. As we shall see later, once a pupil is predominantly typed in a stable form, a number of important processes are set in train. At this point we need only mention the two basic characteristics of the stage of stabilization. The first of these, 'type fusion', refers to the fact that the teacher's knowledge of the pupil is woven into a complex and relatively coherent whole. The outcomes of the elaborative stage—the multiple typings, the specification of the conditions under which typical acts occur, the elaboration of motives—are brought together into a coherent and clear characterization. At this point the teacher is able to talk about the pupil at considerable length and may find it very difficult to 'summarize' the pupil in a few words or in a short description. The second element in this stage is 'type centralization', where some aspects of the typing are made more central to the pupil than others. The typings are ordered into a hierarchy of significance for the understanding of the pupil, some typings being treated as of central significance and others being regarded as peripheral. For instance, two pupils may commit very similar acts of a deviant nature but one pupil is regarded as 'really difficult' and the other as 'difficult, but he's O.K. underneath really'. The first pupil is regarded as centrally, pivotally or essentially deviant,[1] whilst the second pupil is seen as peripherally deviant and centrally 'normal' or 'conformist'.

Our particular interest is in 'deviant' pupils who have reached the stage of stabilization. This will be illustrated by three case-studies of pupils, one in the third year and two in the fourth year. These pupils are examples of deviant pupils who are given diffuse or general deviant labels such as 'nuisance' or 'troublemaker'. Such 'difficult' pupils appear to have three characteristics. The first is that their deviant conduct is of variegated form. That is, they commit a wide range of deviance. More specific labels or typings are used to describe the detail of their deviant conduct, but it is the sheer range of deviance which drives the teacher into using a diffuse typing whenever he wishes to make a summary statement about the pupil. The second characteristic is the persistence of the deviant conduct. It is not regarded as a temporary phenomenon, as in the case of newcomer deviance or in the case of those pupils who are seen as 'passing through a difficult phase'. The deviant conduct is seen as a relatively permanent and central feature of the pupil; it continues now as it did in the past and as it will probably do in the future. The third characteristic, related to the second, is that the deviant conduct is *irremedial;* there is little the teacher can do about it. The teacher is concerned to remedy the deviant conduct both in the short-term and the long-term. In the short-term, the teacher's objective is to handle each deviant act at its point of occurrence in such a way that it is stopped immediately and a recurrence in the immediate future is inhibited. In the long-term, the teacher's aim is to cure the pupil of his deviant behaviour and to convert him to being a 'conformist' or 'good' pupil. A pupil is irremedial when the teacher fails in both objectives, but especially in the second. That is to say, the teacher may manage some degree of short-term control but never manages to eradicate the deviance. Teachers, of course, vary in their ability to achieve short-term control. It is rare for a teacher to find one of these pupils utterly beyond control, but whilst one teacher may find him extremely difficult to handle from lesson to lesson, another teacher may have worked out sufficiently successful short-term strategies which at least allow him 'to cope' with the pupil. Yet all the teachers agree that these deviant pupils are impossible to change. The quality of irremediality is fully conveyed in this extract (about a deviant pupil who is not one of the case-studies), which also reflects many of the processes we have discussed earlier and anticipates many of the issues which will be examined in the next chapter.

I.   Then you said, 'Who's that? John, turn around.'
T.   Yes, it was John, a small dark-haired boy, a very queer
child. I confess failure with John. He's very, very immature and
he makes noises, silly noises, squeaks and screams, and I cannot
stop him. I just don't know. I'm at my wits' end with him. He's
such a baby and if I threaten to do anything to him he cries,
and I'm a bit soft-hearted and he's a beautiful little boy as well,
really. Great brown eyes and lovely dark hair and an innocent
look on his face. But he's a dreadful child to have in a class.
He's a nuisance. He pesters and teases them and does nasty
things like kicking them off the chair and poking them with his
ruler and he's always telling tales on them. With most of them—
I've a lot of nuisances with [another pupil], we've come to terms
now; I had to find my own way of dealing with him as well,
because he's terribly noisy and bombastic, and each child—well,
the problems in a class, I don't mean the really dreadful social
problems, I mean the noisy ones, the lazy ones—they all need
individual handling, and John, well I've tried everything I could
think of and I just cannot make him behave himself, I can't get
him to behave himself. I probably could make him if I slippered
him every time, but to me it wouldn't solve anything because he's
a nuisance outside as well and it would only solve the problem
for the moment. I think this child, his trouble is he's very
immature because he's treated like a baby at home. . . . It's
attention he needs and affection, I think, but you see if I do that
he plays on it. If I do give him attention he clamours for the
whole lesson and that's not fair on the others. I've got
twenty-seven in here. I can't spend the whole time with John,
but it's just one of those problems that teachers have. The other
children don't like him because he tells tales. . . . At the moment
I'm not able to do anything about John. I've sat him on his own;

I've sat him with other pupils; I've given him a lot of work to do; I've gone over every single thing with him—and the trouble is he's quite bright but he's lazy, but he knows if he's lazy I will shout at him. Occasionally he'll do a marvellous piece of work but that is just for a few days and then that wears off and he has to be naughty again. . . . He's an irritating child too. I must confess that I can't like him, you know, I can't feel—I feel sympathetic towards him but he never responds, you see, whatever I do, so that it gets that there are so many others wanting your attention, you know, and needing it, that you don't give it to the ones who don't appreciate it, or rather don't respond to what you're doing. I like them all really, even the ones who hate me and irritate me, I do like them. Because they're children there's something very charming and fresh about them—I mean the boy you sat next to, now he's a most irritating boy, but I can't really get angry with that boy. I can't get cross with him because he's so cheerful and I think cheerfulness is a thing that I take to.

The closing sentences in this interview reveal a common characteristic of these deviant pupils, namely that they are not liked by the teachers. In chapter 6 we saw that likeability is a basic dimension in the typing of pupils, and teachers usually find some pupils much more likeable than others. Yet there are always a few pupils whom the teachers do not like and with whom the teacher finds it difficult to make a warm, human relationship. The teachers find such children surly, resentful, cold, or 'weird'. In some cases, as in the illustration above, the teacher believes that the pupil needs affection and a warm relationship, but then finds that her attempts to make special efforts towards the child are rebuffed. When this dislike arises in the case of a deviant pupil, it appears to strengthen his irremedial status, reinforcing the typing of him as 'difficult' and sometimes creating an additional typing of the pupil as 'disturbed' or 'peculiar'. As we shall see shortly, in case-study number 6, the pupil who is irremedial but none the less likeable redeems himself by this fact.

Once the deviant pupil's 'type' is stabilized, the teacher feels that he knows the pupil, can to a large extent account for his behaviour, and can predict how he will behave in typical circumstances. This confidence in type assessment was amusingly displayed in the course of a teacher interview where the researcher was presenting comments that the teacher concerned had made to pupils, and asking him to comment on his own statements.

I. 'Don't ever come to me and say he's done this or that. You're a nuisance.'

T. This, I'm sure, was to a boy who I could probably put a
name to who I recognize as very often behaving in a manner
which is, leads to difficulties and one of his methods is to draw
attention to other boys who may or may not have done
something which is undesirable and he particularly, of course,
tries to get away with this and possibly thinks teachers are naïve
and consequently draws attention to others thinking to cause
some sort of disruption and I was expressing my dissatisfaction
with him hoping that he will realize that it will not cause the
desired interference with the lesson. I'd put a name to that.
I should say Shaw.
I. As a matter of fact it was Deborah!

In the second of the later case-studies, this teacher talks in similar
terms about Shaw. On the basis of his typing of Shaw, the teacher
expects certain typical acts. The reverse is also true: from the
researcher's description of the teacher's reaction to a deviant act,
the teacher is able to reconstruct the deviant act, assess its typicality
and infer the identity of the perpetrator. Once his typing of a deviant
pupil is stabilized, the links between type-of-pupil, typical-deviant-
act and typical-treatment-of-such-typical-deviant-acts are closely
interwoven in the teacher's common-sense knowledge. We shall
consider the influence of typing on treatment in chapter 8; for the
moment we wish to make a tentative exploration of the consequences
of the deviant typing.

There is a tendency to perceive pupil acts in terms of the type,
i.e. give an interpretation that is congruent with the imputed type.

T. I just told them that I'd had a break-in [i.e. burglary] and he
came and said, 'Let's have a look, Miss.' Well, that's not
Bradley and he said it just like that, you know. Normally he'd
be out of his seat into the stockroom before I could move but
this time he politely asked and went and inspected it with me you
see, had a look round and said, 'Can you see where they got in?'
and so on, and I thought that was odd at the time.

There is a selective sensitivity to pupil acts that are supportive of the
imputed type. Acts that justify the deviant typing or that can serve
as supplementary evidence are noted, remembered and included in
the biography that is imputed to the pupil.

I. Why a tomboy?
T. When you see her knocking one or two of the boys around,
you know. She's not a girl at all I wouldn't think, she's not
ladylike in any way, not at all. Her voice doesn't help. She's got a
very male voice I would call it, very rusty sort of voice like mine.

Once the typing is stabilized, it is unlikely to be changed in the light of apparently incongruent material unless the incongruity is extensive or is constantly re-presented over a long period of time. Incongruent or type-discrepant pupil conduct can be 'explained away' on the grounds that it is superficial and ephemeral.

> T.   For a fortnight there were no complaints at all. Even people
> in the staffroom were saying, 'What's the matter with Shaw,
> is he sick?' because his behaviour had improved. But it went
> off and it never came back.

This 'is he sick?' is, of course, a rhetorical question and a joke for the teachers: they do not think for a moment that Shaw's atypical non-deviant behaviour is to be explained by illness. But the use of this analogy is interesting in that it suggests that the change is temporary (like most illnesses) and is not to be explained by internal changes in Shaw, such as in his motives or attitudes. Shaw's 'real' self remains the same in spite of the surface change, just as sick people are temporarily and superficially 'not themselves' even though they are 'really the same' underneath. Had such a change occurred during the speculative or elaborative stages it might have led to a de-typing; but in the stabilized typing, alternative explanations are sought which do not involve the need to make any fundamental change in the typing. (We are not, of course, seeking to make a value-judgment on the teachers here. Since they know that Shaw-has-been-like-this-in-the-past they have good grounds for not changing the typing without some persuasive evidence.) But were the pupil avowedly making an active effort to change himself, then the disbelief with which his atypical conformity is greeted convinces him, as we saw earlier, that there is no point in attempting to change. If he then reverts to his deviant ways, this serves to confirm the teachers' judgment that the change was temporary and superficial, thus strengthening the teachers' general disposition to doubt any type-discrepant conformity from deviant pupils.

There are other ways in which type-discrepant conduct can be explained.

> T.   Bradley's been so well behaved at the moment that it's
> unnatural. I think that he's putting on an act for me at the
> moment because he's so well behaved.

In this case the teacher explains the conformity by interpreting it as feigned, which in this case is linked with the teacher's perception that the pupil has also been 'less open' of late. By perceiving the conformity as an act of deception, the teacher can retain the stabilized typing of Bradley. Indeed, it is possible that the conformity can be used as a form of type extension, since the changed conduct now shows that Bradley is a deceiver as well.

Once a teacher is confident in his typing of a given pupil, past events can be re-coded under that typing. In these retrospective interpretations[2] the teacher re-interprets the pupil's past behaviour in the light of his current knowledge and reviews his past interactions with, and former knowledge about, a pupil by selectively searching for acts and events which support and are congruent with the present typing. The past is thus reconstructed. In one case in this study, the teacher's discovery that a newly arrived pupil had been in a Borstal institution came as a kind of 'divine revelation' and he is able to re-interpret the past in the light of the newly revealed biography.

> T. I only heard after a fortnight where he'd come from. In fact, the first two weeks I thought he was almost any type of boy, because perhaps he was feeling his way, didn't know the boys in the room and so on. For the first fortnight he was quiet and I thought he was just another boy that had come. We weren't told where he came from and I accepted him until I kept noticing— in later weeks I noticed things, and then we heard where he came from. I had noticed along the corridors, well, I did notice at first, he would walk past people and punch them as he was passing and tap girls on the head with anything he was carrying, paper or a newspaper, so I thought, 'I'll have to watch this boy.'

There is a selective sensitivity to external supportive information derived from other teachers, parents, record cards, etc. Congruent knowledge which is acquired in this way is assimilated into the typing, thereby strengthening it. Incongruent information derived from these sources is less likely to be assimilated or is treated as inconsequential or irrelevant because there is a lack of 'fit' with the teacher's knowledge. Because such information is difficult to weld into the teacher's knowledge, because it does not confirm or support or explain, it is readily forgotten.

> (1) T. I gather from home that he has a lot of his own way, and father doesn't account for much because his father is smaller than he is and I think that this has a lot to do with it.

> (2) T. She's a rebel. I don't mean she's from a bad background, but unfortunate background. I mean she's well dressed and everything, but there's a divorce in the family. It's an unhappy family situation.

Once the typing is stabilized, the teacher assumes that the pupil will continue to be that type of person. The teacher has no reason to anticipate change unless conditions change, either at school or at home. For the most part teachers expect pupils to continue to be-that-type for the rest of their school career. Type transformation, although unlikely as long as these pupils remain in school, may be greatly facilitated by the entry into an occupation and into adult life.

(1) T. I think he's had a very unhappy upbringing, and I'd like to think that the circumstances could be provided where he could meet people who he could deal with. I'm not sure that any of us teachers are quite the right people. Possibly in some sort of adventure setting he might turn out to be a good lad.

(2) T. He'll change when he gets in employment. He'll change then. He's another two years at school. In his last year he could turn out to be a reasonable lad. Next year he'll either make his way by finding the error of his ways and changing, or next year he'll go in the opposite direction. It depends I think on the amount of interest he can get out of school.

As indicated earlier, the outcome of these processes affects the interaction between the teacher and the deviant pupil, and most significantly affects the different treatments accorded the deviant as compared to the conformist. Before considering these in chapter 8, we can show in detail three case-studies of pupils with a stabilized deviant typing, wherein the various characteristics typical of this stabilized state are exemplified.

4 Frankie Bradley—third year pupil in school A

Frankie had been at the school for three years and was in the lowest stream in the third year. We discussed him with six of his teachers, all of whom agreed that Frankie was 'difficult' in the classroom situation.

I. What would you do if Frankie Bradley came late to your lesson?
T. He's a normal troublemaker, he's always in and out of trouble in as many classrooms as he goes to. I don't know how I'd behave until the situation presented itself. I think I would be more aggressive towards him, generally speaking.
I. Because you know him as a troublemaker?
T. I know him as a troublemaker and you've always got to be on your guard against this kind of child.
I. Could you explain a bit more—troublemaker. It's rather a vague term.
T. It is rather a vague term, I agree. General misbehaviour and

general attitude of not doing what the teacher wants him to do.
Wayward I would say, wants to please himself what he does.
Always attempting to get people in trouble by touching, nudging,
throwing and then attempting to blame other people—'I've not
done that, sir, he's done it', or 'Sir, Ashworth's doing this to
you', when you know full well that he himself is doing it behind
your back, although as you never see him, you can't prove this
kind of thing. I feel sure he's the kind of kid who could do this.
I only have them once a week, this particular class, so I don't
really know. Weighing up young Bradley, he's always with the
older boys who are noted throughout school as troublemakers,
he mixes with this type of child. In fact only last week he was
involved in a crowd who were fighting with each other in the
toilets. But wherever there's trouble he's involved in it, but I
only have them once a week so I can't really say.

(Mr E)

Mr E sees Frankie as a 'normal troublemaker'. This is an interesting
construct in that when teachers use the construct 'normal' it is usually
in the sense of 'conformist'. Unfortunately the interviewer asked
Mr E to elucidate his term 'troublemaker' rather than 'normal
troublemaker', and the answer given is in terms of the persistent
commission of variegated deviant acts. However, this does not allow
us to understand the distinction that is possibly implied between the
'normal troublemaker' and the 'non-normal troublemaker'. We
suspect that the term normal is being used to designate the minor
and mundane character of Frankie's deviant acts, in contrast to the
more unusual, dramatic or even outrageous deviant acts that do
occur from time to time in schools. In the following quotation Mr E
elaborates on his description of Frankie's typical acts, and the
imputed typical motives, which constitute 'troublemaking'.

T. Bradley shouts, 'Sir, he's doing this to me', and you know full
well that he hasn't done anything but he wants you to go and
give them a crack or do something. He'll wander around the
room. 'What are you doing, Frankie?' and he'll say he's going
for a ruler or a rubber or something of that nature. You'll say,
'But there's one on your desk, what are you doing here?' and
he'll say, 'I didn't know, sir', and he's got the half-smile on his
face, knowing full well that he did have one back there. Looking
through the window and nudging other kids and saying, 'Look
at that bee out there.'—What it constitutes I don't know, but
it's annoying to the teacher I suppose. . . . I think that he's just
trying to stir up the class and to distract the teacher from what
he is trying to teach them, so that he won't have to do any work.

Here Mr E gives specific examples of the form that Frankie's involvement of other pupils takes and the distractive movements and comments that he makes. The teacher sees this as a reflection of Frankie's disinclination to work, which ties in with Mr E's opinion that Frankie is lazy:

I.   What was he like when you first met him?
T.   Trying to cast my mind back, it's difficult. I found that he wasn't a very industrious worker—that was the first thing that I found out about him. He sat with Dodge first of all and the two of them were a nuisance in the sense that they were always messing about people in front or behind them. This prevented them doing their work. Bradley was worse than Dodge in the sense that he made more noise and seemed to have a cocky attitude but different from Shaw in the sense that he's more cheerful and smiles more often. He's just a general nuisance I would say. He's very small isn't he, that's the thing, so he doesn't constitute an aggressive attitude like the other kids, the bigger kids I mean.

(Mr E)

Although his 'noisiness' and 'cockiness' obviously create problems for Mr E, they are to some extent compensated by Frankie's cheerfulness and occasional smiles. It seems that for all his being a 'troublemaker' he is not seen as a major problem—'He's just a general nuisance.' It is implied that it is only his small physique that keeps him at this tolerable nuisance level. In Mr E's view, were he bigger his aggression would create problems for the teacher. As it is, Mr E is not alone in thinking that this lack of stature helps to keep Frankie's nuisance value at a manageable level.

I.   What's his behaviour like in the classroom?
T.   Well he's very noisy, he shouts you know. He doesn't know when he's shouting. I don't think he realizes he is shouting, it's just his normal voice. Any little thing that another person doesn't agree with what he has said, that really upsets him and he's off then, he's on the top row then, shouting, arguing. I've never had a lesson yet without him arguing at least a dozen times with anybody who'll take him up on a point. Very argumentative, and of course he's not intelligent enough to realize when he's wrong, to accept that he could be wrong on a point. Towards discipline—very resentful, he hasn't got any intelligence to even hold himself back from taking a swipe at you. I have hit him once or twice, he brought his father once; it was in the yard. He was giving what I thought was an exceptional amount of

cheek to other women members of staff, so I gave him a backhand
and he went home. You know he doesn't accept authority.

(Mr C)

Mr C is in agreement with Mr E in seeing Frankie as persistently
and disruptively 'noisy', but Mr C expands on the noisiness by
explaining that it consists of 'arguing', and 'shouting', which he
sees as unintended ('. . . it's just his normal voice'). Mr C does not
mention the variegated deviant acts noted by Mr E, who interpreted
Frankie's deviance as intentional ('to get people into trouble', 'to
stir up the class' and 'to distract the teacher'). On the other hand
Mr C suggests a new element, which is seen as a rejection of the
teacher's authority. As with Mr E, Frankie is seen by Mr C as an
instigator of deviance ('He seems to be the spark in the class'),
particularly in combination with another pupil, Race, between whom
and Frankie there exists a notable friction.

If you've got him calmed down the others will quieten. He seems
to be the spark in the class, sort of sets things off. Now I don't
have them together but when they're in a group of boys, 3E and
3D together, the main trouble comes then between Bradley and
Race who are both of a similar nature and it's like fire and
brimstone then. They can both be very argumentative, they'll
not do what they're told at all, they both require your attention
all the time.

(Mr C)

In the following extract Mr A confirms points already made by
Mr E and Mr C.

I.   What is his behaviour like in the classroom?
T.   Firstly I would say that I find him on the lazy side. He needs
driving. I would say that he's ready for a little bit of mischief,
but I wouldn't call him a noisy individual in a class. Well,
perhaps it would be better if I said that he isn't extremely noisy.
You know he's there, there's no doubt about that, but there are
some who are even noisier; where they think nothing of
shouting across a classroom. I don't think that he is quite as
bad as that. With Frankie I find that in one particular lesson I
take, which is 3D and 3E boys, he and another boy seem to have
a permanent dislike for each other. This is Race and I think that
it's reciprocal this feeling. This is when Frankie would cause
most trouble.
I.   What form does this take?
T.   Just a flare up, you know, the simplest thing can just start
them going. I won't say that I've ever even witnessed something

197

starting, or should I say what has actually started it. It's been in being. They're sort of wielding a T-square at each other or something like that.

(Mr A)

Mr A, like Mr E, regards Frankie as 'lazy' and supports the general consensus among teachers that he is 'noisy', though he does not see him as the worst offender in this respect. In speaking of the 'flare up' between Frankie and Race, Mr A repeats the analogy of conflagration previously mentioned ('spark in the class', 'fire and brimstone'), but he does not see Frankie as the instigator. Frankie's peer relational problems and his poor attitude to work are further substantiated by Mr D, who also sees Frankie as 'aggressive'. In an interview to be reported later, Mr D claims that Frankie would be a 'real bully' if he were bigger.

I.   Bradley?
T.   Bradley, well, that boy he's disturbed in himself, I think.
I think one of his problems is that if he's not going to get his own way then he's not playing and this is it with Bradley.
Many a time I've had to sort Bradley out from the point of view of getting involved with another boy. If he's not grasping the work, if he's doing a good job on a piece of work, then he's happy, but if he comes across the smallest snag, 'I can't do it', that's the thing he'll say. Now in this past three months he's been working on the greenhouse and in this case I've had to leave him with other boys, you see. Now on two occasions he's been in trouble because of another boy provoking him or him provoking the other boy and they finish up having a bit of a get together, you know, and this happened, this has happened when they've been over at the greenhouse and when I've been in my room, so the difficulty is supervision, you see, that's what it boils down to. He's a very aggressive lad is Bradley.

(Mr D)

The impression given in these interviews with four teachers is that Frankie's deviance is persistent and variegated. It is also agreed by these teachers that Frankie experienced problems in his relationships with other members in the class, in particular with Race, and that most of the problems which Frankie presented the teachers in the classroom stemmed from these peer relational difficulties.

Consideration in more detail of the motives imputed by his teachers to account for Frankie's deviance indicates three main kinds of motivational account. The first refers to Frankie's earlier school history, and in particular to his membership of the lowest stream in his year group. Second, there is the influence of his home background, which all the teachers considered to be important. Frankie's father apparently hit him quite frequently, and Frankie's aggression, his nuisance value, and his 'disturbed' personality (Mr D's '. . . he's disturbed in himself') are seen to be a product of this. Third, Frankie's size was considered to be responsible for the emergence of, as well as a limitation on, some of Frankie's peer relational problems.

Although these motivational features are outlined separately here, the teachers in fact presented them in a closely interwoven form in which they account for the current pupil type by reference to the because-motives they saw as important causal factors in the development of this type and to the in-order-to motives which they invoke to explain his present acts.

T.   I have a theory rightly or wrongly, that these kids feel that they're second, third, fourth or fifth best being in the class that they're in, and they automatically think that they're not right, and this doesn't give them cause to learn or to do any learning. Consequently I find that they've got to show off to make their presence felt in one way or another, and I find that Bradley and Dodge do this by putting one over. I mean anything that will disturb you or get you riled or upset and them into trouble, this is one up for them. It seems to me that way.

(Mr E)

T.   He's very difficult. . . . There's some dissatisfaction within himself. In fact there are times when I feel very sorry for him; when he has these sullen moods on him, you sort of look at his face and he looks as though he'd love to injure or even murder somebody, and it's terrible that any child should feel like that, to, you know, bring that look on to his face, but I don't know what it is. I've seen his mother and she seemed interested in him. I complained about his work, that he wasn't doing sufficient and he could do a lot more and she sort of ticked him off and he worked for a bit after that, but I believe his father knocks him about for the fun of it. I don't mean that at all. . . . It's possibly something that's happened at home. I don't know, although his sister was never like that. Jane was always pleasant, and presumably they got the same sort of treatment at home. Well, perhaps it's just a different kind of nature, different kind of personality.

(Miss B)

Note that home background as a motivating force is still retained,

even where evidence provided by the sibling would appear to con-
tradict Miss B's motivational analysis and she is obliged to offer
another possible motive. However, it is retained with much less
certainty than that shown by Mr C.

> T.   Well, he feels that because of his short stature that he must
> project himself in any way he can. You know he feels he must
> come to the top. I think he gets a rough time at home. I don't
> know about this but I believe that his father keeps him well
> under at home, when he's in anyway. This is the reason he stays
> away from home sometimes, he's been out on one occasion
> overnight, so he possibly reacted against that, against authority
> at home. . . . I think they're a little bit disturbed. It's their home
> background definitely. They've been subjected to some very
> violent, I would think, punishment at home, both Race and
> Bradley.

Mr D, however, is less sure of the motivational relevance of Frankie's
home background as known to the teachers. The explanatory power
of this knowledge is reduced in the light of Mr D's recognition that
non-deviant pupils sometimes have a similar home background. It is
this non-selective use of his knowledge of pupils' home backgrounds
which induces problems for Mr D in accounting for Frankie's
deviant conduct in terms of an elaborate, quasi-social-scientific,
causal structure. From Mr D's point of view, the fact that Frankie
'likes his own way' is the 'top and bottom of it'.

> T.   Well I don't know his home background but I think he told
> me, he must get belted around a bit by his father. I think that's
> one thing that might have something to do with it, but there are
> a lot of lads get this sort of treatment at home and they're not
> like that, so you know it may have some effect on him. I think
> he's the type that if he'd been much bigger would have been a
> real bully, but because he's not the size he can't be a bully. He
> likes his own way and that's the top and bottom of it to me, he
> likes his own way, if he doesn't get his own way he's not
> playing, you know.

> (Mr D)

Unlike other teachers, Mrs H does not draw upon home background
to account for Frankie's deviance. For her, the clue to the explanation is to be found in his physical development relative to the other
boys' and his need to assert himself. Like Mr D, she prefers a
'physiological-psychological' explanation to a 'sociological' one.

> T.   You see when it comes to the rest of the class or Frankie I've
> no choice. You know I can't condone Frankie's little foibles

at the expense of the others and they are all growing up and
Frankie isn't, in fact I think what has happened to him, when he
first came here he was quite a little character, he had a Scots
accent and he was a lively little thing and he used to play truant
and he was quite exciting in the first year, you see, and all the
others were fairly conformist at that time, so he was in the
limelight quite a lot and then when they went into 3E, Dodge
was a thin weedy little character and very quiet and very earnest
and Brown was a roly-poly pudding who couldn't defend
himself and Harry Crow was a little scrap of a thing and very
worried about his face and Mark certainly was quiet and
unobtrusive and there were no very strong characters and not
very tough, and then they all grew up and got big and tough
and Frankie stayed as he was and I think that's what's wrong
with Frankie. He's got worse definitely. He can't assert himself
now, you see, the others won't let him, I think this is his trouble.
What can you do about that? That's life, you know.

(Mrs H)

It is clear from these extracts that Frankie's deviant conduct as
described by the teachers is both persistent and variegated. When we
consider how teachers handled this deviance, it becomes apparent
that it was also considered to be irremedial, in both the short-term
and the long-term.

T.   He responds to a reprimand, but this response is not
maintained. . . . He responds immediately but he's
soon at it again. He will shut up when you tell him to shut
up . . . but you've got to keep at him to get anything done,
you see. . . .

(Mr A)

T.   I mean this was the last resort, hitting him. He'd been
shouted at and told to shut up and everything like this but
that had no effect at all.

(Mr C)

T.   If he starts being violent with another boy, if he starts
fisticuffs with another boy, I get hold of him and put him on to
the floor, just get hold of him and push him down to the floor
and then pick him up and say 'Come with me to my room' and
then I give him the works as far as a good telling off is concerned
about it and make him see, if I can, where he's going wrong
and why, and if he starts giving cheek in the end he's going to
get the slipper and that's it, you know if he carries on. I mean,

you just can't put up with it, not when you've so many boys in the class.

I.   How does he react to this?

T.   Well, you see, the first time this happened, oh, he was all over with his hands and things like this but I just got hold of him bodily so that he couldn't move. I find that with boys of that nature you've got to do this to show them that you're in control, because as soon as you start letting them get away with it, well you've lost you know and so you've got to use a physical amount of—well you can call it violence if you want, but I don't call that violence. I call it restraining a lad from doing things.

I.   When you get to the showing him the error of his ways, say when you're talking to him and reasoning with him, how does he react when you're actually talking to him about this?

T.   Well, when I'm talking to him sometimes he'll say, 'Well it was his fault.' You see, it's never him that's to blame in the first place, and then you've got to start trying to explain to him and sometimes you can and sometimes you can't, and then he'll start being cheeky. He might say you know, 'You're always on their side', and things like that, and he'll start being really cheeky to you; and then when he gets out in the class he doesn't stop, so then there's only one thing and that's the slipper. He sulks then and that's it. I don't think we've gained anything by doing that, but at least the class has gained something by doing that.

(Mr D)

I.   Then, 'Will you get on.' I think you were saying this to Frankie.

T.   He's another, he's absolutely hopeless for concentration and willingness to work, so this is necessary at some time during every lesson. I will have to go and look at his book and let him see in no uncertain terms that I want him to do more than he is doing.

I.   Does it usually work?

T.   I don't know that it does because he can be very stubborn but on the other hand I wouldn't just let it go by if I thought he was being lazy because I don't think that's a good thing. I think it's good for him to know I'm watching him and am aware of what he is doing, even though I have to accept his stubbornness and anti-social tendencies at times, although he wasn't bad this morning.

I.   You said last time that Frankie Bradley was probably your worst problem in the class. Would you still say that?

T.   I think he is the most unrewarding to deal with because you
never do find a formula for dealing with him. With the others
you do eventually, but never with that boy somehow. You never
know what mood he is going to be in for a start. You see, it was
sort of half and half today. It certainly wasn't co-operative but
he wasn't in one of those black sullen moods that he can be in
when he comes in determined to cause trouble and today he
wasn't in one of those silly amiable moods when, you know,
you think, 'Why isn't he like this every day?' All the others you
can reach them through the, I don't want to say Frankie is
abnormal, but I was going to say through the normal human
emotions. I don't know whether he is lacking in some component
or what but he does not seem to respond in the same way. You
see Carl Brown for example, you get really angry with him for
the way he will call out without thinking, waste time, lean back
talking and then want all the help you can give him, wants to
monopolize you and yet he wouldn't like to feel really that you
were angry with him, you know, so angry that a link was
snapped sort of thing. In fact I think that would apply to every
single one in that form. They are easy to forge relationships with
but with Frankie it isn't so.

(Miss B)

5   Dave Shaw—fourth year pupil at school A

Dave had been at the school for four years and was in the lowest
stream in the fourth year. He was discussed at length with four of his
teachers, all of whom found him troublesome in the classroom and
obviously disliked him as a person.

T.   My first introduction to Shaw was reasonably quiet but
rather surly in attitude. He didn't want any help or advice from
people and he just appeared to be a surly lad, that's my first
introduction to him. He always appeared to be on the defensive.
I.   Could you explain what you mean by that?
T.   Whenever you went to him he was suspicious or appeared
to be suspicious of you, and your authority presumably, and if
you tried to help him he didn't want any help. He was that kind
of a boy. He just shrugged his shoulders kind of thing, as though
you were trying to trap him into something. It was as though
he didn't want to know you as a teacher. You were different
from other human beings generally, that's how it struck me at
the time.
I.   Could you explain what you meant by surly?
T.   Well, he never seemed to smile or he appeared to be quietly

203

aggressive as though something was smouldering within him.
But I never had any trouble with him in the first term strangely
enough.

I. What's he like now?

T. He's grown in fifteen months bigger and heavier and now
being in the fourth year he feels that he's something of an
authority in a physical sense with other kids and he's the one
who's always in trouble, always starting trouble. Again he
appears to have the ability to be insidious with his stirring—
stirring the kids up and he attempts to keep out of it, but you
know it's stemmed from Shaw. He becomes aggressive when you
approach him, aggressive in the verbal sense; 'What are you
always picking on me for?' that sort of attitude, and you know
that in that group there he's done something.

I. You said he was a good stirrer. Could you give me examples
of the sort of things that he has done to give you that impression?

T. It's always difficult to try to recall things that he's
done. For example, again it's difficult because I take them for
gardening which I have no interest in, and there's twenty-five
pupils in the group all fourth years who've been thrust into
gardening, not because they've opted for it. Now I've got to keep
them confined in a room. Because I don't care for the job,
I'm pretty tolerant with them. So generally I let them do a
drawing or play little games like hangman and that sort of
thing, and when you get four of them together outbursts of
singing and chanting 'United Kings', it's always in the Shaw
area, and you can rest assured that he's done some of it. And
when you go across and you say, 'Now be quiet, let's have some
order. You've got some freedom, for goodness sake try and act
responsibly', 'I've not done anything', says Shaw right away.
But you have an idea in the back of your mind that he's said,
'Come on, let's try to get something going here.' That's only one
incident. If anything is thrown across the room it's come from
that direction and again, he seems to be able to get other kids
to do things. Like young Haworth and Leach, and he's the
master-mind behind that sort of thing. They seem so gullible
and so obvious, that Shaw is the man who's said with his
insidious ways, 'Let's do this or let's do that.' This is what I feel.
And this is nothing that you can pin down but his attitude
generally is one of, 'Who do you think you are, telling me?'
I'm not being very specific am I?

I. If you had to compare him with when you first met him and
now. Has there been any change, and if so what direction has it
been in?

T.   The only change that I have seen is this overt aggression,
this open aggression. He's started standing up whereas before
he was quiet and just smouldered at you, he's now prepared
to stand up and say, 'It's not me' and 'You can't do that to me'.
Argue with a teacher. This is the change that I've seen, but again,
I only take him once a week so it's not a—it doesn't seem to
give me much idea of understanding the boy.

I.   Would you say that he's improved or that he's got worse?

T.   Got worse I should say—got worse yes.

I.   Why should he have got worse in this time?

T.   Only his size I would think. He appears to me to have grown
in stature pretty quickly over the twelve months that I've been
here, and that's the only reason. You see, I don't know his
background. I don't even know him well because of teaching
him, in fact when I taught him in my first year it was only for
one term, then I had to move away and I haven't seen him again
until this year, but now in the staffroom there is a lot of talk
about him. Now whether we are conditioned or not I don't
know, but people who take him regularly often bring him up
and say what an awkward so-and-so he is. But I do find him
like that, and I don't think I would take notice of what goes on
in the staffroom, although I don't know, but I do find him in
my group particularly awkward.

(Mr E)

Although Mr E did not have any 'trouble' with Dave in the early
stages of their relationship, the boy appears not to have made a very
favourable impression on this teacher who (retrospectively) describes him as 'surly', 'defensive', 'suspicious' and 'quietly aggressive
as though something was smouldering within him'. From his present
position Mr E looks back with surprise at the lack of trouble earlier,
since Dave now displays 'overt aggression' and is 'always in trouble,
always starting trouble'. His deviance is perceived as persistent and
variegated, and he is regarded as the insidious instigator of deviant
conduct in other pupils ('. . . You know it's stemmed from Shaw',
'. . . he's the master-mind . . .'). Mr E accounts for this in part as a
product of Shaw's increased size. Whilst Mr E is fully aware that his
view may be 'conditioned' by the frequent staffroom gossip about
Shaw, he asserts that this does represent his own experience of the boy.

Mr K similarly reports that Shaw has become a 'problem' rather
recently and that the main way in which he 'creates problems' is by
instigating other pupils to deviant acts or by blaming others for his
own deviant acts.

I.   Could you tell me when you first came into contact with him?

T. I think I've taught Dave for two years in one of my classes.
I. Did you know anything about him before you taught him?
T. I find it difficult to remember. I find it very difficult to
remember much about him because I don't think he became a
source of any difficulty in the school, anything of a problem to
teachers until this year. And that's been my experience.
I. What's he like now then?
T. He creates problems in a classroom situation. He is often
inattentive and involves other people in activities which seem to
be undesirable to me, and to other teachers in the school.
I don't think that the boy is truthful—I think he tells lies and
involves other members of the class. If he is involved in activities
that I see as undesirable he will attribute it to somebody else
even though it's fairly obvious to anyone that he was the
culprit. If it's a case of throwing a rubber or making a remark,
this kind of thing, he'll hide his face behind his hand and suggest
that it is someone else, all of which makes it difficult to do
anything about.
I. Is this a fairly frequent occurrence with Dave?
T. I think it's a very frequent occurrence nowadays; that he's
often in certain class situations involved. I see him in two
separate circumstances, and his behaviour is different. At present
he is coming to me as part of a CSE group but his behaviour
in that group amongst a different set of children is different from
his behaviour when he is in an option that I take him for, which
is with a lot of other people that are less motivated to want to
please the teacher or achieve some sort of success in our terms.
With those people he can present a difficulty. He gets into
mischief. With the CSE group he has less opportunities because
the others are less easily distracted from their own aims.
I. Could you give details of this involving others? Can you give
any specific examples?
T. I'll hear some remark, possibly some facetious remark, and
from my point of view some undesirable remark, I'll turn to
Shaw and say, 'Did you say that?' He'll have his hand in front
of his mouth and possibly be smirking and look round and say,
'It was so-and-so', naming one of his pals. If I persist, I get this
sort of denial you see, and if one persisted with questions one
could spend a lot of time, waste a lot of time, dealing with these
particular things. So that it is very difficult to strike a balance
between dealing with someone like this and getting on with the
job of giving one's time to the rest of the class. So somewhere a
decision has got to be made and it's not a particularly easy one.

(Mr K)

Mr K appears mainly concerned with the effect that Shaw's behaviour has on the rest of the class. It is the frequent involvement of others and the lying that accompanies this that Mr K objects to, and finds that there are more 'opportunities' for this involvement with the non-examination class, which Mr K sees as 'less motivated to want to please the teacher'.

All teachers commented on the deterioration in Shaw's behaviour during the fourth year, and most of them connected this with the arrival of a new boy called Grimes. This boy had come straight to school A from a Borstal institution. He was a well-built strong boy who had rapidly established a reputation as a fighter and as a disruptive element in lessons. Before Grimes's arrival, Shaw, in the words of Mr K, had been the 'star performer'. After that, teachers felt that Grimes served as a model for Shaw and as a willing partner in disruption.

I. Could you think of the first time you came into contact with Dave?

T. Yes, first year, he was a normal boy then. His brother was in school at the same time and his brother was much smaller than him in stature structure; worked very well did his brother and he followed in the same footsteps to the third year I would say.

I. You say he was a normal pupil at that time.

T. Well, I should say, happen a little bit aggressive, but I should say a normal pupil. I'm convinced the influence of another pupil's played a great part in the way that he's behaving now. He wouldn't be like he is now if it wasn't for the influence of another boy. You see this is because—

I. You can mention the other boy.

T. Well it's because of Grimes isn't it, obviously, I mean you've got Grimes there and he's trying to live up to Grimes's ways of life and that's it. And when I say the influence is coming from Grimes I don't mean from a work point of view. I mean from, the bad behaviour is coming from, partly the other boy.

(Mr D)

T. He does relate specially I think now to Grimes who has come into the school and who is a known—is known to have problems, and who boasts about his stay in Borstal. I say 'boasts of', put that in inverted commas, but who speaks of it and doesn't regard it as anything shameful or disgraceful. He's quite happy to talk about it, and has been encouraged by some teachers to talk about it. Relative to Grimes I get the impression that initially Grimes is physically the master and Shaw thought that he was being put into second place, because he was a known

naughty boy by his classmates, a star performer, but he seems
now to be acquiring the ability to manipulate Grimes. To use
Grimes's physical prowess and his own mental agility, because
he is much more alert than Grimes mentally. If you like he's a
more intelligent boy. . . . His activities relative to Grimes, for
instance, tend to exacerbate difficulties which either would present
separately. They tend to be greater when they are together.
Grimes might have been less of a problem if he hadn't had Shaw
frequently in contact with him.

(Mr K)

T.   I think Shaw saw him as a challenge and I think quite
frankly this is why he's linked up with him. Rather than
challenge him he's linked up with Grimes because he knows he
wouldn't get anywhere. The only person who could tackle Grimes
in the fourth year is Jack Haslam, and he, Shaw knows he couldn't
challenge him as far as physical means goes—But Grimes is not
dim either. Grimes can sort of match him as far as wits goes so
Shaw doesn't lead him round by the nose like he does Jack
Haslam, the same way you see. I think it was a case of if you
can't beat him you'll have to join him. I think quite frankly he
almost wishes he had the same background as Grimes, this is
how I feel about him, you know, so he could sort of have this
tough background, but he hasn't got it.

(Mrs L)

All three teachers agree on the importance of the relationship between
Shaw and Grimes, although they differ on the precise nature of the
relationship. In any event, the arrival of Grimes has led to a
deterioration in Shaw's conduct. Mr D believes that Grimes is
responsible for Shaw's transformation from being a 'normal boy'
who would otherwise have followed in his brother's conformist
footsteps.

The teachers do not seem to be very confident in imputing motives
to Shaw. Several motives are suggested—a 'sense of frustration and
annoyance', 'to show the other kids that he can stand up to
teachers', 'a fear of possible punishment'.

I.   Why does he do these things?
T.   Well, I think that because it's an unusual group that I've
got. They're not interested, and I don't expect them to be.
It's called options and in the first place they were given a choice
but two teachers left—they were doing some craft work I think—
but because these two teachers left they were pushed on to me.
And I think their sense of frustration and annoyance is because

they feel why should they be in this group doing absolutely nothing when they could be doing something more profitable. It's that kind of a group. They don't want to know and I find that Shaw seems more concerned about creating mischief and putting one over against the teachers generally, whatever it may be, whether it's in an aggressive way or a way of stirring up trouble with other kids in a well—anti-teacher behaviour kind of thing. Now why they do it—only the frustration that they feel being in my group, but I'm not so sure. . . . What else could it be? I don't know not being a psychiatrist. . . . I think that one thing that teachers lack is something—understanding of the child's home background, and the way in which he is brought up, if he's any problems—I don't know really. I think that we live in this violent age in the sense that they've got to be top dog in something and I suppose he's being top dog in a physical sense and he's got to show the other kids that he can stand up to teachers to gain their respect. We all have our niches in society and I suppose that his niche is to show kids that he can get away with most things by standing up to teachers.

(Mr E)

I. What motives lie behind this sort of behaviour?
T. Well, when this goes on he's usually relating to some other person in the class, and I get the impression that he is trying to impress them with his own ability to manipulate the teacher; manipulate the situation and score off the teacher or sometimes to score off other lads, which sometimes involves calling them strange names and drawing attention to any short-comings on the part of the other children, physical short-comings possibly, and he will call this out. I know this isn't unusual, giving them nicknames and laughing, to me, rather foolishly when he is doing it. This seems to amuse him highly, but quite honestly I cannot tell you what is going on inside his mind when he does this. One knows that this goes on, and I've seen it in other children quite often, but it leads to difficulty in a classroom situation. I think that he doesn't intend to be seen to accept authority of the kind that I'm talking about. This is the teacher being authoritarian in front of the class. He has to be seen to be capable of creating his own authority of equal standing with that of the teacher, and he's never come to put the teacher in this particular place that we would put the teacher in. In other words this is roles again, isn't it? He sees his own role as rather special relative to the teacher, and as different from that of the other kids, and this is where the difficulty arises.

I.   What about his telling lies?

T.   Quite honestly I find this very difficult. I suppose we've grown up in different ways. Telling the truth to me was, you know, *Boy's Own Paper* stuff, that I thought was very desirable, but I've got to know over the years that there are people who do tell lies. Now without using any psychological terms, all right, we do know that this does exist and I think that he is one of the people to whom telling lies is not of any significance. The words he uses are for his own convenience at the moment, and he will give any answer that suits his requirements. There is no such thing from his point of view as the truth as I see it. He doesn't accept that there is any reason for saying a particular thing: if he wants to say something, then expedience is the chief activating factor.

I.   What is the expedience directed towards?

T.   Well, in this case, obviously it could be to avoid possible punishment, a fear of possible punishment, which has happened in the case of anything serious that has happened. I can't think of a specific instance, but I'm sure that I'm not imagining this, that Shaw is involved in things like throwing water in the toilets. It's difficult because teachers are brought up to believe that there is such a thing as truth and it is difficult for them to accept that quite often there are people who will say things without any appearance of wrongdoing, and they will quite happily tell what we call lies. In graver circumstances the psychologists would give this a name, but I think that we tend to think that the transition from the norm, pure norm, to psychopathy is a sort of sudden one. There must be grades of this and a lot of these kids are sort of well along as far as grading goes. Sort that out!

(Mr K)

All teachers' treatment of Shaw's deviant acts suffered the same fate, in that they failed to prevent the repetition of these acts in subsequent similar situations. This persistence and irremediality led to a hostility between Shaw and his teachers that was more strongly marked than that between Frankie and his teachers. Favourable comments were limited to some suggestions of latent intelligence, but no teacher in any way suggested a liking for Shaw as a person.

T.   He would tell a lie even when it was obvious that he couldn't maintain the lie.

I.   Have you ever actually been in that situation?

T.   Oh yes! When I've spoken to him about making remarks and so on, I've never, and still don't have any doubt. The question is not whether he did it or not, it's what to do about it? To continue to question him, to get him to admit it, seems to me to be a worthless exercise. There is just no point in going on as has happened, and as does happen, in a classroom quite often. To get on to him till he owns up is a nonsense to me. I've seen this going on and to me it's an utter waste of time. . . . I'm sure that from time to time he is punished by people, I don't know how. I know that he's been sent to have the slipper and so on, but in my experience he accepts it and it goes on, and at some future occasion the same thing happens. It has little effect upon his subsequent behaviour because physically I don't think that it hurts him all that much and I think that this kind of treatment only makes him a little special in the eyes of his mates and of course this is one of his original intentions. This is my thesis. Being the one who goes to the Head and either gets a dressing down or the slipper doesn't do him any harm at all. He comes back reinforced in his intentions.

I.   Does this affect the way that you eventually come to treat him?

T.   You know, and I know, that it's inevitable that it does. I would hope that it wouldn't make me forget that I'm trying to help the lad ultimately, and that anything I do is directed to this aim, and that I'm still capable of praising anything that he does that is praiseworthy. This is the hope of course, that his patterns of behaviour will be modified.

I.   Having heard the hope, can we come back to the reality?

T.   The reality is that you try to do this and you watch it, and this is one of the disappointing things about teaching; that very often one feels that one is gaining some success, then very shortly afterwards the original pattern of behaviour recurs and this is when teachers become disheartened. I'm not saying that it doesn't happen to me but I hope that I can understand it a little better than I would have done twenty years ago.

I.   Does it ever reach the stage where you say, 'Oh blow it, it's only Shaw'?

T.   It reaches the stage where I say this but I never mean it. I might well say this to myself, but I should feel that I was being less than dutiful, I was doing less than I ought to do. I may find that under certain stresses that I'd had enough. I'd hope that I didn't, but this obviously does happen to us, and we're not entirely adequate for the things that we're asked to do from time to time. I should think that everybody that's involved with training teachers and dealing with teachers should accept this, that teachers are the same sort of human beings as the children

and they have pressures and so on, and they have weaknesses.
I've got mine and you've got yours.

(Mr K)

One of the problems of irremedial pupils, as Mr K notes, is that
attempts at control can be counter-productive. The only effect of
physical punishment—which most teachers treat as a last resort—
is to 'make him a little special in the eyes of his mates' and to
reinforce him in his intentions. Like most teachers, Mr K knows that
many treatments have proved to be ineffective ('a worthless exercise'),
and he is unable to find a long-term 'cure'. Disheartened and disappointed, he copes as best he can, striving to remember 'that I'm
trying to help the lad ultimately'. Mr E's experience is very similar.

T. I generally shout at him, 'What are you doing that for?'
and 'You're supposed to be responsible'. There's a tendency for
him to laugh behind his hand and snigger and that kind of thing.
On one occasion I did drag him across the table when I got
particularly angry and his buttons fell off his coat and he said,
'I'm not having this. You'll have to pay for this. You'll have to
sew the buttons on', and I said, 'If you don't sit down they'll
have to pay for you—a new Shaw.' I was getting so angry.
Two or three of the lads got up around him, to defend him I
suppose. But it's generally an aggressive attitude that he adopts.
He does react in that way.
I. Any other reactions?
T. Yes. Well, he's the injured party—you shouldn't do that to
him. And I've told him that if I treated him the way people
would outside he would have something to complain about.
But I said that because we are teachers we have to be very careful
about our attitude to you and yet when people try to respect you,
give you some liberty, you don't know how to react to it. You
don't know how to behave in a responsible manner. He does
generally always show a sign of aggression. I've never known
him to be friendly. I don't think I've ever known him to be
friendly.
I. Why is he so unfriendly?
T. Well I don't know why he might behave in this way but let
me give you one example that sticks in my mind. I said,
'Well, Dave, today—' and I put my arm round him and he
shrugged it off and another occasion I said, 'Well, son, what can
I do for you?' 'Don't call me son, you're not my dad.' This is
the kind of thing, and I was being perfectly sincere, well friendly
if you like—well I just was, so that's all I can say, but those two
incidents, that attitude.

I.   Well what lies behind this attitude?

T.   I don't know quite frankly, but I've often thought of saying, 'Look, Dave, why? Why do you want to create this friction and trouble? Why do you want to be anti all the time? Why never a positive contribution from you? Why not meet me part way?' Because I do feel that with my attitude I do go three-quarters of the way to meet the kids, particularly in this particular group because of the class [lesson] that I don't like and they don't like so I've got to bend over backwards, and I'm conscious of this and I've often thought of saying, 'But why, Dave, why?' I don't know. Maybe it's because of my lack of experience as a teacher. I've not got close to him. He doesn't want you to help him. He doesn't want to befriend people, or should I say that he doesn't appear to want that. He doesn't seem to respond to you when you try to be kind and understanding to him, he has to be aggressive all the time. That's the way I find him.

(Mr E)

Perhaps no teacher conveys better the teachers' experience of being 'at their wit's end' when confronted with the irremedial deviant. Mr E notes that he makes many moves towards the boy ('I do go three-quarters of the way', 'I've got to bend over backwards'), but his comprehensive list of questions remains unanswered, the desired response is not forthcoming, and the deviant acts persist.

6   Alan Pearson—fourth year pupil at school A

Pearson had been at the school for four years and was in one of the lower streams in the fourth year. All of his teachers found him troublesome, mainly because of his talkativeness and his 'fooling about' in lessons. His case is interesting in that although he was similar to Shaw and Bradley in his irremediality, this was redeemed by his likeability, which was indicated by all his teachers. Although various teachers referred to him as 'talkative, doesn't get on with work, laughs, clowns, giddy, nuisance, on the fringe of a disruptive element, unsteady, noisy, jester and a comedian', none of them showed the same resentment towards him that they did to Shaw and Bradley. Teachers indicated two main reasons for their different reaction in the case of Pearson. First, his deviant acts were relatively minor, but above all were performed in a pleasant manner. He was seen as 'smiling, jolly, laughing, pleasant' in his deviance, with none of the 'surliness, aggressiveness, sullenness and violence' that was typical of the way in which Bradley and Shaw committed their deviance. Second, he could be handled in the short-term if not converted in the long-term, whereas with Shaw and Bradley neither long-term nor short-term treatments had any effect on their subsequent behaviour. This amenability to discipline in the short-term is much appreciated by teachers because it allows them to achieve their immediate objective of getting through the lesson with the minimum amount of interruption, even if it does little to convert their recalcitrant pupils to the 'paths of righteousness'.

I.   What about Pearson?
T.   Oh dear! Well, Pearson is a peculiar boy. He's as pleasant as they make them in any approach to him. If you reprimand him he will accept it in a good spirit. If you have a private chat with him he'll accept it and you think that you've won him over. And hitting him doesn't make a scrap of difference, and yet, despite all this, he's not the type of lad that you could really fall out with. Almost a likeable rogue. He's not the type of lad in class to offer any resistance to reprimand. Aggressiveness— I don't think this is in his nature at all. He has a pleasant smile with it you know. He's not a quiet boy. When I say that, I mean he's not a reserved individual. He's always ready to have a natter and a laugh you see. He's a jolly individual. I've tried all ways with Pearson, talking to him, thumped him on occasions, I've had private chats with him. I might have sent him once to the deputy head, but I've tried to win Pearson. I've tried to beat him myself, but I haven't succeeded. Pearson, at Open Night I was talking to his father, the first time that I'd seen him incidentally, and we had a good chat. His father was just as affable as his son. 'I know exactly what you mean,' was the answer I got. 'I don't think that he likes Maths. I'll take what you say and have a talk with him. I'll see what can be done.'

(Mr A)

T.   He can be a bit of a nuisance. If he's not interested he'll not put his mind to it, and he'll fool about in class. I think he's genuinely sorry afterwards. When there's anything gone wrong, he knows that he's done wrong. The trouble is that he doesn't seem to know when to draw the line between, you know, a bit of a joke, and it gets more serious. . . . He's a likeable rogue you know. We have one or two like that.
I.   How do you define a likeable rogue?
T.   Well you know it's like these films nowadays you see, not so much the hero type nowadays but the villain of the piece who is a villain but yet you're in sympathy with him. This against authority thing, it's the 'in' trend. I think it's because you laugh at them that you let them get away with so much, because they

do it with a smile on their face. I don't think they would be vindictive. It's just a current trend I think.

(Mr C)

I. What was he like when you first met him three years ago?
T. Just a chubby-faced boy, pleasant, hard working and nothing out of the ordinary I don't think.
I. What was his behaviour like at that time?
T. Just average. In the fourth year, that's when he started getting a bit unsteady. He liked to make a noise. He worked all right but the work could have been better if he put his mind more to it rather than concentrating on doing a bit of playing. He has an aptitude towards my subject, and really is quite good, but I did notice that he liked to be the comedian or the jester. . . .
I've given him pep talks on the importance of being serious and getting down to some hard work, but this had no effect on this boy. I'd have him up for a friendly talk and he'd understand the situation and promise to behave, but it didn't last very long.
I. How does he react when he gets his pep talk?
T. Very well indeed. Of course he has a natural smile which doesn't help him in times of trouble, but when he realizes that it is very serious that smile goes, but it soon returns. It seems to be a natural smile, I don't know whether you've noticed that. He listens well and he agrees with what I say and he's very mannerly. He seems to be an intelligent boy who understands the reasoning and so on and then he obviously throws it to the wind after a time.

(Mr J)

We now have a much better conception of the complexity of the stabilized type. Although deviant pupils may be classified together under the diffuse label of 'troublemaker', there is nevertheless a uniqueness about every typing when pupils are considered as individuals. Deviant pupils emerge as distinct individuals, each with his own methods of deviating on particular occasions and for particular motives. Yet they are all 'trouble*makers*' for they all present the teacher with practical problems. There is a certainty and confidence to the teacher's knowledge of these pupils which, based on multitudinous events a few of which are remembered but most of which are soon forgotten, has been built over time into a coherent and resistant characterization. The hesitancy, the tentativeness and the ambivalence that was so marked in the earlier stage of speculation has been succeeded by the conviction of stabilization. It is this complex stabilized typing which can be readily used by teachers, as we saw at the end of chapter 5, in the evidencing of deviant acts. Since the

H

typing is an integral part of the teacher's common-sense knowledge of the classroom and the pupils, he can use it in ambiguous situations to 'fill in' what the pupil is doing and for what motives. In the same way, this common-sense knowledge constantly informs the ways in which teachers formulate methods of handling or responding to deviant acts.

I.   'Featherstone, how many have you done?' What made you say that?

T.   I asked that question because he's lazy, terribly lazy, and I knew that this was on his conscience [an earlier incident] and I knew he was in trouble and I thought, 'That's it! He's so sullen and so resentful he'll not work. He'll just think, "I'm not doing this." '

I.   Did you look up and see him not working?

T.   Yes, he was sitting sullen; and you see I'm careful with that boy from the health point of view. I don't know whether you know but he's got something rather peculiar wrong with him. The boys told me he'd gone to the hospital; he goes regular. Something about the blood doesn't reach his brain when it should, or something. He does look odd at times. He looks a bit like an epileptic at times, I don't know whether you've noticed. Sometimes not so much concentrating, a bit of a glassy look and he came back and told me, 'I had to go to the hospital, Miss, I've been ill.' I said, 'Yes, I believe so.' So I try to think of that because he could turn out to be violent. He's had several bad fights. He has got such a violent temper and I wonder if he can help it. You know, the very fact of the blood not reaching the brain is a bit of a worry, isn't it?

It is to such intricate constructions of the teachers' treatment of deviant acts that we can now turn.

8   *Reactions to deviance*

In this book our predominant concern has been with two questions: how does a teacher come to define a given pupil *act* as deviant? and, how does a teacher come to define a given *pupil* as deviant? Writing as phenomenologists working within the labelling theory tradition, we have sought to answer these questions by examining: the nature of classroom rules; the means by which they are brought into play, and how the members know that they are in play; how the teachers then fit observed pupil acts to the rules by the use of evidential rules and strategies; how teachers come to know that a pupil is a certain type of person. In short, we have tried to explicate some of the common-sense knowledge and interpretive work whereby teachers are able to define acts and actors as deviant.

Although it is evident in much of the data we have presented, we have so far given no direct attention to the action the teacher takes as a result of making such definitions. Given that acts or actors are defined as deviant, what does the teacher actually do about it? This is the issue of the reaction to deviant conduct or deviant persons. Many questions immediately spring to mind when one raises the issue of reaction or treatment. The most obvious, at least in the mind of teachers and educationists, is that of the effectiveness of the treatment. In this chapter we shall not be addressing ourselves to this problem. But before the teachers amongst our readers close the book with an understandable, and perhaps not totally unexpected, disappointment and confirmed cynicism about research enterprises, let us explain why. To be able to answer questions about the effectiveness of treatments assumes that in classrooms there are *n* number of offences which can be treated by *n* number of possible treatments that are at the teacher's disposal. The question then becomes: what is the most effective or 'best' way of linking deviant acts and treatment? The anticipated answer would then take the form: if a teacher is faced with offence X, then the most effective way of handling it is by Y treatment. But such questions and anticipated answers make some very important presuppositions which we must expose. First, there is the presupposition that we can classify offences. We have shown in earlier chapters that teachers can describe a single act in various ways and see it as a breach of different rules. The teachers themselves do not possess or use a precise, clear and unambiguous terminology for describing deviant acts, though their terminology is perfectly satisfactory for their own practical purposes. In contrast, a research scientist's terminology or classificatory scheme would have to be precise, clear and unambiguous. We are sceptical that such a terminology is possible—for much the same reasons that it is not possible for teachers. At best the researchers could develop a slightly more refined classificatory scheme whose tenability would rest upon a high degree of agreement between different coders. But this would tell us little about how they are able to code deviant acts at all. In this they would presumably rely upon the same common-sense that the teachers themselves use. But since they would assume, rather than explicate, that common-sense knowledge, there would be a massive communicative problem when they reported their findings back to the teachers. This is so because the teachers would have to translate back the classificatory scheme of the researchers into their own everyday classificatory system, yet there would be no guidance on how this translation would be achieved. Second, there is the presupposition that we can classify treatments. Exactly the same argument applies here, with the same consequences. Third, there is the presupposition that there is some specifiable linkage between the offence and the treatment. If the question were about the effectiveness of treatments, then part of this linkage would involve some criterion by which effectiveness was to be judged. This criterion raises the issue of the motives behind the treatment. What constitutes an effective treatment if the teacher's motive is to punish the pupil might no longer be effective if the teacher's motive were to inhibit the pupil from committing the act again. The researcher would need to specify the criteria by which he himself would judge a treatment to be effective; but how would these criteria relate to the criteria being used by practising teachers?

So we see that to ask or to answer these undoubtedly fascinating questions involves important assumptions and problems which we neglect at our risk. If we do neglect them, then there is a real danger that the researchers will discover that their answers are simply not meaningful to the teachers, and/or that the teachers are quite unable to incorporate the findings into their everyday practices. In other words, the immediate, if apparently less dramatic, priority is the exploration of the common-sense knowledge by which the teachers themselves do forge a link between a deviant act and their subsequent reaction to it. Such an analysis might serve as a foundation for later researches of various kinds and might also provide a means whereby any findings could be translated back for usage by teachers.

Our task, then, is to explicate how teachers formulate reactions to pupil deviance. We assume that when a teacher decides to react to a pupil act which has been defined as deviant, he employs some common-sense knowledge by which he is able to forge a link between the deviant act (offence) and the actor (offender) in a way that permits him to decide that a particular reaction is relevant and appropriate. Part of this common-sense knowledge, of course, consists of the teacher's ability to decide that some reactions are likely to be more effective than others. In some instances, the teacher may deliberate at length before deciding on a final overt reaction to a deviant act; in other instances, especially where it is a question of 'routine deviance', the teacher's reaction may happen very quickly indeed and without much conscious deliberation. But in all instances the teacher is nevertheless drawing upon his common-sense knowledge which allows him to formulate some reaction to the pupil act that he has interpreted as deviant.

Before proceeding with this analysis we shall report briefly on the sources of our data. Our principal method was to observe a lesson and from these observations to extract those teacher statements and/ or actions which consisted of a reaction to a deviant act. Clearly this hinges on our ability as observers to recognize reactions when we see them. For us a reaction consisted of some action by the teacher which carried within it an imputation of deviance. (In earlier chapters we dealt with the problems of our own common-sense knowledge by which we as researchers were able to recognize these deviance-imputations.) We then reported the reaction back to the teacher at a later stage, asking for his commentary upon what he did. As material presented in earlier chapters shows, we often merely quoted what the teacher had said, and the teacher was willing to make a commentary upon his action without any direct question from us. On other occasions we reported the teacher's statement back and then asked why the teacher had said or done something. Whatever method we used, the teachers always imputed some motive to us for reporting these events to them or for asking for some commentary upon what had occurred. This motive, presumably, was that we were interested in understanding the events which we were investigating. More interesting, however, is the question of what we were asking for, rather than why we were asking. In reporting the teacher's statement back to him for commentary, it is clear that we are asking teachers to 'display' to us. But often we did not actually tell the teacher precisely what we expected him to display—and we did so intentionally. In consequence the teacher always had an interpretive problem. He had to provide a commentary on his own conduct which he could assume would be seen by us as an appropriate, relevant and meaningful answer to our unspoken question. In fact, it is clear from teachers' commentaries that they imputed a wide range of implicit questions to us. Sometimes the commentary would be about the act, sometimes about the actor, sometimes about their own thinking and motives. All the commentaries have one element in common; they all take the form of teachers' attempts to explain or justify their actions. As far as possible we tried to minimize the evaluative overtones to these conversations, by suggesting that we ourselves were not making evaluative judgments on the teachers and were not interested in making personal judgments about whether or not the teacher had said or done the 'right' thing. Nevertheless, all the teachers' commentaries consisted of explanations and justifications, which has an important bearing on their status as evidence.

Some of the data reported in this chapter came to us 'incidentally' rather than in response to a direct request for some commentary upon the teacher's observed act. For instance, a teacher might be talking at length about a particular pupil—data which for us were likely to be most relevant to typing—but in so doing would disclose the kinds of reaction that he did take or had taken towards this pupil's deviant conduct. We have made full use of data deriving from such 'incidental' sources.

One difficulty in adopting these methods of data collection is that the technique of reporting back an observed event to the teacher for commentary assumes that an overt reaction to the deviant conduct is the only grounds for our knowing that the teacher has made a deviance-imputation. It necessarily ignores those possible situations in which a teacher might define a pupil act as deviant but decide to make no overt reaction to the deviance. We, as observers, cannot detect such events, since nothing observable actually occurs. Sometimes during our observations we would note that both the teacher and ourselves had noticed the act, but the teacher had made no overt reaction to it, even though we would have expected the teacher to define the act as deviant because it seemed to us to infringe the rules in play. How could we explain this? It is possible that the teacher had not in fact noticed the act and that our belief that he had was mistaken. Another possibility is that he had noticed the act but had not defined it as deviant, so our expectation that he would see the act as a breach of the rules in play was mistaken. A third possibility was that he had defined the act as deviant but for some reason had chosen not to make an overt reaction to it. We were on occasions able to follow up these possibilities with a teacher. However, other instances of a deviance-imputation without overt reaction came to our attention from other sources. For example, a teacher might be making a commentary on an overt reaction and in so doing might mention some earlier acts of the pupil which the teacher had defined as deviant but to which he had not made an overt reaction.

We are led to recognize the distinction between definitional and reactional processes. The definition of a pupil act as deviant does not necessarily result in an overt reaction. Given that the pupil act is defined as deviant, the teacher has to decide whether to make an overt or a covert reaction. In other words, the teacher has to decide whether or not to make an open intervention. So we shall conceptualize the reaction as a two-step process.[1] First, the teacher must decide whether or not to make an overt reaction—we shall call this the problem of 'intervention'. Second, given that the teacher has decided to intervene, he must decide what particular form this intervention is to take—we shall call this the problem of 'treatment'.

We shall begin with the problem of intervention. Our examination of the data on this topic suggested various possible ways of organizing and conceptualizing the teachers' commentaries. We do not have space to report—nor are our memories sufficiently accurate to recall —the various analytical lines we explored. The analytical scheme which we are presenting here is the one which we found to be most satisfactory, by the criteria of its relative simplicity and parsimony, its ability to comprehend the data we had at our disposal, and most of all its ability to meet the postulate of subjective interpretation and the postulate of adequacy as proposed by Alfred Schutz (1953).

Deviance in classrooms, as in society generally, is essentially about the problem of order. On the one hand the rules define the boundaries of this order and deviance from these rules threatens the order. On the other hand, there is a danger that reactions against deviance can, paradoxically, disrupt rather than preserve the order. This paradox is reflected within the sociology of deviance. The functionalists from Durkheim to Erikson emphasize that the moral order is strengthened and reasserted by the negative sanctioning of deviant conduct. The labelling theorists, in contrast, emphasize that the control of deviance can amplify the deviance and undermine the order that it is intended to preserve. At the prescriptive level both are concerned with offering justifications for intervention or non-intervention.[2] It is our contention that the principles underlying these justifications offered by social scientists are precisely the same principles which underlie the common-sense thinking about intervention among ordinary members of society.[3] In relation to our study of deviance in schools, we can conceptualize the formulation by teachers of solutions to the intervention problem as reflecting these two potentially conflicting justificatory principles. These principles underpin and provide the rationale for the rules of the classroom; and they are also used for formulating reactions to breaches of the rules. The first principle is that which is emphasized by the functionalists; the second principle is that which is emphasized by the labelling theorists. It is the tension between these two principles which must be resolved by those persons confronted by the problem of intervention.

The first principle we shall call the moral principle. A rule can be established and justified by an appeal to this moral principle on the grounds that the regulation of social order enjoined by it promotes and reflects certain moral values. Such rules, and the values from which they are derived, are seen by members to be inherently 'right', 'good', 'proper' and 'just'. The nature of 'authority' in the classroom is often discussed and debated by teachers in such moral terms, and these moral values are inevitably reflected in, for example, the teacher-pupil relational rules operated by a teacher. The second principle we shall call the pragmatic principle. A rule can be established and justified by an appeal to this pragmatic principle on the grounds that it provides an efficient and effective way in which teachers and pupils can realize their goals, carry out their activities or perform their roles within the classroom. Such rules appertain not because they are 'right' but because they 'work'. They are established by trial and error and they are readily changed in the light of experience. In practice, of course, most classroom rules can be justified by an appeal to both principles. To describe an act as 'wrong' is to invoke either or both principles. But the description of an act as 'wicked' draws predominantly on the moral principle, whereas the description of an act as constituting a 'nuisance' draws predominantly on the pragmatic principle.

We shall use these two principles and the potential conflict between them—bearing in mind that they are constructions created by us rather than being the 'natural' first-order constructs of the teachers themselves—to elucidate the dilemma inherent in the teacher's decision whether or not to intervene. In defining an act as deviant, the teacher is drawing on the moral principle. An act which breaks a rule—whether or not that rule is justified primarily in moral or pragmatic terms or by a mixture of both principles—is nevertheless a breach of that rule even though it has minimal 'disruptive' value for members' pragmatic pursuits. That is, it produces few consequential problems that prevent members from doing what they are supposed to be doing. In this sense the act does not damage the pragmatic principle. Yet in a technical sense it remains a breach of the rule with reference to the absolutism of the moral principle; a deviant act does not lose its deviant status merely because its consequences are non-disruptive. Also by the moral principle, the teacher ought to do something about the act; it cannot be allowed to pass unremarked because to do so would be to jeopardize the very moral foundations by which the rule is justified as well as the notions of justice involved in the enforcement of rules. The tension between the two principles arises because if the teacher does make an overt reaction to a deviant act which has minimal disruptive value, that overt reaction may itself become disruptive. On the other hand, if the teacher prefers non-intervention, then the lack of reaction potentially threatens the moral status of the rule that has been broken. In this sense we can posit two 'ideal type' teachers—moralists and pragmatists. The moralists sacrifice pragmatism for morality, since they are prepared to intervene in the case of many deviant acts which themselves are of little consequence in pragmatic terms and risk creating a disruption by that intervention in order to preserve morality. The pragmatists sacrifice morality for pragmatism, since they are prepared not to intervene in the case of many deviant acts which are of little consequence in pragmatic terms, and thus ensure that no disruption is created by such an intervention. This is achieved at the risk of undermining the rule's moral status. We are not, of course, interested in assigning teachers to one or other of these two 'ideal types'. Our interest rather is in showing that all teachers face this dilemma of the tension between these two principles and that they must find solutions to this dilemma on every occasion that they face the problem of whether or not to intervene.

The pragmatic principle may arise in various forms in the life of schools, but we shall concern ourselves with one form which is particularly dominant in lessons in classrooms. We shall call this the 'time-flow principle', because this construction derives directly from members' own constructs. We shall show how the pragmatic principle of time-flow is used by teachers to account for their decisions over the problem of intervention.

> T. I expect purposeful behaviour in the sense that if there's a
> group of two, one of them will come and get it [equipment] and
> take it back to the desk and carry on from there. I don't expect
> anything else to happen then. They will stop from time to time for
> talks with another group, with other boys, and this is almost
> unavoidable I should think because it could only disrupt the lesson
> if you insisted that they were not to do this. I mean I will accept
> various contact between them, some sort of interplay between the
> kids on the way back to their desks. Provided that they were
> obviously going fairly quickly, that they were not stopping and
> forgetting what they'd come for then I shouldn't do much about it.

The teacher explains that he must tolerate a certain amount of deviant conduct, since to enforce a strict conformity to the rules as

would be required by the morality principle would necessitate interventions which would themselves be disruptive. Morality yields to
pragmatism, for morality could be upheld only at the cost of disrupting the time-flow by which teachers and pupils can 'get on' with their
work. The teacher must calculate whether or not to interrupt the
time-flow. He must be able to gauge when the intervention, disruptive though it is, will be less disruptive than permitting the
deviant conduct to continue unremarked. He must also be able to
gauge when his intervention is more disruptive than the deviant
conduct he wishes to control. He must also be able to judge when he
must make a disruptive intervention in the interests of the morality
principle. How the teacher decides whether or not to intervene, and
the common-sense knowledge upon which such a decision is based,
is the problem we must pursue. In making these decisions, the
teachers emerge as highly skilled strategists, as the following extract
shows.

I.   Peter appeared not to be following. . . .
T.   No, he wasn't. They were, you'd got your back to them, they
were looking, they kept looking. You see I didn't say anything to
them because I didn't want to disturb the others, you know, you
don't want to disturb the flow but there was a little bit of play
between each other, looks and giggles, you know.
I.   Yes, one wonders how you gauge this—whether to intervene
or not—
T.   Well, I mean sometimes they catch your eye and they have got
the sense to stop because you look. But if they don't stop and it
gets worse then you have got to stop the class. I mean, I don't like
to stop a class. In a class discussion if you see two boys not
attending to the discussion at all and having their own little
private thing, there again I'll try and catch their eye to sort of stop
it so that I don't stop the whole class because it's something you've
got to gauge but if it gets too bad you have got to stop it.
I.   So does that mean if you try and stop it without stopping the
flow but you don't succeed—
T.   I stop the flow then, I have to do, yes. They will respond
sometimes to a look or you know. And they know that I don't
want to say, I don't want to stop the class but when it, when they
don't stop then of course I have got to stop the class.

Here the teacher employs a non-verbal and non-disruptive control
technique to inhibit the deviance. Only when the preferred first form
of treatment fails is the teacher willing to resort to a control technique which disrupts the time-flow.
   Given that the teacher's motive is to preserve time-flow as one

means of maintaining order during lessons in classrooms, on what grounds and by what common-sense knowledge does the teacher decide for or against intervention? The first feature which we shall consider concerns the nature of the deviant act. In essence the teacher's judgment rests upon his perception of the seriousness of the act. Seriousness is a two-dimensional concept. Some of the classroom rules are held to be more important than others. 'Fighting' is typically considered to be a more serious offence than 'talking', just as in society 'murder' is considered to be a more serious offence than 'speeding'. It appears that teachers organize classroom rules into some sort of hierarchy by which some rules are thought to be more important than others. If importance is the first dimension of seriousness, the second dimension concerns the perceived consequences of the act. This is used to distinguish different examples of what are technically the 'same' offence. In society we rate 'bank robbery' as more serious than 'petty theft' though both are cases of 'theft', and we rate the consumption of 'hard' drugs as more serious than that of 'soft' drugs though both are cases of 'drug offences'. In school, teachers differentiate between acts in terms of their consequences in a similar way. They estimate the consequences of the deviant act on the teacher, on other pupils, and on the pupil himself. Thus 'loud talk' by a pupil which prevents the teacher from speaking and other pupils from listening is rated as more serious than 'whispering' because the latter prevents only two pupils from listening and does not prevent the teacher from speaking. In short, offences which break minor rules and have few consequences are defined as 'trivial' offences, whilst those which break important rules with wide-ranging consequences are defined as 'serious' offences.

When the deviant act is defined as 'trivial', the teacher often prefers non-intervention, since intervention would be more disruptive than allowing the offence to continue untreated.

(1) T. In the teaching situation, have you got time to do it? If somebody pokes somebody with their elbow, you can say, 'stop it'; but you don't really have time to have a little inquest on all the pros and cons of a minor incident such as this. The only time that you have a major inquest is when there has been a serious disturbance in the class. I think that most teachers do their best to keep the level of disturbance down, it just depends on how many years you have been teaching. But somehow you stop the level of disturbance getting too far. You nip it in the bud as soon as possible.

(2) I. Are there times when you see pupils breaking rules but you take no action?

> T.   Let's say one's actions are modified. Even doing nothing
> would be an action in this case, wouldn't it? Perhaps not
> seeming to do anything would involve the teacher making a
> decision just as much as doing something. So if one decided
> that Jimmy was moving around but it's not necessary to do
> anything about it, he's not interfering with anybody else, he
> may be missing something, one feels it's much better to let
> Jimmy miss it of his own choice rather than stop the whole
> class and draw attention to it.

When the offence is defined as 'serious' the teacher will intervene and,
as we shall see shortly, select an appropriate form of treatment. The
line between intervention and non-intervention cannot be sharply
drawn. It is difficult—for teachers and for us—to specify when a
'trivial' offence becomes a 'serious' offence. Clearly some kind of
'threshold' is involved, above which offences are serious and require
intervention and below which offences are trivial and are ignored.
The acts are ignored in the sense that they do not result in an overt
reaction from the teacher, but they do not pass unremarked. They
are still defined as deviant acts, and come to constitute 'subreactional' deviance as discussed in chapter 6. These thresholds vary
between different teachers, partly because of their different rule
hierarchies and their different estimations of the consequences of
deviant acts. We are also persuaded that there are contextual factors
affecting these judgments. Teachers refer to the crossing of this
threshold when they talk of an act being 'too much' or 'too aggravat-
ing' or 'over-stepping the mark'.

> (1) I.   Could you tell me anything about how much noise there
> would have to be before you said that?
> T.   It was a maths lesson and it varies with each lesson. I don't
> lay down hard and fast rules. This morning they had a great
> deal of difficulty. I'd had a class lesson before when I'd done
> all the talking and they were doing metrics and so on and found
> it difficult. I'd gone through it and I wanted them to do it and
> I know they were finding it difficult and I know that perhaps
> they could help each other with it so I was prepared to put up
> with a little bit of noise but I felt they were getting too noisy
> and they were shouting and at that time these three boys who
> are brighter ones had got on and they were on to problems and
> they were getting very excited about it. They were working
> together which is a good thing as far as I am concerned
> because they are three who are on a level in their maths and
> they can work together but they were discussing this and also
> there was a little bit of shrieking coming from over here where

there were two boys at the back there who should not have
been sitting together anyway, who moved and talked to each
other when I separated them earlier and they were making a
noise. It varies, I can't give you a measure, it's up to the
children. If I feel that they are working well then that's fine
but if I feel that they are losing something by the noise and
they need to be quiet then I will make them be quiet. This
morning I knew they needed to make a noise because they had
to do it with each other to sort it out. It's essential in a non-
streamed class. You see, I can't teach every child individually
and I have to rely on them, not really helping each other, but
often talking it out and that, and if you could have heard them
individually they were having arguments, 'No it's not', 'Yes it
is', 'You don't do it like that', 'The point's that way', that's the
sort of thing that's going on and it's necessary to part of the
maths lesson. So I can't really give you a measure at all, it's
just an instinctive thing. I know when it's getting too loud and
they're interrupting each other.
I.   Your remarks seem to suggest it's a certain type of noise.
T.   It got slightly louder, it's very difficult, again it's a thing I
don't even measure myself, I just know when the noise has got
or is getting too loud. I do it before it gets too much.

(2) T.   The difference is between what they call the hum of activity
and just uncontrolled noise. I don't have a very quiet
classroom. I don't think I ever had even when I taught infants.
I think this is something to do with a teacher's personality. I
am not a very quiet personality so therefore I tend not to have a
very quiet classroom, but I don't think it is uncontrolled noise.

Teachers also operate such thresholds with respect to individual
pupils. These thresholds derive from the teacher's typing of the
pupil, and if the typing is stabilized then the type-related threshold
becomes a relatively permanent feature of the teacher's common-
sense knowledge of intervention in the case of that pupil.

T.   Always difficult to decide when to take action and when
not to take action. Martha is the biggest person in the class, the
largest in size. She is a compulsive talker, very similar to Lee.
I can't treat people equally in the sense that they are all
different. If you compare Martha with Richard, I can't think
of his surname, little Richard who never says anything in class,
I think I allow a person like Martha a bit more liberty conversation-
wise. Whether this is right or wrong I don't know, but that's what
I do and I try to weigh up the situation as I see it.

Given that Martha is typed as a 'compulsive talker', the threshold of intervention is set at a 'higher' level than in the case of Richard, who is typed as 'quiet'. Interestingly, this concession to pragmatism raises problems of morality and justice for the teacher. Because of the way in which she has been typed, Martha is given a relatively permanent greater licence to deviate than is Richard, but in other cases the threshold is adjusted on a more temporary basis to take account of temporary contingencies. One example is the teacher's assessment of the pupil's 'mood' at the time of the act.

I. Why do you think they need to do these sort of things?
T. I don't really know why. It is just something you know as a teacher and I just think it's something they need. I have been bumbling along with 3E all this time and I think it's something they need to do. Bradley particularly, he is destructive, he has this streak in him which is frustrating. I'm no psychologist but it's just what I have learned from college. He has this destructive streak and sometimes if he comes in, like today I knew he wasn't going to do anything, perhaps you didn't notice or you didn't think it was any of your business but he didn't do anything during that lesson at all until the end and then he produced something very good. But before that he had a great sheet of drawing paper which he folded up, you probably saw he was cutting strips and it's very hard work doing it, he had it folded into about eight folds and he cut it with the scissors. But he needs to do this sort of thing, to just get whatever it is out of his system if he has had a bad time during the day, which he invariably does because he's such a monkey. I think he's the worst one for that sort of thing.

In a second example, the threshold is adjusted on the basis of the teacher's perception of the pupil's 'emotional state', knowledge of which the teacher acquired incidentally from another member of staff.

I. In fact I wondered why you hadn't said anything to Steve Roberts earlier on in the lesson.
T. Well, I didn't want, I thought perhaps they might settle down and, you know, carry on and I, well, you see I had heard that day about Roberts, about the father you see, and I didn't want to upset the boy, but I don't think he was upset, I think he, you know, I thought, 'I'll have to be careful with Steve if that's the position this week', because George [another teacher] had told me you see, [Steve's brother] had told him the day before so George told me at home, you know about it so I thought I had better be careful with Steve so that's probably why I didn't speak to Steve before, and

you know I thought I mustn't speak sharply to him because he
might be upset. He may not even know, you never know, he may
not even know. He didn't seem to me unhappy yesterday. I was
keeping, I was looking at him, I was watching him to see whether
he, you know, I was sort of mentally thinking well, how is he and
how shall I treat him if he's like this, but to me he didn't seem as if
he knew. He wasn't upset, did you think so?

I. He didn't seem upset to me but—

T. No, I didn't think he was upset. I shall keep my eye on him
in future, but you see George had told me. That's why I was being
a bit careful with Steve yesterday . . . you just can't expect a boy
to concentrate on school work when he is thinking about what goes
on at home. You can understand inattentiveness then but it
wasn't that yesterday, I'm pretty certain it wasn't, it was just the
two of them, a bit of by-play between the two of them, but that
was the reason I didn't go sharply on to him because I had got it in
the back of my mind what George had told me about him so I was
sort of watching him yesterday.

We have seen that part of the teacher's conceptualization of an
offence as 'serious' was grounded in the immediate consequences of
the act as perceived by the teacher. But in addition the teacher also
makes an estimation of the predicted course of a deviant act were it
to be left untreated. There are three ideal typical forms of this
predicted course: the act might 'peter out' and disappear of its own
accord; the act might persist at the same level of seriousness; or the
act might escalate into a more serious act in that the consequences
become more disruptive. If the teacher suspects on certain grounds
that the act is likely to 'peter out', then intervention becomes
unnecessary. A common example is 'talking'. Although there may
officially be a 'no talking' rule in play, teachers anticipate that some
pupils will exchange a few words with other pupils on non-work
matters; but they also assume that such conversations will typically
'fizzle out' of their own accord after a few moments. They are seen
to serve as a temporary respite from work rather than as likely to
develop into an extensive conversation. When the teacher decides
not to intervene because he predicts that the act will soon 'peter out',
he is able to follow a 'wait-and-see' strategy. If the act does not 'peter
out'—showing that his prediction of the act's course was wrong—it
then becomes a case of persistence; the acceptable if strictly deviant
'brief chat' becomes a conversation which is going on for 'too long',
so the teacher can now resort to intervention. The third predicted
course of the deviant act is escalation. In this case the act would
become more serious if left untreated.

I. You grabbed hold of him and told him to get out.

T. It was Owen again. He was doing something ridiculous to the boy next to him with a ruler. I think he was poking him and hurting him. It was necessary. I know that if I left them any longer there would be murder done.

Thus this teacher justifies her intervention on the grounds of her predicted escalation. Another form of escalation arises, not when the act itself becomes more serious, but when the deviant act 'spreads' to other pupils. We might call this escalation by contagion.

(1) T. I called his attention to that [talking in a loud voice] because if he'd got away with that then there's no reason why Tim Birdsall shouldn't start, and he really has got a penetrating voice. I was nipping it in the bud before it started.

(2) I. So how do you handle him when he is performing his mischiefs?

T. In every possible way. Sometimes I do very little if it's not causing much disruption, because the disruption would be much greater if I did something noticeably about it. Sometimes I shout at him, if I think that he should be aware that there is some authority, if I feel that it is necessary, and sometimes I shout at Fritz so that the rest of the class will not catch it. In other words they will be aware that what Fritz is getting away with is not applicable to them, there's something special about Fritz. It's probably extremely unjust but sometimes it is necessary to put the good of the majority in front. So that while Fritz may be getting away with it often from his point of view, he may be being allowed to act differently from the majority, perhaps from time to time it is necessary to re-establish the teacher's position, and I perhaps shout at Fritz and make him sit down and so on. Exercise the old-fashioned sort of authority.

We can see how this teacher uses the notion of escalation by contagion in his commentary—he actually uses the words 'catch it'. But note that this feature is deeply embedded in a more general discussion which clearly exemplifies the tension experienced by this teacher between the principles of morality and pragmatism. Thus the feature we have called the estimation of the predicted course of a deviant act is seen to constitute part of the common-sense knowledge by which the teacher is able to resolve the tension between the two principles in making his decision about intervention.

This common-sense knowledge provides the essential foundation of the teacher's skill in making decisions about intervention. If, with regard to the predicted course, the teacher estimates that the deviant act will persist or more probably escalate, then the teacher's early intervention serves to 'nip it in the bud'. In this way future problems are anticipated and forestalled. To make a non-interventionist decision rests upon the teacher's capacity to predict that the act will 'peter out'. If the teacher's predictions are inaccurate, then he will intervene in situations where the act would have 'petered out', and will not intervene when the act would have escalated. So we can see that the teacher must acquire considerable knowledge about acts, actors and contexts upon which the exercise of these skills and strategies rests.

Given that the teacher has decided to intervene, he then has to select a specific control technique which will constitute the treatment of the deviant act. Once the teacher has decided that he 'must do something about it', he has to decide precisely what he is going to do about it. Our interest is not concerned with these control techniques as such. We do not intend to analyse, categorize or classify the particular forms of the treatment. We shall, instead, depict teachers' common-sense knowledge which structures the decision-making. Our interest is in the formulation of the decisions about treatments, rather than in the particular treatments that are decided upon. We can, of course, gain access to the grounds on which decisions are made only by asking teachers for commentaries upon decisions they did (or might) make.

We shall see that the tension between pragmatism and morality inheres in decision making about treatments just as it did in the intervention problem. At the pragmatic level, the teacher is concerned to select a treatment that 'works', that is, which inhibits or stops the deviant act, at least in the short-term. We shall term this feature 'effectiveness'. The teacher is also concerned to select a treatment which produced as little disruption as possible to himself, the offender, and the rest of the class. Additionally, deviant conduct must be stopped with the least possible damage to the time-flow of the lesson. In other words, the treatment must not only be effective, but also 'efficient'. A teacher may have at his disposal a wide range of control techniques which would be effective in stopping the deviant act, yet some of these would be highly inefficient in their disruptive effect on the lesson. This acts as a severe constraint on the teacher's selection of an appropriate technique.

I. How would you get this order?

T. Many ways I do this. Shouting, other times I sit quietly and just lean back and take my specs off and put my feet on the desk until they all realize that something is wrong, that teacher is sat there, and then they're quiet. But this takes much longer than shouting, because it takes ten minutes before they all realize I want some order.

Whilst effectiveness/efficiency is a pervasive feature of treatment selection, the common-sense knowledge exhibits many other important features. The teacher does not possess a stock of knowledge of efficient treatments which can be applied irrespective of the deviant act, the offender, and the context. Teachers recognize that a technique sometimes 'works', but sometimes does not. In this sense every treatment is a risk, a calculated guess which is validated only when the outcome—the pupil's reaction to the treatment—is known.

(1) T. They did respond as a matter of fact. I didn't know whether the noises would stop and allow me to get on, but they did as it happened. It worked today, but it might not tomorrow.

(2) I. Then you said, 'If you two don't pay attention you'll be split up.'
T. It sounds like a terrible threat, doesn't it? Well, they like to be together and I must say that splitting them up, putting them at different ends of the room, doesn't always work and in fact I never carried out the threat this morning. Well, I suppose it might have a certain value, it's one of those threats that might work and might not. It didn't this morning, and that's about all there was to it.

In the face of this uncertainty, the teacher draws upon other features of his common-sense knowledge in order to maximize the potential effectiveness of a selected treatment. In particular, he makes use of his typing of (that is, his common-sense knowledge about) the offender(s) involved in the act. This is because part of this typing consists of knowledge of the predicted reaction to the treatment.

(1) I. Just after this there were some other girls, you looked up because I think you heard some other people chattering, but you didn't say anything.
T. Well, I do that frequently and that's enough, my face is enough, if I just stare at them they know, I don't need to speak. With an easy type of girl, not the ones who are less disciplined —they will defy you sometimes and keep on talking and I would have spoken in that case. I can't remember which two they were but I only needed to look.
I. Wouldn't a look have been sufficient for those two girls at the back who you told to stop giggling?
T. I doubt it, they like to attract attention.

(2) T.   Now Higgins, he's a lazy type. But Daltry, whilst he can
enjoy a bit of fun, he also knows that he's got to do some work.
He has some ability and he uses it. But not without prodding.
From time to time I have to have a little word in his ear, bring
him to book and let him understand that things are not going
past unnoticed. And generally speaking I can manoeuvre him
just by talking to him. Fatherly talks.

(3) I.   What is your objective in talking to him and settling him
down?
T.   Obviously we come into a lesson, no matter what the
subject is, to get something done, to get something over and
with a disturbance like this if you tried thumping them
around you'll infuriate them further and finally get nothing
done. Whereas with Frankie I've found that sorting him out
like that, getting him settled down, some little progress can be
made after that. I think that if you tried the heavy hand with
him it could possibly go the other way. I've tried the other
method and I've found that it doesn't always pay. I don't think
that you have a set answer. If you take ten boys, well ten
children, I don't think that you have a set answer to deal with
every individual case in the same way.

(4) I.   I hope you will accept this in the right spirit, but why did
you keep returning to Robert? Somebody watching might have
said you were getting at Robert this morning, you kept coming
back to him a lot.
T.   I was picking on Robert in one sense. Robert needs very
special attention to make sure that he knows that he can't get
away with anything because otherwise he's wasting his time.
He is supposed to be taking GCE next year and unless he's
prepared to change his attitude he's not going to do as well as
he should. He is capable of doing much better than he would if
left alone so I was chivvying him up, if that's the word you use.
His performance may improve; it will not improve if I leave him
to do whatever he is doing, so by picking on him I'm possibly
hoping that he's annoyed with me and to get the better of me,
he will have the right answers in the work to be sought. He's the
sort of person it might work with. I think he's well aware of the
reason why I'm doing it and he has to make a protest because
this is one of his responses, and he makes a protest but I don't
think he expects me to take his protest seriously, so that
ultimately I hope that he'll realize that he's got to get down to
work. If he gets down to work and doesn't get involved with
other people then he'll not be picked on, so that I will not

repeatedly ask him questions and I shall probably go round the class more evenly and ask questions.

The teacher's knowledge about pupils includes not only knowledge about the differences between pupils but also knowledge about the variations in the conduct of the same pupil on different occasions. Pupils are held to have 'good days' and 'bad days', 'good moods' and 'bad moods', which can affect treatment selection.

I. Why did you phrase it in that way? Why didn't you say 'Shut up making noises'?
T. Well you have to vary it a bit you see. You can tell Frankie to shut up and you can give him a clip over the ear if it gets too bad but you have just got to vary it with Frankie.
I. Why is that?
T. Well, he is very difficult. There are some days when he won't tolerate any kind of discipline or authority at all. Now today wasn't a bad day, he was in a fairly amicable mood. I don't like bad relationships if I can avoid it, but there are times when I do have stand-up battles with Frankie and I do say, 'Sit down and shut up', and I sometimes push him down. . . . I don't think he responds to praise, well at least not in the way that some children do, it isn't a spur to going on and doing better things, he really doesn't care whether I think his work's nice or not.
I. What does he respond to?
T. Well, it has to be one of his good days. Sometimes he'll respond to a bribe. Somebody offered him a bar of chocolate at the end of the term if he didn't truant for that term and the silly little thing hadn't the sense to realize that a whole term's solid attendance just wasn't worth, you know, the bar of chocolate wouldn't be worth that much to him. But he kept it up for a term and I can get deep concentration when I'm giving sweets. We play bingo sometimes to test tables, and I can get deep concentration then if there is a sweet in the offing.
I. [Indecipherable]
T. No, I don't think so, except you have always got to be ready to be friendly with him, no matter what mood he comes in with.

In the examples of treatments examined so far, the teacher is quite confident about the deviant nature of the act being committed by the pupils. The problem is not what the pupil is doing, but what to do about what the pupil is doing. Yet as we showed in chapter 5, it frequently happens that the teacher is suspicious, rather than convinced, that a deviant act is taking (or has taken) place. As was pointed out in that chapter, the teacher attempts to resolve this by the use of evidential strategies. In one sense these evidential strategies can themselves come to constitute a form of treatment. The highly skilled way in which a teacher can combine the two is demonstrated in the use of the rhetorical question as a treatment-cum-evidential-strategy. The most common example is the query, 'What are you doing?' If the teacher is merely suspicious that a deviant act is taking place, then the question serves as a useful evidential strategy for it requires that the pupil provide some account of his activities. On the other hand the question does not have the force of a direct accusation; if the pupil is not indulging in deviant conduct, he needs only to explain his action. But the pupil knows that the question is often a deviance-imputation rather than a genuine question. If he is not being deviant, he can reply 'Nothing, sir', which of course means nothing deviant. If, however, the pupil is being deviant, he reads the question not as an enquiry but as a treatment, that is, as the equivalent of a command to cease being deviant. In this case he understands that he need not relate to the teacher the nature of the deviant activity, but merely stops being deviant without making any verbal reply. The teacher can thus treat a deviant act of which he is only suspicious with great efficiency; if his suspicions are wrong, then he will be told so with relatively little loss of time, and if he is right, the pupil will stop. The strength of this technique is that since the teacher can, and often does, use it when he is convinced that the pupil is being deviant (thus using it as an equivalent of a command), the pupil who is the target of the rhetorical question is never sure whether the teacher is suspicious or convinced. It is therefore dangerous for the pupil to risk denying that he is being deviant, since if the teacher is in fact convinced, his denial will only make matters worse. Again the teacher's common-sense knowledge about the pupil influences the use of the technique. Its use is dangerous in the case of pupils who are typed as liars, since they are expected to offer denials as the response. In such cases the use of the rhetorical question is potentially highly inefficient, since the lesson can become disrupted by the ensuing debate between the teacher who is convinced that the pupil was being deviant and the pupil who made a denial and then persists in maintaining the denial. So with some pupils the teacher may be unable to use the rhetorical question either as an evidential strategy or as a treatment. It is only with certain pupils who are typed in given ways by the teacher that the marvellous ambiguity of the rhetorical question can be efficient.

Not infrequently the teacher judges the treatment to be ineffective: the pupil does not desist from his deviant act, or turns to another act which is also deviant. In such cases the teacher's estimation of an appropriate treatment has been inaccurate. Normally the teacher 'follows up' this failure either with a 'strengthened' form of the original treatment (e.g. saying the same words in a louder voice or a more menacing tone) or selects an alternative treatment (e.g. telling the pupil to change seats in place of ordering him to stop talking).

(1) I.   You'll try something else if it doesn't work?

   T.   Oh yes. Supposing I did it tomorrow and he didn't respond to that then I'd be quite willing to walk over menacingly and stand there and see whether that worked and if it didn't then sort of hustle him about a bit.

(2) T.   I'd spoken to them earlier on, in fact when you probably didn't hear me when I was going round saying, 'Cut it out. There's no need to talk like this.' I had warned them a few times and at the end I thought this is ridiculous, it's getting out of hand so I thought I'll bring some order here and Gray had made one or two statements about he'll thump me, pretending for me not to hear but I obviously heard what he said and I thought the only way to bring order is to shout and to rap somebody round the head and this is what I did.

(3) T.   He hit a kid in this class so I got up and walked over to him and said, 'Look, pack that in or else you'll have me to deal with', and he laughed in a very cocksure manner, you know. So I got hold of his arms, and he is strong, let me tell you that. I could feel the power behind this young kid's arms, but I thought, 'It's him or me. I can't take a step back in this situation', so I put my face close to his and I said, 'Look . . .' and I forgot what I said but it was pretty aggressive—that I'd knock his block off or something like that, and he was reasonable after that—reasonable in inverted commas!

There are also important contextual constraints on the selection of the treatment. For instance, a teacher cannot send more than one child at a time to stand outside the classroom in the corridor. A single use of this treatment satiates the technique, for to put two pupils in the corridor makes the treatment less punitive and risks that the two offenders will indulge in further deviance in the safety of the unsupervised corridor.

As usual pragmatism is tempered by morality. Many teachers are aware that heavily punitive techniques could be effective and efficient, but they cannot be justified because of important moral considerations. This is not to say that teachers do not sometimes adopt treatments which to them are morally unjustifiable, but when they do so they typically define their own conduct as deviant and 'normalize' it with accounts such as 'I'd lost my temper'.

T.   If you realize that the methods that you were adopting are not achieving success the teacher may get a bit desperate and eventually adopt some method that would possibly not seem reasonable in the first instance. You hope that it's all been very carefully weighed up and that it's done for the benefit of the child and not to relieve the teacher's feelings, but there again, teachers are human beings and you might find an exasperated teacher. You'll never find me exasperated of course! You can put that in inverted commas!

But such exceptional treatments only serve to emphasize the taken-for-granted moral considerations implicit in routine decision-making. Our research suggests that teachers possess an elaborate theory of punishment. This relates to our earlier discussion of the 'seriousness' of offences in that punishments must be made to fit the crime: the more serious the offence, the more punitive the treatment. This aspect of our research is unfortunately rather neglected. However, it is our impression that in the case of relatively minor or routine offences, the punitive aspect of the treatment is subsidiary to the pragmatic considerations of 'getting on with the lesson'. In the case of serious deviant acts, many teachers appear to feel constrained to make the treatment more censorious and punitive than may be necessary for the efficient inhibition of the offence: pragmatism yields to morality.

One interesting situation where morality yields to pragmatism is when the teacher faces a new class for the first time, especially where the teacher and the pupils are new to one another. Here the teacher may be intentionally more punitive than normal for a temporary period. The teacher is aiming to establish his authority by being 'tough', thereby deterring pupils from committing deviant acts. The teacher's normal moral conception of justice is temporarily modified in the interests of long-term pragmatic objectives.

T.   I let them know that I don't approve anyway. At first, you know when I had them at first I used to dole out lines and things like that but I found that that isn't, er, necessary in the same way.
I.   How do you mean?
T.   Well, you know if I look as though I'm annoyed it usually is enough now, whereas at first they didn't believe that I was going to punish them and so I had to punish them to let them know that I did mean it and since then they've, they know when they've gone too far—with the exception of the odd one or two who are a bit insensible, you know, they don't remember from one day to the next too well, the slower ones, but generally speaking they're pretty good.

Another major moral consideration affecting the selection of the treatment is that the punishment must fit the offender as well as the crime. In this the teacher once again draws upon that common-sense knowledge which comprises his typing of the offender. For example, the teacher may decline to use a treatment on the basis of its perceived consequences for the pupil. Only from an elaborated conception of the pupil is a teacher able to make such a prediction.

> T.   I think there's something physically wrong about him, and I do try to remember that when I'm dealing with him, because I think he could lose his temper to such an extent that he could do irreparable damage to himself.

As we saw in chapters 6 and 7, the typing of a child involves the imputation of typical motives and a 'causal structure' which lies behind those motives, such as home background. These motives are taken into account in treatment selection.

(1) T.   With Sally I would be more lenient [if she came late to lessons].
  I.   Why would that be?
  T.   From her home background. She comes from a particularly bad background. I'm led to believe, I don't know this, but the family generally is noted throughout the school as being in need of protection, if you like. She seems to be a loner in the sense that kids tend to take advantage of her and call her scruffy and dirty and that type of thing. Maybe it's my sympathetic mind but I would be more lenient with her.

(2) T.   Bradley's father beats him black and blue when he's home sometimes, so what difference would it make if I hit him, or anybody else [hit him] come to that. He's so used to it that it doesn't have any effect on him.

(3) T.   I think that he is performing more for the benefit of the class than anything else, to seek his own place. I should say that he's insecure. We read these things and say these words, but I think that the lad is insecure and seeking to establish his position. It's very difficult to remedy this, to make him behave like the others because you can't put back what has been lost over a number of years, you can't just devise a scheme. I know people purport to do this, but you can play about with the most seriously disturbed, but these are only slightly abnormal but they're the bigger problem because there are a lot of people like these in schools. You don't spend a lot of time with them. We've got to try and make them fit into groups and we're squeezing all the round pegs into the square holes.

Unfortunately we don't modify the holes; we modify the pegs, don't we, if they don't fit? I've only just thought of that but you can use it!

Here we see how teachers have to some extent absorbed the analytical schemes and diagnostic vocabularies of sociologists of education. Doubtless they are beginning to do the same with labelling theory.

An important feature of the imputation of motives consists of the attribution of intent. In some cases the teacher may be unsure about the intentionality of the deviant act. If the act was not committed deliberately, but from ignorance or by accident, then although the teacher is constrained on pragmatic grounds to make some reaction, the treatment would not, on moral grounds, be punitive. The inference of intent is often made on the basis of contextual clues but the teacher's typing of the offender is also relevant here.

I. 'Do you know you're whistling, Derek?'
T. Yes, I sometimes think you know, I mean I can hum when I'm
working or reading to myself and I thought now it may be that
he's not doing this, or trying to attract attention, it might be that
he doesn't really know he's doing it; and I thought if he does know
he's doing it he knows he ought not to be doing it. So I thought I'd
give him the benefit of the doubt.

A pupil who is typed as deviant, and who is assigned typical motives for intentionally committing disruptive acts, might not so readily be given 'the benefit of the doubt' in the absence of clarificatory contextual clues.

This brings us directly to the issue of the teacher's treatment of pupils who are typed as deviant. What is the relationship between the treatments meted out to pupils who are typed as deviant and the treatments meted out to other offenders who are not so typed? Given that the deviants commit more deviant acts than others (the quantitative difference) and that they commit them for imputedly different motives (the qualitative difference), how does this affect the selection of treatments? Are the treatments in themselves different? And if so, what is the relationship between the common-sense knowledge by which these treatments are generated and the common-sense knowledge of treatment as we have so far explicated it? We have shown that typing is an important feature of the common-sense knowledge underlying treatment; we must now address ourselves to the impact of this feature in the case of pupils who are typed as deviant.

In our analysis we shall make use of the concept of 'avoidance-of-provocation'. Stebbins (1970) developed what he called the 'avoidance-of-provocation hypothesis', in his symbolic interactionist analysis of disorderly behaviour in classrooms, to account for the fact that the teachers often make no overt reaction to some forms of disorderly conduct. His argument is essentially the same as some of our earlier analysis.

> It is reasonable to hypothesize that the teacher prefers to avoid provoking [pupils] if the conduct is merely whispering that is not disturbing the class as a whole. . . . It appears that teachers regard the misconduct of [some students] as a lesser evil than that which might result should they oppose it.

In our terms, this refers to the fact that teachers often ignore deviant acts which are 'trivial' on the pragmatic grounds that intervention would disrupt the time-flow of the lesson. We shall show that a particular version of avoidance-of-provocation is used by teachers in the treatment of pupils who are typed as deviant. It rests upon the usage of the pragmatic principle described earlier but it is an extension of it in that it rests upon certain features of the teacher's common-sense knowledge that these pupils are deviant pupils. We shall also show—which Stebbins does not—that this concept can be used to link this analysis with some of the central concepts of labelling theory.

We saw in chapter 7 that the pupils who emerge as deviant pupils are distinguishable in terms of four features: generally, their deviance is variegated, and it is persistent, they are seen to be irremedial, and they are often not likeable. Irremediality, which is the most relevant aspect here, refers to the difficulties experienced by teachers in devising efficient or even effective treatments for deviant acts committed by these pupils. The pupils are often characterized as 'difficult' and this is often synonymous with 'difficult to handle'. At best, teachers are able to 'cope': the deviance is never cured, but neither does it become utterly uncontrollable. To typify a pupil as irremedial is to assign him to a special status. This means that teachers' encounters with such pupils are not expected to be very satisfying, especially where the pupil is not likeable; and when the encounter involves the control of deviant conduct, the teacher does not expect the outcome to be successful. In the light of these expectations it is not surprising that the teacher tends to avoid social interactions with these pupils. The trivial offences of deviant pupils, as in the case of all pupils, are ignored by the teacher in order to preserve time-flow. But their specialized status, deriving from the ascription of irremediality, means that these pupils lose the status of being 'normal' pupils. The teacher adopts an attitude to them which is guarded, suspicious, wary, cautious, apprehensive, and even fearful. This is the attitude induced in others by persons who have been defined as pivotally or essentially deviant. The teachers speak of these pupils in terms of 'I am suspicious of him' or 'I tread warily with him'.

Avoidance-of-provocation as defined by Stebbins is certainly used in relation to these pupils—

> T.   Well, his noisiness, of course, is interfering with others often, because it is directed at others, shouting to somebody across the class, so that one needs to draw attention to it, his attention to the fact that he is disrupting the class. If the class could ignore his noise then I would ignore it too, and in so far as it is not noticeably causing anybody else to get involved, I ignore it. It's only when it is obviously involving other people that I'm worried. The noisiness itself is not something that I particularly object to. This is an outlet that he finds and if he could do this freely and get on with his work, then I would not be unhappy at all.

—but it extends far beyond this. The deviant pupil is generally avoided in that the controls, especially in relation to work, to which normal pupils are subjected are withdrawn. Indeed, they are often not expected to do any work at all. The teacher simply loses interest in whether or not they undertake any school work. The only restriction the teacher attempts to impose on them—usually with only partial success—is that they do not interfere with the teacher or other pupils. Often this takes the form of a tacit bargain, by which the teacher agrees to leave the pupil alone provided that he in his turn leaves the teacher and other pupils alone. From the teacher's point of view this is a reasonable pragmatic solution in that he knows that any attempt to make the pupil work (and thereby stop being deviant) will be at best ineffective and at worst counter-productive.

> (1) T.   Well, as I say she'll do anything for me and providing I don't force her hand she's not any trouble for me. Perhaps if I pinned her down and said, 'Right, you're going to do that', then we might have trouble then.

> (2) T.   I sort of knew instinctively today that he wasn't going to do anything, so while he was quietly doing that, well, you know, that was quite all right by me. It just causes a lot of fuss if you try and make him work. Maybe it's quite wrong. This isn't discipline to some people but I know Frankie well enough now to know what he will do and one might as well accept it. There are sixteen or seventeen others who need attention as well so it is perhaps as well to leave him.

> (3) T.   You know how I treat him. I just don't bother. I just give

him work to do and I don't bother whether he does it or not, so long as he's quiet. We've come to this agreement.

In effect the teacher raises his interventional threshold. Were a similar deviant act to be committed by a 'normal' pupil, the teacher would intervene. But when the pupil is typed as deviant, the teacher avoids intervening until the deviant act is so disruptive that the teacher feels he has no pragmatic choice but to intervene, or until the act becomes so non-disruptively serious that he feels obliged to intervene on moral grounds.

The teacher's grounds for avoiding intervention are manifold. The most obvious of these, in the case of the older boys, is fear of physical retaliation.

> T.   Grimes realizes, I'm sure he does, that if he's going to cause trouble, that nobody's going to get hold of him, really. Now he'll accept punishment, but with a bit of a grudge, like everybody else, but I'm afraid people let him get away with it too much because of the size of him. . . . Well, for a beginning he's a very tall boy. He's very well made. He's no puppy fat on him at all. It's all muscle.
> I.   I can see with Grimes he's a lad almost as big as I am [six feet tall] and obviously as you say he's very well made as well. Do you think that it is possible that there is an element of fear when teachers are trying to handle him? That they are a little bit afraid of what might happen?
> T.   They're afraid of Grimes, yes, I'm certain. I'm certain that most people don't want to have any trouble with him and he gets away with most things because most people don't want that. They might not tell you this openly, but I'm afraid I just don't care. If he did turn on me, I mean he'd most probably finish up the worse off, but this is only because of age and knowing a bit more than he knows, not because of any other reason.

The pupils are aware of the possible existence of these fears.

> I.   Do you think that they might be frightened of you?
> Shaw.   I don't know. I don't think that they're frightened that we might start bawling at them or summat. One or two women teachers are not bothered about it, but I can't see the men teachers being scared. They might not deal with you themselves but I don't think that they're too scared. You get one or two that are getting scared. I think Mr —— is scared and Mr —— is getting a bit old now. Since Jim Grimes has come, before Jim come, you couldn't say owt to him, but he [Jim] said, 'I'm getting sick of you and if you ever touch me, I'll break your neck.' That's the first time that I ever heard anybody say it to him. He said, 'I'm just waiting for you

to hit me, then I'll break your neck.' I think that he's getting a bit
frightened because he's knocking on a bit, because when I first
come here he used to punch holes out of us when we were in first
year.

There are more subtle grounds for the avoidance of intervention.
On the basis of his knowledge that the pupil is irremedial, the teacher
anticipates that any treatment he accords the pupil is very unlikely
to be effective. On the contrary, he knows that his intervention may
well exacerbate the deviance, delay the teacher and distract the class.

(1) I.   When he denies responsibility for things that you're sure
that he's done, how do you handle the situation?
T.   It's obviously variable, but in most cases I say: 'Well,
we'll not waste any more time about it, let's get on with what
we're here to do.' Not let him make a big issue of it.
I.   When you do this, what are you attempting to do in
handling him in that way?
T.   I'm attempting to dispose of the problem as rapidly as
possible. Not particularly concerned with the effect on him,
except to convince him that he's wasting his time if he's trying
to attract attention. I'm trying to minimize the effect that it has
on the rest of the class by not letting him get into an argument
with me as the teacher so that we can get on with it and that the
class will then tend to be less influenced by what he's doing and
more by what I'm doing.

(2) I.   Why do you say that this is opposition?
T.   Well, any delay is inconvenient. If it's a case of he's picked
up someone else's pencil and they ask for it back, and you say,
'Give it back to him', the longer it takes the bigger the
disruption in the classroom. Though he may eventually give it
back, he'll make some show before doing it. He might in fact
refuse to give it back and you can either start an argument
which could stop the whole lesson, because everybody else
would stop to listen, or you tell the other boy, 'Pick up
another' and ignore the man. This is again where you're trying
to make a judgment between imposing authority on someone,
or with letting the class get on with what it is here to do.
Possibly it's not important that you impose authority on this
person so much. Some would see it differently and say that the
most important thing of all is to make him do as he is told; it
depends how one sees one's own role in this. We're in a very
difficult area of course.

As this second teacher notes, intervention often creates, at the pragmatic level, more problems than it solves. There is also the danger that the pupil's reaction to the treatment will create additional problems at the moral level, such as the pupil's acceptance of the teacher's authority. Moreover, intervention against deviant pupils raises problems affecting other moral considerations which themselves are not directly related to deviance. In teaching a class a teacher is presented with many demands on his time from the pupils. There is a moral consideration in this distribution of his time between pupils, namely that each pupil is entitled to his 'fair share'. Doubtless teachers operate in the belief that some pupils need more time and attention than others in particular ways or on particular occasions. Nevertheless, the teacher is able to define a limit beyond which a pupil's demands or needs would become excessive. The time required to make the deviant pupil work or refrain from deviating is seen by the teacher as greatly exceeding this limit. Moreover, since he anticipates an unsuccessful result to such a time expenditure, the teacher sees it as 'wasted' time. It is preferable to let the pupil 'waste his own time' rather than that of the teacher and other pupils.

(1) T.   In the workshop Shaw just doesn't do anything. You see, you've got to decide sometimes how much time you're going to spend on this lad because you've got the rest of the class. You can't spend all the time with him, and so you just let him go. You just say, right, so long as he's not doing anything, not upsetting anyone, he's just sitting there talking, well, leave him till I've got round the class and go back to him again and say, 'Now have you decided what you want to do?' . . . [If you're not careful] he's getting attention more than the other kids; the other kids are suffering for it. They're bound to be because you're spending more time with that sort of boy.

(2) T.   The objectives in the lesson are quite often to pass on a body of knowledge and the obvious requirement is that that should be achieved with respect to the greatest number of pupils in the class that it is possible to do so. Consequently, if one or two pupils require one to spend a large proportion of one's time with them, not moving towards this objective, then you've got to stop and think as to what you can do about it. Dealing with Fritz is one of the things. One has to stop from time to time and say, 'What shall I do about Fritz? How can I cope with Fritz, do something for him, and still get on with the primary objective?' These lads, some of whom will be taking exams in three years' time, how can I achieve this end and at the same time cope with Fritz who's obviously got some rather special requirements? Can I deal with a group of this

kind that has these extremes? Or possibly the one extreme at one end! This is my problem.

(3) T.   I'll hear some remark, possibly some facetious remark, and from my point of view some undesirable remark. I'll turn to Shaw and say, 'Did you say that?' He'll have his hand in front of his mouth and possibly be smirking and say, 'It was so-and-so', naming one of his pals. If I persist I get this sort of denial, you see, and if one persisted with questions one could spend a lot of time, waste a lot of time, dealing with these particular things. So it is very difficult to strike a balance between dealing with someone like this and getting on with the job of giving one's time to the rest of the class. So somewhere a decision has got to be made and it's not a particularly easy one.

From the teacher's point of view the use of avoidance-of-provocation will be successful provided that the deviant act does not escalate, that is, it either 'peters out' or merely persists. But on some occasions the deviant act does escalate. If the pupil is unaware that the teacher has noticed the act and is adopting an avoidance-of-provocation reaction to it, then the deviant act may escalate 'naturally'. For instance, if the pupil is talking and he is not aware that the teacher is making any kind of reaction to that talk, then the talk may 'naturally' become more extensive or louder, which from the teacher's point of view would constitute escalation. On the other hand, the pupil may be aware that the teacher has noticed the act but, on the basis of the lack of overt reaction against it, infers that the act has not been defined as deviant. He is therefore entirely free to continue with the act.[4]

If, however, the pupil does recognize the teacher's lack of overt reaction as a case of avoidance-of-provocation, then the pupil knows that the teacher has defined the act as deviant but has deliberately decided to take no overt action against it.[5] This perceived deliberate lack of overt reaction from the teacher may itself create a problem for the pupil. We shall examine shortly how the pupil resolves this problem and the consequences of that resolution. How this problem arises at all is only partially explicated in the brief analysis that has just been given. The members' own accounts elaborate on our analysis in that they specify the pupil's motive for the original deviant act, whereas our analysis does not.

In their accounts, deviant pupils frequently specify their motives for deviant acts as attempts to annoy the teacher.

P.   Some lessons we just go in for to get them aggravated, you know. We just keep talking and they just shout at you and sometimes you get sent up to the office. Just get them aggravated, do what we want to do.

If the deviant act, which is committed on the basis of the pupil's avowed motive to annoy the teacher, is reacted to with avoidance-of-provocation, then the pupil has failed in his objective, since the lack of overt reaction gives the pupil no grounds for believing that he has succeeded in annoying the teacher—though covertly the teacher may indeed be annoyed. So from the pupil's perspective the problem resulting from the teacher's adoption of avoidance-of-provocation consists in his belief that his attempt to annoy the teacher has failed.

A somewhat different picture emerges when we examine the teachers' accounts. We saw in chapter 7 that the motives which the teachers impute to deviant pupils are enormously varied. At times they do impute the motive to annoy, but more typically they impute the motive of attention-seeking. The teachers believe that deviant pupils are seeking attention from the teacher and/or from their peers. The typicality of this imputed motive perhaps derives from its congruence with the known features of the pupils' home circumstances which are usually seen as 'disturbed' or 'deprived'. Because deviant pupils imputedly receive too little attention at home, they are seen to express this need for attention through deviant activity in school. Thus deviant pupils are held to 'need' attention in two senses; they need attention in the sense that it would be beneficial to them were they to receive it, and they also need it in the sense that their actions are an expression of their demands for it.

(1) T.　If he gets into trouble, at least you notice that he's there and you talk to him, you see, even if you are telling him off.
I.　I wonder why.
T.　Well, there's a lot of them do, isn't there? You know, as long as you notice them it doesn't matter if you are giving them a good hiding. There's a lot of kids like that.
I.　Yes, I've heard this but I've never understood it.
T.　No I don't. I mean it's not the sort of thing I would do myself you know, but they do it, definitely, you know. Well then, little Barry, it's the one who's in hospital at the moment, does anything to make you talk to him all the time, even if you are angry with him, you know. Funny—mm. . . .

(2) T.　He's a rather peculiar boy. Again he needs—if I can ignore something some time, that doesn't matter, then he's going deliberately to try and get my attention, then I will do. I mean, sometimes you'll hear a snigger. I don't let him know that I've seen it, because if I have seen it, I have to—er—do—but it's

better sometimes not to see it rather than interrupt what I'm
doing. Because if the rest of the class are quiet, I don't want to
draw attention to him, but this is what he wants. He likes
attention. I think he does it as a deliberate thing, though I
think that it's best to ignore some things with him. I believe
that his home background isn't terribly good. He's got some
difficulties there. . . . If you ignore it, then it sometimes settles
down, but he does like attention.

If we take the teacher's account of the pupil's motives as the 'correct'
one, then pupil acts imputedly motivated by attention-seeking which
are reacted to by avoidance-of-provocation fail in their objective.
Whatever the motive for the original deviant act, whether it is to seek
attention or to annoy, if the teacher reacts to it with avoidance-of-
provocation, then that act will from the pupil's point of view appear
to have failed in its objective. The pupil has a problem.

We shall now show that this problem and its resolution provides a
dramatic illustration of that central concept in labelling theory,
Lemert's notion of secondary deviation. Lemert suggested that
secondary deviation occurs when the social reaction to a deviant act
creates a problem for the actor which may be resolved by the commission of further (or secondary) deviant acts. The motive for the
secondary deviant act is no longer the same as the motive for the
original deviant act, but is now oriented to the solution of the problem created by the social reaction. In his analysis Lemert saw the
social reaction as some form of social control, such as punishment,
stigmatization or segregation. In our case, where the social reaction is
avoidance-of-provocation, the social reaction consists of *a lack of*
social control.

The effect, however, is the same—the generation of secondary
deviation. The pupil can most easily resolve his problem of not
succeeding in obtaining attention or annoying the teacher by the
commission of further deviance, whose motivation has been affected
by the avoidance-of-provocation response he evoked in the teacher.
For instance, if the pupil's original motive was to get attention, the
teacher's failure to provide it may arouse a resentment in the pupil,
so that subsequent further deviant acts are motivated by a strengthened determination to obtain attention and to express the resentment experienced as a result of the teacher's avoidance-of-provocation
reaction. These secondary deviant acts take the form of escalation
which will continue until the teacher is forced by the seriousness of the
pupil's deviant conduct into an overt reaction of social control. To
take an example from one of the teacher's commentaries given earlier,
the social control may take the form of a 'good hiding', nevertheless

the pupil has succeeded in his objectives. We may summarize this interactional process as:

1. Pupil commits (for whatever motives) a deviant act→
2. teacher takes avoidance-of-provocation reaction→
3. pupil experiences a problem as a result of being ignored→
4. escalation of deviance to resolve that problem→
5. renewed avoidance-of-provocation from the teacher→
6. alternation of 4 and 5 until→
7. teacher makes overt social control reaction.

For example:

T.   Well, I think that it is better than when I do take strong action, in that quite often he's not as effective with what he's doing if I take little notice of it. Unfortunately, sometimes to reinforce his position he will make his activities less acceptable. He will do something more unacceptable in order to create a situation. So that if I've let him get away with say sliding a ruler down the desk and doing nothing about it, I may find that the next time he will grab somebody else's and slide that as well. Here again one has got to choose a path.

Thus we see that paradoxically the avoidance-of-provocation reaction can itself constitute a provocative act from the pupil's point of view: the teacher's reaction has effectively exacerbated the deviant conduct it was intended to control.

We tentatively suggest that this may have significant consequences for the pupil. During his early deviant acts, which evoke avoidance-of-provocation reactions from the teacher, the pupil is apparently being allowed considerable licence to indulge in deviance. Eventually the teacher responds to the escalated deviance with a 'strong' social control reaction, since from his point of view the immediately preceding act constitutes 'the last straw' which forces him into overt reaction. Not only has his attempt to use avoidance-of-provocation been unsuccessful, but also his final overt reaction takes account of the accumulated deviance which had earlier been ignored. But from the pupil's point of view this ultimate reaction appears to be disproportionately 'strong' in relation to the immediately preceding act. It is thus made easy for the pupil to claim that he is being treated unjustly and being 'picked on'—which is a common claim of deviant pupils. Surely the pupil is likely to perceive that he is in some kind of special status. When the teacher uses avoidance-of-provocation reactions to him, the deviant pupil knows that were his act committed by a 'normal' pupil the teacher would make an overt reaction to it. He is 'different' by virtue of the frequency with which the teacher adopts avoidance-of-provocation towards him. He is also 'different' by virtue of the overt reaction he finally evokes, which is more 'punitive' than that which is accorded to 'normal' pupils who commit similar acts.

Our analysis of teachers' reactions to deviant acts committed by deviant pupils has carried us, almost imperceptibly, to questions which are of a very different order to those with which we began this chapter. The 'natural' direction of the analysis leads to two questions. The first is concerned with the pupil's experiences of the teacher's reaction, whereas our original question was directed to the analysis of how teachers formulate reactions. As we made clear in chapter 2 this research is predominantly about teachers. We have presented data from pupils on occasions, but generally we have been much more concerned with teachers' understanding of pupils, rather than with the pupils themselves and their understanding of teachers. The second question now being raised concerns the long-term consequences of the differential treatment of pupils typed as deviant. Again, this is a very different kind of question. To answer it we would need extensive data from pupils who had been systematically followed throughout their school career.

These are important questions, and ones which derive directly from a labelling theory approach to deviance. Indeed, they were on our original list of research topics which we formulated prior to the field work and presented in chapter 2. In the event—like many other questions on that list—they were topics which we kept 'at the back of our minds' but which were never systematically brought to the forefront of our activities. The reason for this is that our paramount concern was progressively centred on the analysis of deviance-as-it-occurs-in-lessons. We became more and more absorbed with the study of 'routine deviance'—those relatively undramatic and fleeting episodes that are so characteristic of classrooms everywhere. Yet in these ubiquitous and taken-for-granted episodes, which in themselves are apparently of little significance and which hitherto have in consequence remained unexplored, are encapsulated the fundamental features of the phenomenon of deviance: action is rule governed; rules are broken; rule-breaking is evidenced; persons are typified as deviant; reactions to deviance are made. It is easy enough —as most labelling theorists have done—to pass over 'routine deviance' and its explication. We too could have ignored this issue and addressed ourselves directly to the more conventional questions, for which labelling theory provides a host of well-developed concepts. Since such broader issues were 'at the back of our minds' we did collect some relevant data, but this material was acquired incidentally, as it were, in the pursuit of other more immediate problems.

For example, in our interviews with deviant pupils we were furnished with material which fitted into labelling theory's concept of stigmatization. These pupils said things which could be used to amplify the notion that typified deviants sense that they are held under surveillance, are victimized, are subject to false accusation, and perceive that there would be no point in trying to reform themselves because the teachers would not believe that any change was genuine. We obtained some information on the differential treatment to which deviants are sometimes subjected, for instance being placed 'on report', whereby a pupil carries a card from lesson to lesson which is then signed by the teacher in charge. But in all cases our information was too sketchy and too insubstantial to bear an adequate analysis. We made the difficult but necessary decision to discard this material. Other topics that can be derived from labelling theory, such as the 'career' of the deviant and the contingencies of such deviant careers, were not pursued by us because we were in each of the two schools for too short a period to be able to track individual pupils for a sufficient period of time.

Some topics, on which there is an existing literature, were not so easily or readily put at the back of our minds. A good example, deriving from Werthman's and Kounin's very different researches, is the existence of significant differences among teachers in the amount of deviance, the kind of deviance, and the source of deviance that occurs in lessons. Like every researcher who has been an observer in schools, we were struck by the enormous differences between teachers in the ways lessons were conducted and individual pupils were handled. Our search for the common elements among teachers in their common-sense knowledge of deviance blunted our analysis of, but not our sensitivity to, differences between teachers with respect to rules, the evidencing of deviant acts, the typing of pupils and reactions to deviance. Such an analysis is undoubtedly needed and the lack of it in this book merely underlines the limitations of our work.

Finally, there are many concepts which analysts of educational as well as deviance phenomena have used extensively but which make no appearance in our work. The concepts of social class and organizational variables such as streaming are cases in point. These have become central concepts in the sociology of education. Our own judgment would be that they have become *too* dominant, for in using them one attends to certain kinds of question and produces a particular form of analysis, most commonly a functionalist analysis. As yet we have very little in the way of phenomenological approaches which use these concepts or offer an alternative analysis of phenomena that have traditionally been examined in terms of these concepts. We certainly would not wish to argue a priori that our own analysis cannot be related to such concepts or to studies that use these concepts; it is simply that we did not attempt to do so in this book.

To have addressed ourselves to all these issues would have inevitably meant that we had to neglect others. Here is one of the central dilemmas of every researcher: in choosing some questions, and some methods by which to answer them, he must ignore others. We made our choice on the grounds of what we regarded as the 'logical' priority of some questions over others. We assigned this priority to certain phenomenological questions which underpin much of labelling theory rather than to those issues with which labelling theorists have been most preoccupied. Other researchers would doubtless have selected other questions as more fundamental, more interesting, or perhaps as more 'practical' in their potential for policy applications. Our selection was based on the belief that the answers (however provisional) to certain questions would help to establish the necessary foundations on which the answers to other questions could more fruitfully build. The later questions on our list, which we did not examine, are to us just as interesting as the earlier questions, which we did examine. It is only time that prevented us from building on our own foundations.

9 Some implications

This book was written with two kinds of reader in mind—social scientists and educationists. Given their somewhat different interests in our work it might seem appropriate to have two sets of implications, one set for social scientists and one set for educationists. In fact our so-called double audience consists of five (not mutually exclusive) groups: academic social scientists with a strong interest in deviance but little interest in education; academic social scientists who have a major interest in education; teachers who are concerned with the initial or further education of teachers; student teachers who follow courses in social science applied to education; and practising teachers who spend their lives teaching pupils or students in schools or colleges. The members of these five groups will have different interests in our conclusions as they relate to (1) theory—the implications of our work for the conceptualization of deviance and for the labelling theory perspective, (2) research—the implications for future research into deviance and into classrooms, and (3) practical applications—the implications for the provision and development of practical help for teachers, student teachers and teacher trainers.

For social scientists working in the area of deviance, we believe we have accomplished more than simply making an application of existing labelling theory to a new substantive area. Whilst we regard our own work as only a beginning, we have drawn attention to the importance of what we call 'routine deviance' in contrast to the kind of deviance implicit in the criminological model. We believe we have also shown the fruitfulness of asking phenomenological questions which have been ignored because of the dominance of symbolic interactionism in labelling theory.

The classroom is but one of a wide variety of settings where routine deviance takes place and can be studied. In particular it is important to research into deviance in those settings where the relationships between the members are less formal and less sharply differentiated in terms of power than is true in classrooms. Only when such further substantive studies are conducted shall we be able to judge the extent to which our own theorizing is relevant at the level of formal theory. We began our research with a list of questions derived from labelling theory and criticism of it; we end our research with a further set of issues that arise from our analysis.

Rules. What are the rules that regulate social conduct in these other social settings? How do members conceptualize the rules? How do these conceptualizations of members relate to sociological formulations of the rules by writers such as Goffman and Denzin? How are these rules taught and learnt? How do they emerge and decay? How do they come into play on particular occasions? Are there many forms of switch-signal? How do members know that a given rule is in play?

Deviant acts. How do members accomplish conformity to and deviance from the rules? How useful is it to conceptualize such conformity and deviance in terms of the members following or breaking normative and technical implemental rules which underpin those rules? How do members perceive the conformity or deviance of others? Is the notion of implemental rules a useful device for conceptualizing the common-sense knowledge by which a member is able to define (recognize) an act as deviant or conformist? What other interpretive and evidential practices and strategies are used by members in making deviance-imputations?

Deviant persons. Is our theory of typing generalizable to other settings of routine deviance? How useful are our proposed stages—speculation, elaboration, stabilization, transformation—in analysing deviant person-formulation in other settings? Are factors such as the sibling phenomenon unique to one substantive area or are there equivalent or related features in other settings? How do members explain or account for the emergence of a given type of person? How do members use their knowledge of deviant types of person in making deviance-imputations, and in accounting for deviance?

Reactions to deviance. In what form are deviance-imputations made? How is it possible that a wide range of utterances can be used to make the 'same' deviance-imputation? How do members recognize a deviance-imputation? How do members distinguish deviance-imputations from other kinds of utterance? How do members recognize different utterances as having the same deviance-imputational meaning? On what occasions and on what grounds do members keep their deviance-imputations covert? Is our concept of sub-reactionality generalizable? Is our distinction between intervention and treatment generalizable? What is the common-sense knowledge that underlies intervention decisions? What is the common-sense knowledge that underlies the selection of overt reactions or treatments? Are the principles of morality and pragmatism universal features of this common-sense knowledge?

Clearly there is relatively little overlap between these questions and those which we posed in chapter 2. Our own judgment is that we have emerged from the field with a more interesting set of questions than the set with which we entered it.

For academic educationists we hope that we have demonstrated the fruitfulness of applying labelling theory to deviance in school. In education this perspective of deviance has been used much less frequently than other psychological and sociological theories. This neglect cannot be justified. Our own work develops no more than a few of its potentialities. So many other avenues for research in schools within the labelling theory approach remain undeveloped by us that it would be superfluous to re-state them. Additionally we have sought to show the more general value of applying the phenomeno-logical perspective to the study of classrooms. Phenomenologists are increasingly active within education (cf. Young, 1971), but there is still a severe shortage of empirical studies. Our own general con-tribution (as opposed to the more specific analysis of deviance) has been the analysis of teachers' and pupils' common-sense knowledge relating to classroom rules, which is but one part of the members' common-sense knowledge. Academic researchers have on the whole badly neglected these mundane common-sense features of life in the classroom, in spite of the renewed interest shown in classrooms by the pioneering 'micro' studies of such different writers as Holt (1964), Henry (1966), Hargreaves (1967, 1972), Kohl (1967, 1970), Jackson (1968), Rosenthal and Jacobson (1968), Smith and Geoffrey (1968), Barnes (1969), Lacey (1970), Good and Brophy (1973) and Nash (1973), all of which reveal the massive contribution made by Waller (1932). Much of this writing can be said, implicitly or explicitly, to be a symbolic interactionist analysis of classrooms and as such points to the potential scope of the application of the phenomenological perspective which poses more fundamental questions. Symbolic interactionism is limited by its own major concepts. In particular, there is a need to move beyond the highly constrictive application of the concept of 'role' to the analysis of teacher and pupil conduct, since the more fundamental questions are simply ignored in studies which use concepts such as 'role performance' or 'role conflict' or 'role socialization' as the key analytical tools. The growing preference for the concept of 'rule' in place of the concept of 'role' (Winch, 1958; Cicourel, 1970; Harré and Secord, 1972; Mischel, 1974) allows new questions to be posed and new analyses to be made. We believe that our own work on teachers' and pupils' common-sense know-ledge of classroom rules by which teachers are able to make deviance-imputations, pupils are able to recognize certain utterances as deviance-imputations, and teachers are able to utter them in the knowledge that pupils will be able to recognize them as such, makes a contribution not only to the study of deviance and of classroom deviance but also to the more general phenomenological analysis of life in classrooms. Moreover, we believe that this work can be linked with, and provide an important foundation for, symbolic interactionist writing where there is a strong emphasis on teachers and pupils as 'strategists' (cf. discussion by Hargreaves (1972), pp. 154–98). For instance, much interest has been shown in the concealment strategies of pupils and the counter-strategies adopted by teachers. Our own analysis shows that these rest upon a hitherto unexplicated common-sense knowledge, shared by teachers and pupils, that (1) certain rules are in play, that (2) each knows that the other knows these rules are in play, that (3) certain acts constitute conformity to or deviance from these rules, and that (4) the teacher will act against deviant conduct. It is on this basis that (5) pupils attempt to undermine the teacher's ability to recognize deviant acts by adopting concealment strategies, that (6) teachers develop rules for recognizing (and means for investigating) certain pupil acts as attempts to conceal deviant conduct, and that (7) pupils are able to negotiate deviance-imputations where they believe that the teacher has not directly evidenced their deviant conduct. It is through such phenomenological elaboration that the nature of the strategic work of teachers and pupils can be more adequately analysed.

In our own work in secondary schools, this shared common-sense knowledge was taken for granted by teachers and pupils. We were unable to analyse how this common-sense knowledge is acquired in the first place. Our work clearly points to the need for research work in primary schools, along the lines of the associated research currently being conducted by Anne Proctor, of St Martin's College, Lancaster, into teacher-pupil interaction during the first few weeks of a reception class in an infants' school.

Similarly, there is a need for research into the acquisition of this common-sense knowledge by new teachers. Many trainee teachers feel that large portions of their courses on the psychology and sociology of education are of little relevance to the classroom work of practising teachers. The students' pleas for more 'practical help' are usually ignored. Clearly if extensive research findings into the common-sense knowledge of experienced teachers, and its acquisition by beginning teachers, were available, then we might be in a much better position to satisfy some of the demands made by student teachers without resorting to the 'tips for teachers' that have no explicit relationship to psychological and sociological enquiry.[1]

To practising teachers our analysis of teachers' common-sense knowledge will almost certainly appear to be 'obvious'—and teachers have frequently complained that social scientists make a profession of telling them what they already know. But if we can succeed in providing a mirror in which teachers can look at themselves—and if the image in the mirror is not too distorted—then the teachers are free to decide whether the image is or is not to their liking. We would hope that in making what is taken for granted more explicit to teachers we might be helping them, should they so choose, no longer to take it for granted. There will always be a common-sense knowledge of teaching (as of any other action), but there are many forms this common-sense knowledge can take. It is here that the phenomenological researcher may be able to help the teacher to choose.

Having briefly outlined some of the general implications of our work in its relationship to other analyses of classroom life and to the directions of future research, we now wish to turn to the more practical implications of our work in connection with classroom deviance, for our research was intended primarily as a contribution to the study of deviance rather than to the phenomenological analysis of the classroom. There are, of course, some general implications of labelling theory for teachers which are not directly related to our own work. For instance, since according to labelling theory deviance rests upon the existence and enforcement of rules, the way to abolish deviance is to abolish the rules. True though this may be, it is no more possible completely to abolish rules in the classroom than it is in any other area of human life; as long as there are human relationships there will be rules regulating those relationships. More to the point is the implication that deviance will be reduced if the number of rules is reduced, and it may well be that in some schools some of the rules could be abolished without any serious consequences. If a rule is not strictly necessary or does not serve any really important purpose, might not its abolition—and the abolition of all its associated deviance—be in the interests of all? Rules are always more easily made than unmade; and the same is true of deviance. In particular, teachers might devote greater attention to examining the pupils' perspectives on rules, for they may not always understand or share the teachers' justification for rules. Research has shown (Werthman, 1963; Hargreaves, 1967) that where teachers enforce rules which are seen by some pupils as illegitimate, the enforcement of the rules may provoke an entirely unintended and unanticipated widespread deviance. Because the pupils see a rule as illegitimate does not mean that the rule must be abolished, but it does mean that the teachers should consider very carefully whether that rule is a necessary or important rule which is worth maintaining in spite of the deviance it provokes. In Britain, the enforcement of school rules against long hair for boys is a case in point. In the event most schools had to abandon or alter the rule; but this change was often made only after its enforcement had done extensive damage to teacher-pupil relationships.

The reduction of school and classroom rules to a minimum is a valuable preventive measure that teachers could take. It is because prevention is highly preferable to cure that the work of Jacob Kounin (1970) is so important. Kounin was concerned to identify those features which might explain the differential incidence of pupil deviance in lessons conducted by different teachers. It is part of the common-sense knowledge of teachers that some classes are more 'difficult' than others to all the teachers, and also that some teachers have fewer 'discipline problems' than other teachers even with the same class. Kounin's analysis is directed at the individual differences between teachers and he identifies a number of classroom managerial techniques which can increase or reduce the extent of pupil deviance. One important area is that which is described as 'movement management', which is concerned with the means by which the teacher initiates, sustains and terminates the different activities enjoined on the pupils during a lesson. Two examples are what Kounin calls 'dangles' and 'flip-flops'. A dangle occurs when the teacher begins an activity, then leaves it 'in mid-air' by turning to another activity, and then finally returns to the original activity. For instance, the teacher begins a question-and-answer session, suspends this to investigate the absence of a pupil which he has just noticed, and then returns to the question-and-answer session. A flip-flop occurs when the teacher terminates one activity, begins a second activity, and then returns to the first activity. For instance, the teacher tells the pupils to put away the spelling books and to get out the arithmetic books, and then asks the pupils about their work in spelling. Kounin shows that there is a positive correlation between the number of dangles and flip-flops and the extent of pupil deviance, and the implication is that if the teacher can reduce the number of, or entirely eliminate, dangles and flip-flops, then the extent of pupil deviance will be reduced. This analysis has a clear relationship with our own concepts of subphases in the lesson proper and the effecting of transitions between them by means of switch-signals. In our terms a flip-flop occurs when the teacher switch-signals the end of one subphase, initiates the subsequent subphase, and then jumps back into the original subphase. Our analysis would explain the increase in pupil deviance on such occasions in terms of the pupils' confusion about the rules in play, since we showed that the rules are known to be in play by pupils because they have learned that certain rules are brought into play with particular types of subphase. Different subphases have different rules, and if the pupils do not know which subphase is operative at a given time, then they do not know which rules are meant to be in play. In this respect our analysis elaborates that of Kounin, for we have given much more careful attention to the structure of switch-signals and their relationship to rules in play.

The practical implication of Kounin's work as well as our own is that we must conceptualize switch-signalling as an important social skill of teachers, the successful exercise of which can serve as an important preventive measure against deviance. Student teachers and teachers who are experiencing discipline problems could be trained to observe the successful use of switch-signalling in other teachers and to rectify their own faults in this respect. This could be particularly important with the new teacher, since here the pupils have not learned what rules are to be in play during a particular subphase, since different teachers impose different rules in the same subphase. The implication is that the new teacher should tell the pupils very clearly what rules are in play in different subphases and then switch-signal in a clear manner. Switch-signalling is simply part of the common-sense of teaching which teachers 'pick up naturally'—or fail to do. By making this common-sense knowledge more explicit, it is possible to examine it and to teach it to student teachers.

It is sometimes popularly held that labelling theory proposes that deviance would disappear if we all stopped labelling. On examination this assertion reduces to the notion that all rules should be abolished or remain unenforced. We have already stated that in our view this is absurd and impossible. We also mentioned at the beginning of the book that there has been too little research into those situations where the effect of labelling is to create effective social control rather than the promotion of deviance. It is unquestionably the case that the labelling by teachers of some pupils, or some pupil acts, as deviant ensures that the pupil will not commit such acts again. As yet it is not possible to specify the conditions under which the labelling can have positive effects (reduction or elimination of deviant conduct) rather than negative effects (the development of deviant identity and an increase in deviant conduct). Given that preventive measures are imperfect and that some deviant conduct will inevitably occur in classrooms, which are the teacher reactions to such deviance that are most likely to reduce subsequent deviance? Among practising teachers there appears to be little more than vague folk-wisdom ('Well, what I do . . .'), and among social scientists there are the humanistic approaches of writers such as Redl and Bettelheim as well as the (to us) morally repugnant applications of behaviouristic psychology in the form of techniques of behaviour modification.

Since labelling theory offers an analysis of how people come to be deviant, it also potentially offers some possible methods of reducing deviance. One possibility is that acts rather than persons should be the focal point of the labelling. For if the act rather than the person is subject to the definition of deviance, then the offender has some means of 'normalizing' his conduct, that is, of dissociating his act from his 'real' self so that his act is seen to be 'out of character'. It is by such normalization or neutralization techniques—'I wasn't myself when I did that'—that most of us can cope with the many minor acts of deviance that we commit in our everyday lives. They are not merely excuses for deviant conduct; they help us to maintain our self-image as essentially non-deviant. It is when a person believes that he really is deviant that the commission of further congruent deviant acts is facilitated. The implication is that if the teacher insists on labelling only the act and carefully avoids labelling the person as deviant, then the pupil will find it easier to define his deviant acts as atypical of himself and will find it easier to avoid such conduct in the future. On the other hand, if he is labelled as a deviant person by the teacher, then the pupil is more likely to type himself as a deviant person and indulge in those congruent deviant acts that the teacher expects of him and that he expects of himself. Moreover, if the teacher can focus on the act rather than the person, then he is less likely to type the pupil as deviant—and therefore less likely to communicate his typing to the pupil—and the less he types the pupil as deviant, the easier the teacher will find it to focus on the act rather than the person. In other words, if teachers could systematically, and from an early stage, focus their deviant definitions on acts rather than persons, then many of those processes which facilitate deviant pupil careers, especially the teacher's typing of a pupil as deviant and the pupil's self-typing as deviant, could be powerfully inhibited. This means that the teacher would need to develop a highly self-conscious, sceptical attitude to staffroom discussion and pre-labelling of certain pupils as deviant and to the use he makes of the sibling phenomenon, both of which we have seen to be important factors in the teacher's typing of deviant pupils. A teacher cannot forget what he hears in the staffroom, nor can he forget his experience with a pupil's elder brother(s); but he may be able to reduce their influence upon him.

Our analysis of typing by teachers shows that within a week or two after first meeting a new pupil many teachers are prepared to speculate that he will possibly or probably become a deviant pupil. It is not surprising that they should anticipate that some pupils may emerge as 'difficult', but this speculation nevertheless sets in motion certain processes such as surveillance ('I'd better keep an eye on him') as well as attempts to confirm and elaborate the speculative typing. Thus the sibling phenomenon alerts the teachers to the fact that a pupil may prove to be 'difficult' like his brother and when he does behave in that way, the sibling phenomenon explains the 'difficult' conduct and apparently confirms the reasonableness of the teachers' provisional typing. Of course the teachers hope that their speculations are wrong and are willing to de-type and re-type the pupil in the light of his conduct, but it does seem possible that in subtle ways the teachers selectively search for supportive evidence of deviance and perhaps even communicate their typing to the pupil. Certainly once the deviant typing is elaborated and stabilized, then the teachers will not be easily persuaded that a pupil is non-deviant. At this point the focus is on deviant persons rather than deviant acts, and the deviant pupil is assigned a special status and subjected to particular treatments, as we saw in chapter 8. All this can facilitate the pupil's self-typing as deviant and undermine his motivation to change which he believes will be discounted by the teachers. The implication is that the teachers might be able to inhibit the development of deviant careers—which is what they want to do—if they can avoid typing a pupil as a stabilized deviant, which probably means actively avoiding the development of speculative and elaborative deviant typings. This does appear to happen, though the best evidence comes not from our own research, where there was little emphasis on individual differences between teachers, but from the study of Jordan (1974). This is not so much an application of labelling theory, but a symbolic interactionist examination of the perspectives of a group of deviant boys and of their teachers. In reporting this work we shall take the liberty of reformulating the analysis in a way that is compatible with our own concepts, just as we did with Kounin's work. Jordan outlines two types of teacher which we might term as 'deviance-provocative' and 'deviance-insulative'. The first type of teacher finds that the deviant pupils behave in highly deviant ways in his classroom and his handling of them serves to exacerbate their deviance. The second type of teacher finds that the same pupils present relatively few problems in his classroom and his handling of them serves to inhibit their deviance.

The deviance-provocative teacher believes that the pupils he defines as deviant do not want to work in school and will do anything to avoid it. He thinks it is impossible to provide conditions under which they will work; if they are ever to work then the pupils must change. In disciplinary matters he sees his interaction with these pupils as a contest or battle—and one that he must win. He is unable to 'de-fuse' difficult situations; he frequently issues ultimatums and becomes involved in confrontations. He considers these pupils to be 'anti-authority' and is confident that they are determined not to conform to the classroom rules. The deviants are neglected in lessons and punished inconsistently, whereas overtly preferential treatment is accorded to the conformist pupils. He expects the pupils to behave badly and makes many negative evaluative comments upon them, both to them as well as to colleagues in the staffroom. The pupils are referred to a higher authority when they refuse to comply. The derogation of and laughing at pupils is common, and he is highly suspicious of them because his experience has shown that they cannot be trusted. He avoids contact with such pupils outside the classroom. The pupils are blamed for their misconduct. Since he believes the pupils are resistant, hostile and committed to their deviance, they are seen as potential saboteurs and he refuses to believe that any signs of improvement are authentic.

The deviance-insulative teacher believes that these pupils, like all pupils, really want to work. If the pupils do not work, the conditions are assumed to be at fault. He believes that these conditions can be changed and that it is his responsibility to initiate that change. In disciplinary matters he has a clear set of classroom rules which are made explicit to the pupils. He is firm with pupils and believes that this is what they prefer. He makes an effort to avoid any kind of favouritism or preferential or differential treatment; he also avoids confrontations with pupils. He rarely makes negative evaluative comments on pupils who misbehave. When he punishes deviant conduct, he allows the pupils to 'save face'. He does not derogate them in the classroom—or in the staffroom where he often springs to the defence of a deviant pupil who is being discussed. He is highly optimistic, in contrast to the fatalism of the deviance-provocative teacher, and confidently assumes that pupils will behave well and co-operate with him. He perceives all the pupils as potential contributors to the lesson and sees the unpredictability of the deviant pupils as a potential source of change. He encourages any signs of improvement. Whereas the deviance-provocative teacher dislikes the deviant pupils and considers himself unfortunate in having to teach them, the deviance-insulative teacher claims to like all children and considers it a privilege to work with any pupil. He respects and cares about the deviant pupils and tells them so. He enjoys meeting them informally outside the classroom, where he can joke with them and take an interest in their personal problems. He trusts them.

In our own work we did not detect such sharp differences between the teachers—possibly because our main interest was not in finding such differences. Nevertheless, the differences specified by Jordan are relatable to our own analysis. It is clear that what we have called the deviance-provocative teacher swings inconsistently between morality and pragmatism. At times he will be highly moralistic about an instance of deviant conduct and will 'make an issue out of it'. At other times he will be highly pragmatic, abandoning the deviant pupils by extensive use of avoidance-of-provocation. These pupils are given a highly stabilized deviant typing; change is not expected and any signs of improvement are distrusted and discounted. As the deviant typing is so highly resistant to change, reactions to deviant conduct are focused not on the act but on the person, who is derogated. The deviant typing is fully communicated to the pupil. In contrast, the deviance-insulative teacher is a pragmatist in that he avoids disrupting the time-flow for minor deviant conduct, but he does not take this pragmatism to the point of extensive use of avoidance-of-provocation with deviants. He is a moralist in that serious misconduct is dealt with consistently and fairly, but he avoids confrontations with pupils about his authority. More significantly this type of teacher is on principle opposed to the notion of a stabilized deviant typing, which he never applies to any pupil. He does not ignore the deviant conduct of these pupils, but he constantly believes that they are 'not really like that'. It is therefore natural that he should focus on acts rather than persons and make an active search for signs of non-deviance to support his belief in their non-deviant identity. The deviance-insulative teacher simply does not make the usual transition from the imputation of deviant acts to the imputation that the person is deviant. For him, the recognition that pupils commit deviant acts does not provide grounds for defining those offenders as deviant persons. In other words, his common-sense knowledge of deviance has an unusual structure in that he does not follow the common logic whereby if a person commits deviant acts he is therefore a deviant person. This has crucial consequences. The deviance-provocative teacher has accepted this logic and so interprets signs of improvement as inauthentic because such an interpretation is compatible with his stabilized deviant typing. To the deviance-insulative teacher, who never develops a stabilized deviant typing, it is the deviant conduct which is seen as inauthentic and atypical and the signs of improvements are interpreted as expressions of what these pupils 'really' are and what they really want to be. The difference between the two types of teacher is not merely that one is more open to the possibility of type transformation than the other. That to the deviance-insulative teacher deviant pupils never become stabilized deviants in the first place is the outcome of a different common-sense knowledge of classroom deviance and a different set of wider assumptions about human nature and education—a different 'philosophy of life' and a different 'philosophy of education'.

The deviance-insulative teacher, it appears, would not take issue with the advice offered by Tannenbaum (1938), one of the earliest labelling theorists.

There is a gradual shift from the definition of the specific acts as evil to a definition of the individual as evil, so that all his acts come to be looked upon with suspicion. In the process of identification his companions, hang-outs, play, speech, income, all his conduct, the personality itself, become subject to scrutiny and question. From the community's point of view, the individual who used to do bad and mischievous things has now become a bad and unredeemable human being. From the individual's point of view there has taken place a similar change. He has gone slowly from a sense of grievance and injustice, of being unduly mistreated and punished, to a recognition that the definition of him as a human being is different from that of other boys in the neighbourhood, his school, street, community. This recognition on his part becomes a process of self-identification. . . . The young delinquent becomes bad because he is defined as bad and because he is not believed if he is good. There is a persistent demand for consistency in character. . . . The process of making the criminal, therefore, is a process of tagging, defining, identifying, segregating, making conscious and self-conscious; it becomes a way of stimulating, suggesting, emphasizing and evoking the very traits that are complained of. . . . The person becomes the thing he is described as being. Nor does it seem to matter whether the valuation is made by those who would punish or by those who would reform. In either case the emphasis is upon the conduct that is disapproved of. . . . Their very enthusiasm defeats their aim. The harder they work to reform the evil, the greater the evil grows under their hands. The persistent suggestion, with whatever good intentions, works mischief, because it leads to bringing out the bad behaviour that it would suppress. The way out is through a refusal to dramatize the evil. The less said about it the better. The more said about something else, still better.

The deviance-insulative teacher has already accepted this advice, and much else besides, as part of his common-sense knowledge of classroom deviance. The labelling theorist is making explicit what some teachers—but not all teachers—already know.

There is a massive psychological and sociological literature which can be used to explain why some pupils are 'deviant', 'difficult' or 'maladjusted' in classrooms. We do not dispute the 'truth' that is embedded in that literature, but we would assert that this is only a partial truth. We have shown that this social scientific literature has been taken over by teachers to 'explain' deviant conduct and that the social scientific vocabulary has become part of the explanatory vocabulary of teachers, whether it is sociological ('He comes from a bad home, you know') or clinical-psychological ('He's maladjusted, you know'). The difficulty is that this literature, whilst helping teachers to account for deviance in classrooms, offers relatively little practical help. On the contrary, it is our impression that it increases the teachers' sense of fatalism and powerlessness, for there is indeed very little they can do to change home environments and they cannot make claims to be psychotherapists. Labelling theory, and analyses such as ours which derive from it, also expose no more than part of what we call the truth. It provides no panacea for classroom deviance; on the contrary it asserts that deviance, like rules, is an essential feature of social life everywhere. But it does provide an analysis of classroom deviance which contributes not only another explanation of the phenomenon but also some insights which can help to generate means of reducing deviance. Social scientists are primarily interested in explanations; teachers, student teachers, and teacher trainers are primarily interested in solutions. We hope that we have interested both groups and provided a link between one kind of explanation and some kinds of solution.

Notes

Chapter 1   A critical introduction to labelling theory

1 The key authority on scientific paradigms is Kuhn (1962). For the discussion of different paradigms in sociology, see Wilson (1970), Douglas (1971) and Filmer (1972), and in social psychology, see Harré and Secord (1972) and Armisted (1974). There are considerable variations in the terminology used by different writers. For instance, Wilson contrasts 'normative' with 'interpretive' conceptions of interaction, whereas Harré and Secord contrast 'mechanistic' or 'behaviouristic' models of man with 'anthropomorphic' or 'ethogenic' models. In our own discussion we have preferred the terms 'positivistic' and 'phenomenological' since these appear to be the ones that are most widely used.

2 On the problematic status of official statistics of deviant behaviour see Cicourel and Kitsuse (1963a) and Douglas (1967). There is now an extensive sociological literature documenting the social construction of official statistics, summary and discussion of which may be found in Box (1971) and Bottomley (1973).

3 It is not surprising that labelling theorists should neglect this attenuative or deterrent consequence of labelling, for one of their main objectives is to document the neglected alternative possibility, namely the amplificatory effect of labelling. But it can reasonably be claimed that labelling theorists have then neglected the traditional wisdom that social control inhibits deviance, as some critics (e.g. Mankoff, 1971) have noted. The 'fashion' in social science is perhaps changing, and the pendulum swinging away from labelling theory. We ourselves would recognize the truth contained in both positions, but our main interest as phenomenologists is in the ways in which these positions are held by members. Our own work demonstrates that the teachers certainly believe that their attempts at social control in the classroom situation can indeed reduce the incidence of deviant conduct, but they also are aware of the amplificatory consequences of labelling as is shown in chapters 6 and 7. That both these theoretical positions, and the conflict between them, are embedded in the common-sense knowledge of teachers is demonstrated in chapter 8.

4 Those who have alleged that labelling theorists have failed to give an adequate causal analysis of deviant behaviour include Gibbs (1966), Mankoff (1971) and Taylor, Walton and Young (1973). The criticism

has some force in that labelling theorists are sometimes unclear about the causal status of their theory. The difficulty is that it depends upon what one means by the term 'causal analysis'. In terms of Matza's (1964) distinction between 'hard' and 'soft' determinism, most labelling theorists would show a strong preference for the latter variety. Whereas there is a consensus in favour of causal analysis among the positivists, there exists a variety of views among social scientists working within the phenomenological paradigm. Some phenomenologists would appear to reject any attempt to construct a causal analysis of deviance.

5 The earliest critic of labelling theory to point out this logical flaw in Becker's analysis was Gibbs (1966).

6 Paradoxically, this logical flaw passes unnoticed by Becker, in spite of his recognition of the significance of self-labelling—'Even though no one else discovers the non-conformity or enforces the rules against it, the individual who has committed the impropriety may himself act as enforcer. He may brand himself as deviant . . . ' (1963, p. 31). The importance of self-labelling is noted by Gibbs (1966), Lorber (1967) and Mankoff (1971), though only Lorber (1967) recognizes the subtlety and range of the concept. Pollner (1974) examines the ethnomethodological implications of this flaw.

7 This is what might be called a paradigmatic criticism, i.e. comes from a different paradigm rather than from within the same paradigm. The critical debate between different paradigms is often sterile because each paradigm makes different sets of assumptions which permit certain questions and exclude others. So some of the positivistic criticisms of labelling theory are rejected by labelling theorists because such questions are not legitimate or relevant questions from within the paradigm they have adopted. Thus there is a difficulty in integrating labelling theory with structural explanations of deviance. The critique of labelling theory by Taylor, Walton and Young (1973), who have an apparent preference for structural explanations, would have been clearer and perhaps fairer had they distinguished internal (i.e. from within the same paradigm) criticisms from external (i.e. from a different paradigm) criticisms. We ourselves would not a priori reject such structural explanations, but as phenomenologists our major interest would be in the use of such structural explanations by members (including, of course, sociologist members such as Taylor, Walton and Young) as ways of making deviance accountable.

8 See, for example, the debate between Denzin, and Zimmerman and Wieder, in Douglas (1971); see also Warren and Johnson (1972).

9 For example, see Cicourel (1972).

10 For example, Sykes and Matza (1957), Matza (1964), Scheff (1968) and Goffman (1971).

Chapter 2 Deviance and education

1 The psychometric approach has been predominantly concerned with the measurement of individual differences with respect to ability, personality,

etc. Clinical psychologists use and develop these measures as diagnostic tools. Traditionally, clinical psychologists have used various forms of psychotherapy, but in recent years they have often turned to behaviour modification techniques which are based upon behaviourist psychology, not psychometrics or theories of psychopathology or psychotherapy. The psychological approach to deviance is not easy to summarize in a short space without some degree of distortion, which is a common fault of sociologists' descriptions of the psychological perspective. We are not, of course, offering a critique of the psychological approach; it is being mentioned by us for contrastive purposes only. Our simplified picture of this literature is, we think, preferable to ignoring it completely.

2 Fisher's (1972) research, entitled 'Stigma and deviant careers in school', would appear to be an apparent exception to this. In our view the author misunderstands and distorts labelling theory, and develops an argument that is replete with illogicalities and other deficiencies. In this note we can do no more than point out some of the most outstanding defects of the work. Fisher attempts to test in a school situation the 'claim by deviance theorists that a public deviant label generates special and consequential difficulties for the person'. In fact what labelling theorists assert is that the application of a deviant label may create problems for the offender which may be solved by the commission of further deviance. Fisher transforms this notion into a hypothesis, which is never explicitly formulated, that pupils who are delinquents on probation (i.e. the deviant label) will experience special problems (which are not at any point specified or examined) and these will be reflected in the performance assessments of these pupils by teachers (though why this should be so is never revealed). In other words, Fisher attempts to test an inadequately formulated hypothesis, based on a distortion of labelling theory, by positivistic methods (namely, correlations between performance scores and delinquent status) which seem inappropriate to the problem. He declines to make an analysis which is congruent with the process view so dominant in labelling theory; it is perhaps for this reason that he utterly neglects the relevant contributions of Werthman (1963) and Cicourel and Kitsuse (1968), and is concerned with a court label (i.e. official delinquent) rather than the teachers' own labels for deviant pupils or the teachers' reactions to the court label, which would be central phenomena for a labelling theorist. It is perhaps understandable that a positivist should misunderstand and misapply theory in this way; but it is astonishing that his work should betray so many deficiencies by his own positivistic criteria. For instance, there is a confusion between cause and correlation; there is a complete absence of appropriate statistical tests; the measures of ability are crude; there are serious deficiencies in the assignment of pupils to control and experimental groups. In short, we completely reject this work as an adequate test or application of labelling theory, and so we also reject the partial support of labelling theory that is offered in the results.

3 Cf. Glaser and Strauss (1967);

So often in journals we read a highly empirical study which at its conclusion has a tacked-on explanation taken from a logically deduced theory. The author tries to give his data a more general sociological meaning as well as to account for or interpret what he found. He uses this strategy because he has not been trained to generate a theory from the data he is reporting.

In our experience this is also strikingly true of higher degree theses. In effect the creativity of the young researcher is often stultified. Similarly, many research assistants become 'slaves' who collect data for their superior, the 'theorist'. Such forms of research training are, in our view, inherently deficient and destructive of talent.

4 See note 6 (this chapter) and note 1 (chapter 1).
5 See Goldthorpe (1973) and Benson (1974).
6 The distinction between qualitative and quantitative methods is in fact not a sharp one, in that so-called quantitative methodologists must employ so-called qualitative methodologies to code their data into quantitative forms. The particular interest in qualitative analysis among phenomenologists is well represented by Bruyn (1966), Garfinkel (1967), McCall and Simmons (1969), Filstead (1970), Denzin (1970), Douglas (1971, 1972) and Lofland (1971). See also Churchill (1971) for a programmatic statement of ethno-methodological interest in quantitative methodologies.
7 A recent example is the work of Nash (1973).

Chapter 3   Rules in school

1 This is not to say that all the rules in the criminological model are written down in a carefully codified form. Most of these rules are written down, at least in the form of cases and judgments, but there is enormous variation in that many rules are left implicit in such cases and judgments whereas others are carefully codified into 'laws'.
2 For an example of an attempt to construct such a set of guidelines in a different context see Scott (1968).
3 On this issue of topic and resource see Zimmerman and Pollner (1971). See also Wieder (1974) for an attempt to explicate the researcher's common-sense resources as a topic for analysis.
4 The need for greater theoretical and empirical analysis of interpretive rules, which are neglected in traditional sociological formulations, has been cogently argued by Cicourel (1970). Cicourel's own developing thinking in this respect is reflected in his change of terminology from 'basic and normative rules' in the early version of the paper (1970, 1972) to 'interpretive procedures and normative rules' in the later version (1973b). We entirely agree with Coulter's (1973) comment that 'Cicourel's own inventory of "interpretive rules" looks hardly like rules members might formulate for conceptualizing concrete actions or utterances; in fact they are simply Schutz's postulates for orderly intersubjectivity'. Having come to the same conclusion independently, we are attempting to rectify this in our own work, especially by the concepts of 'evidential

rules' and 'evidential strategies' in chapter 5. We use the terms 'interpretive rules' and 'interpretive work' in an embracing way to cover both
the more universal, fundamental and invariant features examined by
Schutz and the (as it were) less basic, more specifically contextual
interpretive work undertaken by teachers in making deviance-imputations. In neglecting the former in favour of the latter, we are aware that
we have also failed to specify the relationship between the two. We
hope to rectify this later in a separate publication.

5 That pupils frequently react to teacher utterances of which they are not
the intended target is one example of the 'ripple effect' as defined by
Kounin and Gump (1958).

Chapter 4 Rules in context

1 This is Goffman's (1963) term, and refers to picking one's nose, cleaning
one's fingernails, various forms of 'fidgeting', daydreaming and dozing.
In an auto-involvement a person is excessively self-absorbed at the
expense of the attention that should be paid to other persons present.

2 This problem has been noted by other writers:

> Any series of actions which a man may perform can be brought
> within the scope of some formula or other if we are prepared to make
> it sufficiently complicated. Yet, that a man's actions might be
> interpreted as an application of a given formula, is in itself no
> guarantee that he is in fact applying that formula (Winch, 1958, p. 29).

> In sociology there has long been a tendency to pay lip service to
> 'norms of action' whilst leaving it quite unclear how such norms or
> rules are grounded in everyday courses of action. As soon as one
> focuses upon that issue, it becomes clear that we are very ignorant of
> the presuppositions of rule use, and the ways in which rules are used
> not only to guide conduct but to bring conduct into some scheme of
> interpretation. Moreover, there are vexed issues about the ways in
> which an analyst might go about *formulating* rules that members
> might be claimed to be following. One must avoid treating action-
> *in-accord-with*-a-rule as action-*governed-by*-a-rule, since one can
> easily bring some course of observed activity under the auspices of a
> rule-like formulation without such a formulation expressing the state
> of knowledge of the member doing the activity (Coulter, 1973, p. 142).

> An analyst faced with the task of inspecting an array of classified
> behaviours of residents in order to generate theoretically a set of rules
> or conditions which would produce those patterned behaviours could
> easily do so. He would find, however, that without the guidance of
> resident talk, he could have many competitive sets of rules and
> conditions, and he would have no way of arguing which single set
> among the many were, in fact, operative in the setting (Wieder, 1974,
> p. 169).

Chapter 5 The imputation of deviance

1 See note 4 to chapter 3.
2 Schutz and Luckmann (1974) suggest that when persons engage in activity they automatically insert themselves in a structure of incompatibilities, of which three kinds are distinguished: ontological, historical and biographical.
3 This is not to say that pupils always fall asleep deliberately. Clearly, pupils may fall asleep unintentionally, simply because they are tired, and in so doing they need not know how, i.e. by what rules, it is possible to fall asleep. However, when pupils intend to fall asleep they generally follow implemental rules for doing so; for example, shutting the eyes, finding a place to rest the head, and so on.
4 Cf. Alfred Schutz (1970), especially pp. 35–45.
5 Retrospective interpretation is defined by Kitsuse (1962) as 'a process by which the subject re-interprets the individual's past behaviour in the light of the new information concerning his deviance'. For a more extensive treatment of the method of this interpretation see Garfinkel (1967), especially chapter 3.
6 An adequate analysis of this example would clearly require us to specify how a teacher knows that a question he puts to pupils is an 'easy' question. This is another aspect of the teacher's common-sense knowledge which is not in itself directly relevant to our analysis. Yet the application of the evidential rule hinges upon this common-sense knowledge in this example. In other words what we refer to as the teacher's 'common-sense knowledge of deviance' constantly interpenetrates with the much wider common-sense knowledge of teachers. For us to demarcate the 'common-sense knowledge of deviance' is an artificial and analytic procedure. We shall argue in chapter 9 for wider phenomenological studies of the common-sense knowledge of teachers; without this, our own analysis suffers inevitable limitations in places.
7 See Scott and Lyman (1968, 1970) for discussion and analysis of 'accounts', which they define as 'linguistic device(s) employed whenever an action is subject to valuative inquiry. . . . By an account, then, we refer to a statement made by a social actor to explain unanticipated or untoward behaviour.' Cf. Mills (1940), Sykes and Matza (1957) and Matza (1964).

Chapter 6 A theory of typing

1 There have been three major approaches to this topic. The phenomenologists have drawn extensively on Alfred Schutz's work on types and this has been linked with the sociological/phenomenological approach to motives (Blum and McHugh, 1971). Social psychologists have approached the topic in the form of person perception, where there have been some major phenomenological contributions (Heider, 1958; From, 1971). Heider provided the foundations for attribution theory in social psychology (Jones, 1972). The third approach is based on the work of George Kelly (1955) on personal construct theory. Each strand has been

developed with a quite astonishing neglect of the other two. The relationship between these three strands is far too complex to analyse in a note. In this book we have drawn most heavily on the first of the three approaches.

2 For some references, see Hargreaves (1972), pp. 156–8.

3 Our findings here come as no surprise; they fully support the literature. We shall take two of these many studies. Hallworth (1961, 1962), in a psychometric study, analysed teachers' personality ratings of their pupils. Two main factors emerged. The first factor, based on the teacher's implicit question, 'How does this child get on with me?', is called the factor of conscientiousness and reliability. It includes traits such as emotional stability, trustworthiness, persistence, co-operation with teacher, and maturity. The second factor, which arises from the teacher's implicit question, 'How does this pupil get on with other pupils?', is called the factor of extraversion, and includes such traits as cheerfulness, sense of humour and sociability. From our point of view this pioneering study has one important failure: it imposes certain constructs or terms in the rating schedule given to the teachers, and tells us little about the teacher's natural or everyday constructs that he uses in his own thinking or conversation. This fault is remedied in Nash's (1973) study, using Kelly's repertory grid test, which elicits the teachers' own constructs in the form of bipolar opposites. With an extremely small sample of secondary school teachers, he showed that the main constructs are:

Bright	— dull
Lively	— lumpish
Likeable	— less likeable
Well-behaved	— less well-behaved
Sociable	— less sociable.

There is clearly a heavy overlap with Hallworth's findings. Nash claims that his approach is phenomenological, but this is a claim we would dispute. Having obtained the constructs from the teachers, Nash then makes comparisons between teachers without checking that the constructs have the same meanings for the teachers, and he also quantifies the constructs in a highly dubious way. More important from our point of view, Nash shows no interest in how these constructs are arrived at by the teachers, but instead spends a whole chapter reporting his own interpretive observations of pupils in the light of the constructs elicited from the teachers. 'The child in the classroom was observed as objectively as possible and . . . his behaviour was reinterpreted as it seemed to be perceived by his teacher' (pp. 29–30). Apart from the inherent absurdity of such a practice, it simply does not help us to discover either the teacher's meanings of the constructs or the way in which they were generated. Nash compounds and confuses his own common-sense knowledge with that of the teacher, instead of attempting to explicate the teacher's common-sense knowledge by analysing the meanings of, and grounds for, as well as the relationship between, the teacher's constructs. Since our interest was in providing a dynamic and process theory of typing, we used the interview method, which seems more appropriate to that purpose than the time-consuming and cumbersome repertory grid technique.

4 This clearly draws upon George Kelly's (1955) notion of the layman as an 'incipient scientist'.

> As a scientist, man seeks to predict, and thus control, the course of events. It follows, then, that the constructs which he formulates are intended to aid him in his predictive efforts . . . each construct represents a pair of rival hypotheses, either of which may be applied to a new element which the person seeks to construe.

A much more extensive treatment of this notion is provided in the work of Garfinkel (1967).

5 We had a serious methodological problem here in that we were unable to make very frequent checks on teachers' developing typings without taking the risk that our questions might actually affect the process of typing. Teachers are not normally subjected to such questions and we were anxious not to create a special research-effect by regular or repeated interviews about these first year pupils. We confined ourselves to two interviews, one in September and one in January, and we did not warn the teachers in September that we would repeat the process in January.

6 Seaver (1973) shows that what we call the sibling phenomenon can create self-fulfilling prophecies with respect to academic attainment.

7 This distinction rests upon a distinction between the covert definition of an act as deviant and the overt reaction to that act. Further analysis will be provided in chapter 8.

Chapter 7 The typing of deviant pupils

1 This notion is a common one in labelling theory. Becker (1963) draws upon Everett Hughes's (1945) distinction between 'master' and 'auxiliary' characteristics. Lofland (1969) writes:

> One of the clustered categories is singled out and treated as the most important and significant feature of the person . . . being dealt with. It is seen as defining the character. . . . That is, there comes to be a *pivotal category* that defines 'who this person is'. . . . The phenomenon of humans adopting a category as pivotal and scrutinizing all other categories in terms of their consistency with it, implies, in practice, that whatever is taken as pivotal *is* Actor—*is* his essential nature or core being.

The topic is also extensively explored by Matza (1969).

2 See note 5 to chapter 5 for a note on retrospective interpretations. Lofland (1969) writes:

> There can begin a process of biographical reconstruction. Whatever may have been the pre-existing selection of facts from the Actor's life

line that supported a view by Others of him as a pivotal normal, there now begins a re-examination of that life line to discover if these selected biographical events are consistent with the prospective reclassification. Efforts are made to render the known facts consistent, either through discounting (or redefining the significance of) what is known, or through undertaking to discover additional facts that support the new imputation.

Many of the features of the stabilized deviant typing could in a similar way be supported with references to the labelling theory literature. Readers who are familiar with this literature will recognize the extent of our debt to it. Readers who are not familiar with the literature will gain more from reading it directly than from reading our notes on it.

Chapter 8　Reactions to deviance

1 The distinction between intervention and treatments is, of course, an analytical one. We do not mean to suggest that the teacher is always conscious of making two distinct decisions. Subsequent discussion will show that, for instance, a non-intervention decision is made because of anticipated problems of treatment.

2 On the implications of sociological theories of deviance for intervention decisions, see Schur (1973).

3 We are fascinated by the relationship between common-sense formulations of deviance and social scientific formulations of deviance. On the one hand, social scientists may be said to derive their theories from 'hunches' embedded in the common-sense knowledge they share with many other non-social scientist members of society. On the other hand, the social scientific theories are then fed back to lay members of society and thus extend and emphasize the common-sense theories from which they were originally drawn. It is perhaps because social scientific theories draw selectively upon certain common-sense notions, that members of society (and social scientists themselves) respond favourably to certain social scientific theories, because they can then be used to legitimate positions which were originally taken up on common-sense grounds. Systematic sociological examination of this topic is urgently needed, not only in the area of deviance, but also in the area of education, since teachers are subjected during their training to courses in social science which may have an important impact on their subsequent common-sense knowledge about education. See also note 3 to chapter 1.

4 That persons will deviate so long as nothing occurs to prevent them from so doing is a major assumption of control theory (Hirschi, 1969, Box, 1971). See also note 3 to chapter 1.

5 Pupils' perceptions of teachers' motives or justifications for the use of the avoidance-of-provocation technique appear to be accurate.

I.　Why do some teachers not take action when they see that you are doing wrong?
P.　Well, some teachers wait till everybody's gone out, then they'll just call you back and have a talk with you, see why you're messing

about and all that. It depends which teacher that it is. Mr ——, I think that he more or less does it then [when it happens] but most teachers, soft teachers like, if they brought it up in front of the class you just start shouting back at them and take no notice of them. But if they say 'Come here' when everybody's gone out—like a teacher started talking to me today, after everybody had went out—you listen to him, just see what he has to say. They're at it, 'Why do you mess about and shout out?' and they say, 'Well don't do it again next week. Try your best.'

I.   But why doesn't he do it when it happens?

P.   Well, he's disturbing all the rest. I don't know if it's right, this, but it could be that he's disturbing all the class, and he can get it through to you better on your own afterwards. It depends how bad it is. Some teachers might see you throw a rubber, or talking, or summat, and they don't bother. They'll just look at you, they'll just look down on you like this. You know that they're watching you, so you just shut up until they're not looking. If it's owt serious, I think they'd come out with it straight away, get on to you straight away.

Chapter 9   Some implications

1 The 'tips for teachers' provided by the tutor rest upon his own common-sense knowledge of deviance (what constitutes a typical deviant act, the phase and relational rules with their underpinning implemental rules, the rules for accomplishing deviant acts and for concealing deviant acts, evidential rules and strategies, methods of imputing deviance, etc.) which he has acquired through his own experience. But the student teachers to whom these 'tips' are communicated share only part of this knowledge derived from their experience as former pupils. It is therefore difficult for the student either to understand or to apply the 'tip' because he has still to acquire the common-sense knowledge upon which it rests. Even where no explicit formulation of this common-sense knowledge is available to the student—which awaits the further explorations of researchers—the student could be encouraged in his conversations with, and observations of, practising teachers to make an explicit attempt to uncover the common-sense knowledge which serves as the foundation for the social skills and actions of the experienced teacher.

Bibliographical index

Figures in square brackets refer to page numbers in this book.

Armisted, N. (ed.) (1974), *Reconstructing Social Psychology*, Penguin. [265]
Bailey, R. V. and Young, J. (eds) (1973), *Contemporary Social Problems in Britain*, Saxon House. [6]
Barnes, D. (1969), *Language, the Learner and the School*, Penguin. [254]
Becker, H. S. (1963), *Outsiders: Studies in the Sociology of Deviance*, Free Press. [3, 4, 7, 8, 12, 21, 266, 272]
Becker, H. S. (ed.) (1964), *The Other Side*, Free Press.
Becker, H. S. (1974), 'Labeling theory reconsidered', in Rock and McIntosh (eds) (1974). [10]
Belson, W. A. (1968), 'The extent of stealing by London boys and some of its origins', *Advancement of Science*, vol. 25, no. 124. [17]
Benson, D. (1974), 'A revolution in sociology', *Sociology*, vol. 8, no. 1, pp. 125–9. [268]
Blum, A. and McHugh, P. (1971), 'The social ascription of motives', *American Sociological Review*, vol. 36, pp. 98–109. [270]
Blumer, H. (1966), 'Sociological implications of the thought of G. H. Mead', *American Journal of Sociology*, vol. 71, pp. 535–48. [10]
Bottomley, A. K. (1973), *Decisions in the Penal Process*, Robertson. [265]
Box, S. (1971), *Deviance, Reality and Society*, Holt, Rinehart & Winston. [265, 273]
Bruyn, S. T. (1966), *The Human Perspective in Sociology*, Prentice-Hall. [268]
Cannon, C. (1971), 'The culture of delinquency', *Times Educational Supplement*, 13 August. [17]
Carson, W. G. and Wiles, P. (eds) (1971), *Crime and Delinquency in Britain*, Robertson.
Churchill, L. (1971), 'Ethnomethodology and measurement', *Social Forces*, vol. 50, pp. 182–91. [268]
Cicourel, A. V. (1964), *Method and Measurement in Sociology*, Free Press. [7]
Cicourel, A. V. (1968), *The Social Organization of Juvenile Justice*, Wiley. [7, 18]
Cicourel, A. V. (1970), 'Basic and normative rules in the negotiation of status and role', in Sudnow, D. (ed.) (1972), *Studies in Social Interaction*, Free Press (also in Dreitzel, H. P. (ed.) (1970), *Recent Sociology, No. 2*, Collier-Macmillan). [254, 268]

Cicourel, A. V. (1972), 'Delinquency and the attribution of responsibility', in Scott, R. and Douglas, J. D. (eds) (1972), *Theoretical Perspectives on Deviance*, Basic Books. [266, 268]

Cicourel, A. V. (1973a), *Cognitive Sociology*, Penguin. [7]

Cicourel, A. V. (1973b), 'Interpretive procedures and normative rules in the negotiation of status and role', in *Cognitive Sociology* (1973). [7, 268]

Cicourel, A. V. and Kitsuse, J. I. (1963a), 'A note on the uses of official statistics', *Social Problems*, vol. 11, pp. 131–9. [7, 18, 265]

Cicourel, A. V. and Kitsuse, J. I. (1963b), *The Educational Decision Makers*, Bobbs-Merrill. [7, 18]

Cicourel, A. V. and Kitsuse, J. I. (1968), 'The social organization of the high school and deviant adolescent careers', in Rubington and Weinberg (eds) (1968) (also in Open University, 1971). [18, 267]

Clegg, A. B. (1962), 'Delinquency and discipline: the role of the school', *Education*, vol. 119, pp. 1239–40. [17]

Cloward, R. A. and Ohlin, L. E. (1960), *Delinquency and Opportunity: A Theory of Delinquent Gangs*, Free Press. [17]

Cohen, A. K. (1955), *Delinquent Boys*, Free Press. [17]

Cohen, S. (ed.) (1971), *Images of Deviance*, Penguin. [6]

Coulter, J. (1973), *Approaches to Insanity*, Robertson. [7, 268,269]

Denzin, N. K. (ed.) (1970), *Sociological Methods: A Source Book*, Butterworth. [93, 268]

Denzin, N. K. (1971), 'Symbolic interactionism and ethnomethodology: a proposed synthesis', in Douglas (ed.) (1971). [93, 266]

Denzin, N. K. (1974), 'The methodological implications of symbolic interaction for the study of deviance', *British Journal of Sociology*, vol. 25, no. 3, pp. 269–82. [7]

Douglas, J. D. (1967), *Social Meanings of Suicide*, Princeton University Press. [7, 265]

Douglas, J. D. (ed.) (1970), *Deviance and Respectability*, Basic Books.

Douglas, J. D. (ed.) (1971), *Understanding Everyday Life*, Routledge & Kegan Paul. [265, 266, 268]

Douglas, J. D. (ed.) (1972), *Research on Deviance*, Random House. [268]

Downes, D. M. (1966), *The Delinquent Solution: A Study in Subcultural Theory*, Routledge & Kegan Paul. [17]

Emerson, R. M. (1969), *Judging Delinquents: Context and Process in Juvenile Courts*, Aldine. [7]

Erikson, K. T. (1962), 'Notes on the sociology of deviance', *Social Problems*, vol. 9, pp. 307–14 (also in Becker, 1964). [4, 6, 7]

Erikson, K. T. (1966), *Wayward Puritans*, Wiley. [6]

Filmer, P., Philipson, M., Silverman, D. and Walsh, D. (1972), *New Directions in Sociological Theory*, Collier-Macmillan. [25, 265]

Filstead, W. (ed.) (1970), *Qualitative Methodology*, Markham. [268]

Fisher, S. (1972), 'Stigma and deviant careers in school', *Social Problems*, vol. 20, no. 1, pp. 78–84. [267]

From, F. (1971), *Perception of Other People*, Columbia University Press. [270]

Garfinkel, H. (1962), 'Common-sense knowledge of social structures: the documentary method of interpretation', in Scher, J. (ed.) (1962), *Theories of the Mind*, Free Press (also in Manis and Meltzer (eds) 1972). [25]

Garfinkel, H. (1967), *Studies in Ethnomethodology*, Prentice-Hall. [7, 268, 270, 272]

Gibbs, J. (1966), 'Conceptions of deviant behaviour: the old and the new', *Pacific Sociological Review*, vol. 9, pp. 9–14. [265, 266]

Glaser, B. and Strauss, A. (1967), *The Discovery of Grounded Theory*, Weidenfeld & Nicolson. [26, 63, 267]

Goffman, E. (1959), *The Presentation of Self in Everyday Life*, Doubleday Anchor (Penguin, 1969).

Goffman, E. (1963), *Behaviour in Public Places* (Free Press). [22, 93, 269]

Goffman, E. (1971), *Relations in Public*, Basic Books (Penguin, 1971). [22, 93, 266]

Gold, M. (1963), *Status Forces in Delinquent Boys*, University of Michigan, Institute of Social Research. [17]

Goldthorpe, J. H. (1973), 'A revolution in sociology?', *Sociology*, vol. 7, pp. 449–62. [29, 268]

Good, T. L. and Brophy, J. E. (1973), *Looking in Classrooms*, Harper & Row. [254]

Gouldner, A. (1968), 'The sociologist as partisan: sociology and the welfare state', *American Sociologist*, vol. 3, pp. 103–16. [8, 10]

Hallworth, H. J. (1961), 'Teachers' personality ratings of high school pupils', *Journal of Educational Psychology*, vol. 52, pp. 297–302. [271]

Hallworth, H. J. (1962), 'A teacher's perceptions of his pupils', *Educational Review*, vol. 14, pp. 124–33. [271]

Hargreaves, D. H. (1967), *Social Relations in a Secondary School*, Routledge & Kegan Paul. [17, 254, 256]

Hargreaves, D. H. (1971), 'The delinquent subculture and the school', in Carson and Wiles (eds) (1971). [17]

Hargreaves, D. H. (1972), *Interpersonal Relations and Education*, Routledge & Kegan Paul. [144, 254, 255, 271]

Hargreaves, D. H. (1975), 'An interactionist approach to deviance in schools', in Ahier, J. and Flude, M., *New Trends in the Sociology of Education*, University of London Press. [21]

Harré, H. R. and Secord, P. F. (1972), *The Explanation of Social Behaviour*, Blackwell. [254, 265]

Heider, F. (1958), *The Psychology of Interpersonal Relations*, Wiley. [270]

Henry, J. (1966), *Culture Against Man*, Tavistock. [254]

Hirschi, T. (1969), *Causes of Delinquency*, University of California Press. [273]

Holt, J. (1964), *How Children Fail*, Pitman (also Penguin, 1969). [254]

Hughes, E. C. (1945), 'Dilemmas and contradictions of status', *American Journal of Sociology*, vol. 50, pp. 353–9. [272]

Humphreys, L. (1970), *Tearoom Trade*, Duckworth. [7]

Jackson, P. W. (1968), *Life in Classrooms*, Holt, Rinehart & Winston. [254]

Johnson, A. C. (1942), 'Our schools make criminals', *Journal of Criminal Law and Criminology*, vol. 33, pp. 310–15. [17]

Jones, E. E. et al. (1972), *Attribution: Perceiving the Causes of Behaviour*,

General Learning Press. [270]

Jordan, J. (1974), 'The organisation of perspectives in teacher-pupil relations: an interactionist approach', unpublished M.Ed. thesis, University of Manchester. [260]

Kelly, G. M. (1955), *The Psychology of Personal Constructs* (2 vols), Norton. [270, 272]

Kitsuse, J. I. (1962), 'Societal reaction to deviant behaviour: problems of theory and method', *Social Problems*, vol. 9, pp. 247–56 (also in Becker (ed.), 1964, and Rubington and Weinberg (eds), 1968). [4, 18, 23, 270]

Kohl, H. R. (1967), *36 Children*, Gollancz. [254]

Kohl, H. R. (1970), *The Open Classroom*, Methuen. [254]

Kounin, J. S. (1970), *Discipline and Group Management in Classrooms*, Holt, Rinehart & Winston. [21, 257]

Kounin, J. S. and Gump, P. V. (1958), 'The ripple effect in discipline', *Elementary School Journal*, vol. 57, pp. 1–13. [269]

Kuhn, T. (1962), *The Structure of Scientific Revolutions*, University of Chicago Press. [265]

Lacey, C. (1970), *Hightown Grammar*, Manchester University Press. [254]

Lemert, E. M. (1951), *Social Pathology*, McGraw-Hill. [5]

Lemert, E. M. (1967), *Human Deviance: Social Problems and Social Control*, Prentice-Hall. [5, 7]

Lofland, J. (1969), *Deviance and Identity*, Prentice-Hall. [7, 272]

Lofland, J. (1971), *Analysing Social Settings*, Wadsworth. [268]

Lorber, J. (1967), 'Deviance as performance: the case of illness', *Social Problems*, vol. 14, no. 3, pp. 303–10. [266]

McCall, G. J. and Simmons, J. L. (eds) (1969), *Issues in Participant Observation*, Addison-Wesley. [268]

McDonald, L. (1969), *Social Class and Delinquency*, Faber & Faber. [17]

McHugh, P. (1970), 'A common-sense perception of deviance', in Douglas (ed.) (1970) (also in Dreitzel, H. P. (ed.) (1970), *Recent Sociology No. 2*, Collier-Macmillan). [13]

Manis, J. G. and Meltzer, B. N. (eds) (1967), *Symbolic Interaction: A Reader in Social Psychology*, Allyn & Bacon (2nd ed., 1972).

Mankoff, M. (1971), 'Societal reaction and career deviance: a critical analysis', *Sociological Quarterly*, vol. 12, pp. 204–18. [12, 265, 266]

Matza, D. (1964), *Delinquency and Drift*, Wiley. [266, 270]

Matza, D. (1969), *Becoming Deviant*, Prentice-Hall. [2, 7, 272]

Mead, G. H. (1934), *Mind, Self and Society*, University of Chicago Press.

Mills, C. W. (1940), 'Situated actions and vocabularies of motive', *American Sociological Review*, 1940, pp. 904–13 (also in Manis and Meltzer, 1967 and 1972, and in Open University, 1971). [270]

Mischel, T. (ed.) (1974), *Understanding Other Persons*, Blackwell. [254]

Nash, R. (1973), *Classrooms Observed*, Routledge & Kegan Paul. [254, 268, 271]

Natanson, M. (ed.) (1963), *Philosophy of the Social Sciences: A Reader*, Random House. [7]

Open University (1971), *School and Society: A Sociological Reader*, Routledge & Kegan Paul.

Phillipson, C. M. (1971), 'Juvenile delinquency and the school', in Carson and Wiles (eds) (1971). [17]

Phillipson, C. M. and Roche, M. (1974), 'Phenomenology, sociology and the study of deviance', in Rock and McIntosh (eds) (1974). [15]

Pollner, M. (1974), 'Sociological and common-sense models of the labelling process', in Turner (ed.) (1974). [13, 266]

Power, M. et al. (1967), 'Delinquent schools?', *New Society*, 19 October. [17]

Rist, R. C. (1970), 'Student social class and teacher expectations: the self-fulfilling prophecy in ghetto education', *Harvard Educational Review*, vol. 40, pp. 411–51. [141]

Rock, P. and McIntosh, P. (eds) (1974), *Deviance and Social Control*, Tavistock.

Rosenthal, R. and Jacobson, L. F. (1968), *Pygmalion in the Classroom*, Holt, Rinehart & Winston. [140, 254]

Rubington, E. and Weinberg, M. S. (eds) (1968), *Deviance: The Interactionist Perspective*, Macmillan (2nd ed., 1973). [2, 6]

Schafter, W. E. and Polk, K. (1967), 'Delinquency and the schools', *Taskforce Report: Juvenile Delinquency and Youth Crime*, President's Commission on Law Enforcement and Administration of Justice, Appendix M, Washington, D.C. [17]

Scheff, T. (1968), 'Negotiating reality: notes on power in the assessment of responsibility', *Social Problems*, vol. 16, no. 1, pp. 3–17. [266]

Schervish, P. (1973), 'The labeling perspective: its bias and potential in the study of political deviance', *American Sociologist*, vol. 8, pp. 47–57. [7, 9]

Schur, E. M. (1971), *Labeling Deviant Behavior*, Harper & Row. [7, 11]

Schur, E. M. (1973), *Radical Non-intervention*, Prentice-Hall. [7, 273]

Schutz, A. (1932), *Der sinnhafte Aufbau der sozialen Welt*, Springer. [157, 158]

Schutz, A. (1944), 'The stranger', *American Journal of Sociology*, vol. 49, no. 6, pp. 499–507. [28]

Schutz, A. (1953), 'Common-sense and scientific interpretation of human action', *Philosophy and Phenomenological Research*, vol. 14, pp. 1–37. [27, 221]

Schutz, A. (1954), 'Concept and theory formation in the social sciences', *Journal of Philosophy*, vol. 51, pp. 257–73. [27]

Schutz, A. (1967), *Collected Papers: Vol. 1. The Problem of Social Reality; Vol. 2. Studies in Social Theory*, Martinus Nijhoff, The Hague.

Schutz, A. (1970), *Reflections on the Problem of Relevance*, Yale University Press. [270]

Schutz, A. and Luckmann, T. (1974), *The Structures of the Life World*, Heinemann. [270]

Scott, M. B. (1968), *The Racing Game*, Aldine. [268]

Scott, M. B. and Lyman, S. M. (1968), 'Accounts', *American Sociological Review*, vol. 33, pp. 46–62. [270]

Scott, M. B. and Lyman, S. M. (1970), 'Accounts, deviance and social order', in Douglas (ed.) (1970). [270]

Seaver, W. B. (1973), 'Effects of naturally induced teacher expectations', *Journal of Personality and Social Psychology*, vol. 28, no. 3, pp. 333–42. [272]

Smith, L. M. and Geoffrey, W. (1968), *The Complexities of an Urban Classroom*, Holt, Rinehart & Winston. [254]

Stebbins, R. (1970), 'The meaning of disorderly behaviour: teacher definitions of a classroom situation', *Sociology of Education*, vol. 44, pp. 217–36. [20, 239]

Stinchcombe, A. L. (1964), *Rebellion in a High School*, Quadrangle Books, Chicago. [17]

Sykes, G. M. and Matza, D. (1957), 'Techniques of neutralization: a theory of delinquency', *American Sociological Review*, vol. 22, pp. 664–70. [266, 270]

Tannenbaum, F. (1938), *Crime and the Community*, Columbia University Press. [262]

Taylor, I. and Taylor, L. (eds) (1973), *Politics and Deviance*, Penguin. [6]

Taylor, I., Walton, P. and Young, J. (1973), *The New Criminology*, Routledge & Kegan Paul. [7, 9, 265, 266]

Turner, R. (ed.) (1974), *Ethnomethodology,* Penguin.

Waller, W. (1932), *The Sociology of Teaching*, Wiley. [254]

Warren, C. and Johnson, J. (1972), 'A critique of labelling theory from the phenomenological perspective', in Scott, R. and Douglas, J. D. (eds) (1972), *Theoretical Perspectives on Deviance*, Basic Books. [266]

Webb, J. (1962), 'The sociology of a school', *British Journal of Sociology*, vol. 13, pp. 264–72. [17]

Werthman, C. (1963), 'Delinquents in school: a test for the legitimacy of authority', *Berkeley Journal of Sociology*, vol. 8, pp. 39–60. [19, 256, 267]

Wieder, D. L. (1974), 'Telling the code', in Turner (ed.) (1974). [31, 268, 269]

Williams, C. J. and Weinberg, M. S. (1971), *Homosexuals and the Military*, Harper & Row. [7]

Wilson, T. P. (1970), 'Conceptions of interaction and forms of sociological explanation', *American Sociological Review*, vol. 35, no. 4, pp. 697–710. [265]

Winch, P. (1958), *The Idea of a Social Science and its Relation to Philosophy*, Routledge & Kegan Paul. [254, 269]

Young, M. F. D. (ed.) (1971), *Knowledge and Control: New Directions for the Sociology of Education*, Collier-Macmillan. [254]

Zimmerman, D. H. and Pollner, M. (1971), 'The everyday world as a phenomenon', in Douglas (ed.) (1971). [268]

Zimmerman, D. H. and Wieder, D. L. (1971), 'Ethnomethodology and the problem of order: comment on Denzin', in Douglas (ed.) (1971). [266]

Subject index

Accounts, 130–3
Amplification/attenuation, 6, 265
Appreciation, 3, 30, 32
Ascribed rule-breaking, 12
Auto-involvements, 36, 75, 269
Avoidance-of-provocation, 239–
    249

Careers, 24, 250, 259
Causal structure, 159, 200, 238
Concealment strategies, 123ff
Criminological model, 21–3, 26,
    33, 252

De-typing, 153ff; and re-typing,
    156f
Deviance-imputations, 23f, 49,
    55f, 93f, 142; categories of,
    49–52; definition of, 52; and
    instructions, 53f; recognition
    of, 51f

Effectiveness/efficiency of
    treatment, 231f, 235
Elaboration, stage of, 145, 152ff,
    171ff; see also Idiosyncratiz-
    ation, Motive elaboration,
    Type extension, Verification
Evidential strategies, 117–21;
    interrogative, 121f; as
    treatment, 235

Filling in, 55f, 58ff, 134ff

Functionalists, 221f, 250

Idiosyncratization, 158
Interpretive work, see Rules,
    evidential, interpretive
Irremediality, 188–90, 201–3,
    210–15, 240f

Labelling theory, 3–16; general
    criticisms, 6f; phenomeno-
    logical criticisms, 10–16;
    symbolic interactionist
    criticisms, 8–11
Likeability, 145, 190, 213f

Morality, principle of, 221ff
Motive elaboration, 158f, 177ff,
    186, 195f, 198ff, 208ff
Motives, 24, 158f, 167, 198–201,
    208–10, 238f
Movement management, 257f

Neutralization, 14, 259
Newcomer status, 154–6, 167

Paradigms, 1–3, 6f, 11, 18, 25,
    27, 30f
Participant-observation, 30
Phases, 65–93; clearing up,
    84–6; entry and settling down,
    67–75; exit, 86–9; lesson
    proper, 75–84; see also
    Subphases

Phenomenologists, 1f, 7, 10–16, 18, 25, 27–32, 254–6
Positivists, 1f, 6, 10, 18, 24–6, 28
Postulate of adequacy, 29f, 34, 221
Postulate of logical consistency, 27f
Postulate of subjective interpretation, 29, 221
Pragmatism, principle of, 221ff

Qualitative methodology, 30

Reactions to deviance, chapter 8; intervention and treatment, 221ff; *see also* Avoidance-of-provocation, Morality, Pragmatism
Retrospective interpretation, 124f, 128, 193
Routine deviance, 23, 27, 49, 55f, 93f, 142, 219, 249, 252
Rules: ad hoc, 91f; classroom, 35ff; evidential, 117ff, of conviction, 118ff, retrospective conviction, 125ff, retrospective suspicion, 124ff, of suspicion, 119ff, type-congruency, 136ff, type-discrepancy, 134ff; implemental, 107ff, 253; institutional, 34f, 92f; interpretive, 59, 91, 116, 253, 268; multiphasic, 92; personal, 34, 36, 43; relational, 93, pupil-pupil, 93, 101–4, teacher-pupil, 93, 95–101; school, 33ff; situational, 34f; suspension of, 89f

Schools, selection of, 30f
Secondary deviation, 5, 247

Secret deviance, 8f
Self-fulfilling prophecy, 140f
Self-labelling, 8, 259
Settling down, 150, 154, 162, 173ff
Sibling phenomenon, 160–2, 167, 180, 184, 200, 253, 259f
Speculation, stage of, 145ff, 253; *see also* Sibling phenomenon, Staff discussion, Standing out
Stabilization, stage of, 145, 186ff, 253, 262; *see also* Type centralization and Type fusion
Staff discussion, 162–5, 180, 205
Standing out, 147ff, 159ff
Stigma, 13, 267
Subphases, 75ff; type 1, 75–8; type 2, 78–81; type 3, 81–3
Subreactional deviance, 168f, 173, 180, 226, 253, 256
Switch-signal, 65ff, 89f, 253

Task-phase, 65
Teachers: deviance-insulative, 260ff; deviance provocative, 260ff
Themes: movement, 46, 48; pupil-pupil relational, 46, 49; talk, 46ff; teacher-pupil relational, 46, 48f; time, 46, 49
Time-flow principle, 223ff
Type centralization, 188
Type extension, 157
Type fusion, 187f
Type permanence, 186
Type transcendence, 157
Type transformation, 186f, 194, 262
Typing, stages of, 145; *see also* Elaboration, Speculation, Stabilization

Verification, 152ff

LC   Hargreaves, David H.
4801
H37   Deviance in
           classrooms

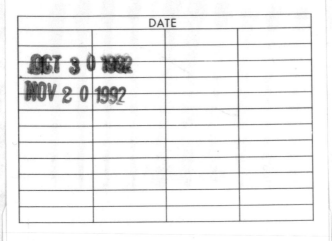

DATE			
OCT 3 0 1992			
NOV 2 0 1992			